TOURING IN 1600

'It should appeal to a large public, if the modern globe-trotter has any curiosity to learn the experiences of his travelling ancestry' *Times Literary Supplement, November 23, 1911*

Touring in 1600 is an extraordinary mixture of travel, history, personal philosophy and literature, charting the development of 'travel' from 1600. E.S. Bates considers the character and class of those men and women who travelled, which countries were in vogue in different periods, where the best inns or markets were to be found and all manner of other topical information. Combining historical reflections with chapters on current practice and what the modern-day traveller could expect, E.S. Bates's unusual masterpiece is here introduced by the highly-acclaimed historian, translator and travel writer, George Bull.

Also in the Century Classics

Voyages to the Virginia Colonies by Richard Hakluyt

To the Inland Sea by Donald Richie

Every Rock, Every Hill by Victoria Schofield

Jerusalem by Colin Thubron

Uttermost Part of the Earth by Lucas Bridges
Introduced by Gavin Young

Coups and Cocaine by Anthony Daniels

Life in Mexico by Madame Calderon de la Barca
Introduced by Sir Nicolas Cheetham

A Sabine Journey by Anthony Rhodes
Introduced by Peter Quennell

Raymond Asquith: Life and Letters
Edited and Introduced by John Jolliffe

Mayhew's London Underworld
Edited and Introduced by Peter Quennell

Journey Into the Mind's Eye by Lesley Blanch

A Backward Glance by Edith Wharton

Muddling Through in Madagascar by Dervla Murphy

Italian Hours by Henry James
Introduced by Tamara Follini

With An Eye to the Future by Osbert Lancaster
Introduced by Richard Boston

Isles of Illusion by Asterisk
Introduced by Gavin Young

Two Middle-Aged Ladies in Andalusia by Penelope
Chetwode

TOURING IN 1600

A Study in the Development of Travel as a Means of Education

E.S. BATES

Introduced by George Bull

CENTURY
London Melbourne Auckland Johannesburg

First published by Constable and Houghton Mifflin
Company in 1911

© Introduction George Bull 1987

This edition first published in 1987 by Century,
an imprint of Century Hutchinson Ltd, Brookmount
House, 62–65 Chandos Place, London WC2N 4NW

Century Hutchinson Australia Pty Ltd
PO Box 496, 16–22 Church Street, Hawthorn,
Victoria 3122, Australia

Century Hutchinson New Zealand Limited
PO Box 40-086, Glenfield, Auckland 10, New Zealand

Century Hutchinson South Africa (Pty) Ltd
PO Box 337, Berglvei, 2012 South Africa

Printed and bound by Richard Clay Ltd, Bungay

ISBN 0 7126 1495 8

CONTENTS

I. SOME OF THE TOURISTS   3

II. GUIDE-BOOKS AND GUIDES   35

III. ON THE WATER   60

IV. CHRISTIAN EUROPE:

    PART I: EUROPEAN EUROPE   95

    PART II: THE UNVISITED NORTH   154

    PART III: THE MISUNDERSTOOD WEST   162

V. MOHAMMEDAN EUROPE

    PART I: THE GRAND SIGNOR   182

    PART II: JERUSALEM AND THE
      WAY THITHER   205

VI. INNS   240

VII. ON THE ROAD   284

VIII. THE PURSE   313

    SPECIAL REFERENCES   381

    BIBLIOGRAPHY   389

    INDEX   407

TO

INTRODUCTION

In 1982 I sent a copy of a book of mine– *Venice: The Most Triumphant City* – to Professor J. H. Whitfield, a scholar who has been especially kind to me over many years. In his note of thanks he asked if I had ever read *Touring in 1600*. I had not; but about a year later, browsing in an enormous second-hand bookshop in New York ('One million books'), I looked up to a high shelf and saw the title, and remembered the recommendation. The book cost me thirty dollars, but any hesitation I felt was soon dispelled by a glance at the 'Illustrations from Contemporary Sources', at the seductive index, and at the quotation opposite the title page: '*Che Dio voglia che V.S., abbia pazienza de leggerla tutta*' – *Pietro dela Valle*. This borrowed invitation to have the patience to read all of E.S. Bates clinched the matter. But who was E.S. Bates?

After consulting various reference books, I set out to find out more about an American author, one Ernest Sutherland Bates, on the mistaken assumption that, as the book had first been published in the United States, the author would have been American. The American's dates were right. He had written many interesting works, including the *Gospel According to Judas Escariot*. But nowhere could I find mention of *Touring in 1600*. I was puzzled. Then by chance, I discovered that *Touring in 1600* had in fact also been published in Britain, by Constable, and was by an Englishman.

Failing to find E.S. Bates in the British *Who Was Who*, I thought, not very hopefully, that possibly the current *Who's Who* would list a Bates of the same family. It was a long shot, but worth a try. Sure enough, when I consulted a copy, the entries under Bates yielded a likely-looking candidate in Sir (Julian) Darrell Bates, an author himself of books with beguiling titles such as *A Fly Switch from the Sultan* and *A Longing for Quails*.

I wrote off at once, and a few days later received his reply: 'Thank you for your letter which I was very glad to get as I am E.S. Bates's youngest son and a loving and lasting admirer of him both as a writer and a scholar . . .'

E.S. Bates, I learned, was the second of three sons of a London cotton merchant who believed in the virtues of trade and commerce and put him into the Westminster Bank. His interests and talents were scholarly and literary rather than commercial, but he persevered as a banker till his father died. His inheritance enabled him to retire, to devote himself to writing and travel. He proceeded to write a series of books, all well-received and well-reviewed, including *Modern Translation*,

Inside Out – an Introduction to Autobiography (in two volumes), *Soviet Asia* and, lastly, *Studies in Translation*, published in 1943. He died in London the following year.

Touring in 1600 was published in 1911, and written while E.S. Bates was still working for the Westminster Bank. He did the writing and extensive research in the evenings, chiefly in the British Museum Library and at the London Library, to both of which, along with Marsh's Library, Dublin, he pays warm tribute in his Bibliography. This Bibliography, and the eccentric original index to the book, are enjoyable for their own sakes: they testify to Bates's application and scholarly instincts (he drew first-hand evidence from over 230 travellers); his rare honesty (square brackets indicate books of which his knowledge was second-hand); his courtesy to the reader (through the conscientious assessment of his sources); and his rather donnish wit (non-contemporary sources he has used, he says, only to decide which of two travellers is the bigger liar). In all these scholarly appurtenances, he is precise but not pedantic.

On the book's first appearance, the *Times Literary Supplement* noticed *Touring in 1600* briefly in its issue of November 23, 1911 (along with books by Hilaire Belloc and W.H. Davies, and the first volume of the Cambridge Mediaeval History). It carried a full review (in just over a column of about a thousand words) on 7 December. Priced at 12s 6d, the book was gently criticised for occasionally perpetrating what has since come to be called a 'dangling modifier' ('Being Lent, they fasted' is not good grammar, scolded the *TLS* reviewer); but it was welcomed as an engaging addition to our knowledge of social life at that period, and its chapter on inns was considered particularly entertaining. Mr Bates's book, the reviewer concluded, 'should appeal to a larger public, if the modern globe-trotter has any curiosity to learn the experiences of his travelling ancestry'.

Not too immodestly, Bates himself draws attention to the fact that, thanks to his researches – which resulted in 'a summary of the experiences and thoughts of scores of individuals, and of the thousands they stand for, over a period of more than a century and extending all over one continent and into fractions of two others' – the 'half-truths' of his anthology were less stereotyped and the detail less hackneyed than in many other books of travel. Certainly, the main virtue of Bates's book is its freshness and novelty, not in its being a travel anthology but in its discoveries and its range. We may all have come across a few quotations from Fynes Moryson, Sir Henry Wotton, or Tom Coryat; but how many from Pietro de la Valle, John Lauder or Zinzerling? And even with the better known, such as Benvenuto Cellini early in the period, Bates closes in on the apposite and the unexpected.

Through shrewdly chosen chapters reporting opinions on emotive topics such as guide-books and perils at sea, religious differences, inns, roads and money, Bates manages to sustain the difficult feat of interweaving without bathos his historical quotations with his own reflections. To judicious and imaginative selection – the rare achievement of the first-rate anthologist – he adds his temperate and timely comment. Bates's tone of voice is not quite urbane – he is a little too self-conscious for that – but it is civilised. He enjoys his own erudition. He enjoys sharing it. He is didactic but not dull. He is a bit of a sceptic, but never a cynic: he laughs with people, whether the foreigner abroad or the native, never at them. There are examples of this in every chapter, but look in particular at the skill with which Bates composes his account (from page 272–283) of the Rabelaisian Innkeepers' Congress at Rothenburg on the Tauber.

To savour experiences of travel we need sour and sweet, a view through the jaundiced eye as well as the benign. If it is done just to shock (Bernard Shaw's 'stupid classic Acropolis and smashed pillars') this can be tiresome; not if it reflects passionate feelings. For Catholics, Protestants, Mohammedans and even perhaps agnostics, the fears and fantasies of one set of believers about another around the year 1600 – a recurrent theme in Bates's early chapters – make suggestive reading: 'William Lithgow is proud to say he quarrelled with companions simply because they were Papists, and had often seized opportunities to tear in pieces the rich garments on images rather than "with indifferent forbearance wink at the wickedness of idolators".' And did you know that the tip of the nose of Mary Magdalen used to be on view near Marseilles?

But for non-sectarian spleen and sarcasm, and

genuine qualms suggesting an Iliad of woes, relish the list of characteristics of sixteenth-century travel tacked on by Bates to end his chapter on guide-books and guides, including the conviction that women should not travel at all, and men not much.

Presenting his studiously mixed raw material, Bates points out that around 1600 the classes of traveller in evidence still, as in Chaucer's day, included the ever-lasting bands of students and artisans, the men of commerce in yet greater numbers, the pilgrims (especially in Rome in Holy Year), the vagabond, with his offshoot the *picaro*, and perhaps the knight-errant, transformed into a *picaro* of high degree. To those still surviving from the Middle Ages, he adds for the years around 1600 the exiles, political and religious, and notes in their absence the missionaries 'occupied at home converting each other at this date, or re-converting themselves . . .'. Then Bates presents his image of the Average Tourist, extinct by 1900, he thinks, because of reference-books, telegraphs and democracy; beginning to abound by 1600 in the form of the person leaving his own country to seek information 'because he was a junior member of the aristocracy, at that time the governing class more exclusively than at present'. He continues: 'in the two half-centuries preceding and succeeding the year 1600, the practice of the upper classes of sending sons abroad as part of their education became successively an experiment, a custom, and finally, a system.'

'Take away that pudding,' growled Winston

Churchill once over lunch at the Savoy, 'it has no theme . . .' E.S. Bates convinces us that his book has a theme; but, thank heavens, he then gets on with letting the ingredients please the palate. It is a book for entertainment and rightly so, since, as Bates exclaims exultantly in agreement with the Elizabethan Thomas Nashe, the straying abroad by the people we meet in its pages was, as it always will be for tourists, 'the sense of the inexhaustible pleasure of travel'. In his rhetorical flourish about the marvellous contacts that travel brings about between the ideas and efforts of millions of persons, he appears to apologise for the 'more trivial details' reported in his book. On the contrary, these are the essence of historical reality: the all-revealing trifle that can bring to life or illuminate a person, a place or a period; and *Touring in 1600* is stuffed with them like a bulging hamper, from the dogs used as hot water bottles to the bits of fur attached to bridles in Italy as a mark of status.

The world that Bates's travellers describe so variously and colourfully was settled enough for regular and increasing travel soon to evolve, for the English, into the Grand Tour. Constantly, as one reads the comments and reports, the surprisingly familiar swaps places with the disturbingly bizarre. Bates mentions the increasing volume of travel made possible by the extent of civilised order and relative peace. But in 1600, too, the Ottoman Empire was still expanding, its conquest of Iraq from Persia still to come, as was the outbreak of the ferocious Thirty Years' War. Russia was not yet a significant European power,

Sweden was formidable in arms. Against this distant background, *Touring in 1600* puts on a superbly animated human show, with some of the best performers.

Where does the book belong on the library shelves? It is History as well as Travel, but is also so full of quotations it might be lodged among the reference books. But *Touring in 1600* vies with accomplished literary works, and yields marvellous observations to compare with those of modern travel writers from Evelyn Waugh to Norman Lewis and Jan Morris, all miraculously capable, transported anywhere, of immortalising what they observe. To my mind, to place *Touring in 1600* with books on the history of travel seems a bit too obvious. It is a one-off, an anthology of exceptional charm and variety (like Maurice Baring's very different *Have you Anything to Declare?*), and an education.

George Bull
1987

"Che Dio voglia che V. S. abbia pazienza di leggerla tutta."

Pietro della Valle, "*Il Pellegrino*."

TOURING IN 1600

CHAPTER I

SOME OF THE TOURISTS

But thus you see we maintain a trade, not for gold, silver, nor jewels; nor for silks; nor for spices; nor any other commodity of matter; but only for God's first creature, which was Light; to have Light (I say), of the growth of all parts of the world . . . we have twelve that sail into foreign countries, . . . who bring us the books, and abstracts and patterns of experiments of all other parts. These we call Merchants of Light.

F. BACON (1561–1626), *New Atlantis.*

FIRST, M. de Montaigne. — When Montaigne found himself feeling old and ill, in 1580, he made up his mind to try the baths of Germany and Italy. So he set out; and returned in 1581. And sometimes the baths did him good and sometimes they made no difference; but the journeying never failed to do what the baths were meant for. He always, he says, found forgetfulness of his age and infirmities in travelling. However restless at night, he was alert in the morning, if the morning meant starting for somewhere fresh. Compared with Montaigne at home, Montaigne abroad never got tired or fretful; always in good spirits, always interested in everything,

and ready for a talk with the first man he met. And
when his companions suggested that they would
like to get to the journey's end, and that the longest
way round, which he preferred, had its disadvantages, especially when it was a bye-road leading
back to the place they started from, he would say,
that he never set out for anywhere particular;
that he had not gone out of the way, because his
way lay through unfamiliar places, and the only
place he wished to avoid was where he had been
before or where he had to stop. And that he felt
as one who was reading some delightful tale and
dreaded to come upon the last page.

So, no doubt, felt Fynes Moryson, for much of
his life he spent either in travelling or in writing
the record of it. Starting in 1591, when he was
twenty-five, he passed through Germany, the
Low Countries, Denmark, Poland, Austria, Switzerland, and Italy, spending his winters at Leipzig, Leyden, Padua, and Venice, learning the languages so thoroughly as to be able to disguise his
nationality at will. Returning through France,
he was robbed, and consequently reached home
so disreputable-looking that the servant took him
for a burglar. He found his brother planning a
journey to Jerusalem. On the 29th of November,
1595, they set out, and on July 10, 1597, he was
back in London, in appearance again so strange
that the Dogberry of Aldersgate Street wrote him
down for a Jesuit. But he returned alone: his bro-

ther Henry, twenty-six years old and not strong,
fell ill at Aleppo, how ill no one knew till too late,
and near Iskenderún he died in his brother's arms,
while the Turks stood round, jeering and thiev-
ing. Fynes buried him there with stones above
him to keep off the jackals, and an epitaph which
a later traveller by chance has preserved.[1]

> To thee, deare Henry Morison,
> Thy brother Phines, here left alone,
> Hath left this fading memorie.
> For monuments and all must die.

Fynes himself hurried home and never crossed
the Channel again. But he extended his knowledge of Great Britain by a visit to Scotland, and
by accompanying Sir Charles Blount during the
latter's conquest of Ireland. Then he settled down
to write all he knew and could get to know about
the countries he had seen, and wrote at such length
that no one till quite recently has had the courage to reprint his account, although what he
printed was by no means all that he wrote. For
this reason his work has remained practically unused, even by writers whom it specially concerns.
It must form the basis of any description of the
countries he saw, at any rate, as seen by a foreigner, going, as he does, more into detail than
any one else, and being a thoroughly fair-minded,
level-headed, and well-educated man, whose knowledge was the result of experience. His day was
not the day of the 'Grand Tourist,' whose habit

it was to disguise single facts as general statements, and others' general statements as his own
experiences.

Yet however irreplaceable may be Montaigne's
subjectivity and Moryson's objectivity, it is desirable to find some one who combines both. Such
a one is Pietro della Valle, of Naples and Rome.
He is the impersonation of contemporary Italy
at its best; of, to use his own phrase, "quella
civiltà di vivere e quello splendore all' italiana,"
and to read his letters is to realise, as in no other
way can be so readily realised, the reason why
Italy held the position she did in the ideas of
sixteenth-century people. If you separate the
various characteristics that account for much of
the attractiveness of his writings; the interest
in things small and great, without triviality or
ponderousness; the ability to write, combined
with entire freedom from affectation; the lovable-
ness of his Italian and a charm of phrase apart
from his Italian, which might even, perhaps, sur-
vive translation; learning without arrogance and
hand in hand with observation; and refinement
and virility living in him as a single quality —
if you isolate these, there still remains something
to distinguish him from contemporary travellers,
the product of gifts and character, it is true,
but only of gifts and character as moulded by
contact from birth with the best of a splendid
civilisation, of which all the gentlemen of Eu-

rope were students, but none but natives gradu-
ates.

Still, in one respect, contemporary travellers
may claim he has taken an unfair advantage. Not
one of them has a romantic love-story as a background to his journeyings; Della Valle has two.
After a twelve years' courtship at home, his intended bride was given by her parents to some
one else. This was the cause of his wanderings.
At San Marcellino at Naples, a mass was sung
and the nuns prayed, the little golden pilgrim's
staff he wore round his neck was blessed, and a
vow made by him never to take it off until he
had visited the Holy Sepulchre.

Thus he became Pietro della Valle, "Il Pellegrino" (the Pilgrim); and started. Venice, Constantinople, Cairo, Jerusalem, Damascus, was
his route; but his next letter thereafter is "from
my tent in the desert": he has disappeared over
the tourist horizon, and become a traveller on the
grand scale. But he returns, and has much to say
on the way back. Meanwhile, in Babylon, he has
met another lady-love, Maani Gioerida, eighteen
years old, daughter of an Assyrian father and an
Armenian mother. Marriage with her was soon
followed by her death; for the remaining four
years of his wanderings he carried her body with
him, laying it to rest in the end in his family tomb:
and married again, this time the girl who had
attended his first wife, alive and dead, Maria

Tinatin di Ziba, a Georgian. And with her he lived happy ever after, and by her had fourteen sons.

Another type of traveller is the philosopher philosophizing. Sir Henry Blount set four particular aims before himself when he started for southeastern Europe with the intention of increasing his knowledge of things human, choosing the southeast because the west too closely resembled England. He went to note, first, the characteristics of "the religion, manners, and policy of the Turks" in so far as these threw light on the question whether they were, as reputed, barbarous, or possessed of a different variety of civilisation. Secondly, to satisfy the interest he felt in the subject-races, especially Jews; thirdly, to study the Turkish army about to set out for Poland; and fourthly, Cairo, which being the largest city existing, or on record, had problems of its own whose solutions he wished to note, much as foreigners might come to study London County Council doings now. This was in 1634.

But besides those who were born travellers and those who achieved travel, there were those who had travel thrust upon them; Thomas Dallam, for instance. Dallam was the master organ-builder of Elizabethan England. When, therefore, the Queen wished to send such a present to the Grand Turk as should assure her outshining all other sovereigns in his eyes and assist the Levant Company (who probably paid for it) in securing further privileges, an organ was the present, and Dallam had to make it and to take it. In 1599 he set out, and in 1600 praised God for his return. He, too, was an excellent Englishman: shrewd, interested, and interesting; and with an ability to express himself just abreast of his thinking faculty. His organ was a marvellous creation; played chimes, and song-tunes by itself, had two dummy-men on it who fanfared on silver trumpets, and, above, an imitation hollybush filled with mechanical birds which sang and shook their wings. The Grand Turk sent for Dallam to play on it, which he did rather nervously, having been warned that it meant death to touch the Signor, and the latter sat so near behind him that "I touched his knee with my breeches. . . . He sat so right behind me that he could not see what I did, therefore he stood up, but in his rising from his chair, he gave me a thrust forward, which he could not otherwise do, he sat so near me: but I thought he had been drawing his sword to cut off my head."

The organ was so great a success that Dallam became a favoured man. One attendant even let him look in at a grating through which he saw thirty of the girls of the harem playing ball, each wearing a chain of pearls round the neck, a ring of gold round the ankle, velvet slippers, a small cap of cloth of gold, breeches of the finest muslin, and a scarlet satin jacket.

Dallam was more in favour than he liked, for he was urged to settle there. "I answered them that I had a wife and children in England who did expect my return, though indeed I had neither wife nor children, yet to excuse myself I made them that answer."

Besides the business man who became a tourist without knowing it, there were the tourists who became so because home was too hot for them. Of their number was William Lithgow, whose "Rare Adventures" is the record of nineteen years' travel, ended in 1620 by the severity of the torture he endured in Spain through being taken for a spy. Although fifty years of age when he started writing his account, a fair sample of his style is,— "Here in Argos I had the ground to be a pillow, and the world-wide fields to be a chamber, the whirling windy skies to be a roof to my winter-blasted lodging, the humid vapours of cold Nocturna to accompany the unwished-for bed of my repose." And this was accompanied by so much second-hand history and doggerel that the printer rebelled and saved us from much more of it. The trustworthiness of his facts may be gauged by his stating as the result of his personal experience that Scotland is one hundred and twenty miles longer than England. On the other hand, he visited more places in Europe than any other one tourist, besides having some experience of Palestine and North Africa; and what he wrote he wrote after he had seen all that he did see. His comparisons are, therefore, worth attention, and these and the personal experiences which his verbiage has not crowded out of his book give it a permanent value and interest to those who have the patience to find them.

All this while we are forgetting the ladies; very few in number, but three at least possessing personality, — two princesses and an ambassador's wife. Princess number one was the eldest daughter of Philip II of Spain, the Infanta Doña Clara Eugenia, who crossed Europe with her husband, to take up the government of the Low Countries, in 1599, and wrote a long letter to her brother about the journey from Milan to Brussels, bright and pithy, one of the most readable and sensible letters that remain to us from the sixteenth century. Princess number two is the daughter of a king of Sweden, who had trouble in finding a husband for Princess Cecily, inasmuch as she would marry no one who would not promise to take her to England within a year from the wedding day; for the great desire of her life was to see Queen Elizabeth. A marquis of Baden accepted the condition, and on November 12, 1564, they started, by which time she had spent four years learning English and could speak it well. The voyage took ten months, the winter was a severe one, and much of their way lay through countries whose kings were hostile to her father and the inhabitants to every stranger. Leaving Stockholm while her relatives expressed their opinion about her journey by lamentations and fainting-fits, she crossed to Finland in a storm, in which the pilot lost heart to the extent of pointing out the rock on which they were going to be shipwrecked. Finland they left in four days, to escape starvation, during another storm; crossed to Lithuania; thence by land through Poland, North Germany, and Flanders, to Calais. Even from here it was not plain sailing, in any sense of the words; the sea was high when she started; all were sick ("with the cruel surges of the water and the rolling of the unsavoury ship"), except herself, standing on the hatches, looking towards England. But it proved impossible to get into Dover and they had to turn back. "'Alas!' quoth she, 'now must I needs be sick, both in body and in mind,' and therewith taking her cabin, waxed wonderful sick." A second time they tried; and again all were sick but herself; "she sitting always upon the hatches, passed the time in singing the English psalms of David after the English note and ditty." But again they had to turn back and again that made her sick, so sick that they thought she was going to be confined, for she had become pregnant about the time of her starting. A third attempt was successful; and on September 11, 1565, she arrived at Bedford House, Strand; on the 14th Queen Elizabeth arrived there, too, to see her; and on the 15th came the baby.

This story ought to end like Della Valle's, that she lived happy ever after; but that cannot truthfully be said, because of what is recorded about Princess Cecily and certain unpaid London tradesmen. Much more would there be to say of her as a tourist, had she written an autobiography; for the rest of her life she continued travelling, spending all her own money on it and much of other people's.

The third, the ambassador's wife, is Ann, Lady Fanshawe. Her travels belong, strictly speaking, to dates just outside the limits (1542–1642) with which this book is concerned, but for all practical purposes may be referred to with little reserve. Her experience was great, for her journeys were even more numerous than her pregnancies, which numbered eighteen; and being cheerful, clear-headed, and sincere in no ordinary measure, her "Memoirs" are almost as excellent a record of travel as of character.

It is a matter for regret that her husband, Sir Richard, has not left us an account of his own, but in this he resembles practically all his kind. There is Sir Robert Sherley, who went ambassador to two Emperors, two Popes, twice to Spain, twice to Poland, once to Russia, twice to Persia: yet of Sir Robert Sherley as tourist, we know next to nothing. So also of Sir Paul Pindar, who says in a letter that he has had eighteen years' experience of Italy; and De Foix, a man greatly gifted, who wished to serve his country as far as possible distant from its Valois Kings, and consequently chose a series of embassies as an honourable, useful form of self-exile. Yet of these last two and others there remains some record by means of men who accompanied them. Part of the travels of Peter Mundy, whose name will often recur, happened in the train of the former; and when De Thou, the historian, paid the visit to Italy which he recounts in his autobiography, it was with De Foix that he went.

Among the exceptions, most noticeable is Augier Ghiselin de Busbecq, a Fleming. After representing the Emperor in England at the wedding of Philip and Mary, he was sent to Constantinople (1556–1562), and afterwards to France. His letters from France that have been preserved are semi-official; of minor interest compared with those from Constantinople, which, not meant for publication but addressed to friends who were worthy of them, in time became printed. They belong to the literature of middle age, that which is written by men of fine character and fine education when successful issues out of many trials have made them wise and left them young. A many-sided man: the library at Vienna is the richer for his presents to the Emperor; many are the stories he tells of the wild animals he kept to while away the hours of the imprisonment which he, ambassador as he was, had to endure; the introducer into Europe of lilac, tulips, and

syringa; a collector of coins when such an occupation was not usual as a hobby. His opportunities, indeed, were such as occur no more; in Asia
Minor coins one thousand years old were in daily
use as weights; and yet Busbecq missed one
chance, for a brazier to whom he was referred
regretted he had not met him a few days earlier,
when he had had a vessel full of old coins which he
had just melted down to make kettles.

Turning from the personalities to the causes of
travel, we find that the class to which Busbecq
belonged, that of resident ambassador, was of
recent growth, and that it, and the tendencies of
which it is one symptom, are responsible for
creating the whole of the motives and the facili-
ties for travel which characterise journeyings of
this time as something different in kind from
those which preceded them. The custom of maintaining resident representatives was developed in
Italy during the fifteenth century, but it did not
spread to the rest of civilised Europe till near the
beginning of the next; German research, indeed,
has even narrowed down the dates within which it
established itself as an international system to
1494–1497.[2] The change was partly due to the
consolidation of sovereignties, which increased
the distances to be traversed between neighbour-
princes, partly to the insight of the three great
rulers who achieved the consolidations, — Ferdinand of Aragon, Louis XI, and Henry VII, who

abandoned the idea of force and isolation as the
only possible policies, and attempted to gain the
advantages, and avoid the disadvantages, of both
by means of ambassadors. Henry VII regarded
them as in no way differing from spies; the most
efficient kind of spies, from the point of view of
the sender; and unavoidable, from that of the re-
ceiver. The latter's only remedy, Henry VII
thought, was to send two for every one received.
This alone, regarded, as it must be, considering
who the speaker was, as indicating what the practice of the future would be, suffices to explain,
even to prove, a great increase in diplomatic movements. But what further compels the deduction
is that the foregoing is reported by Comines, who
was probably, next to Francesco Guicciardini,
the most frequently read historian throughout the
sixteenth century.

Side by side with these official spies was the
secret service; bound to grow in proportion to the
increase among the former, implying a certain
cosmopolitanism in its members, which, again,
implies touring. This class of tourists is naturally
the least communicative of all, but so far as England alone is concerned, if the history of the growth
of the English spy-system between Thomas and
Oliver Cromwell ever comes to be written, it is
bound to reveal an enormous number of men,
continually on the move for such purposes, or
qualifying themselves for secret service by pre-

vious travel. And while there is a certain amount
of information concerning tourists and touring
to be gathered, in scraps, among State Papers
which concern spies as spies, there is a great deal
available, often first-hand, from them during
this period of probation. Many, also, would be
termed spies by their enemies and news-writers
by their friends; persons who are abroad for some
other, more or less genuine, reason, whose information was very welcome to those at home in
the absence of newspapers, and was often paid
for by politicians who could acquire a greater hold
on the attention of those in power by means of
knowledge which was exclusive during a period
when the Foreign Office of a government existed
in a far less definitely organised form than at
present. It was in the course of such a mission
that Edmund Spenser saw most of Europe and
gained that intimate knowledge of contemporary politics which gives his poems a value which
would have been more generally recognised had
not their value as poetry overshadowed other
merits. The traveller, then, still fulfilled what had
been his chief use to humanity in mediæval times,
that of a "bearer of tydynges," as Chaucer insists
often enough in his "House of Fame."

It is worth while turning back to Chaucer's
time to see how far the classes of travellers then
existing have their counterparts in 1600, and how
far not. Omitting students and artizans, as not

varying, the types to be met on the road then may be collected into those of commerce, pilgrimage, vagabondage, and knight-errantry.

With regard to commerce, it may safely be guessed that the absence of the modern inventions for communication at a distance implied, in 1600 as in Chaucer's day, a greater proportional number of journeys in person than at present: and the enormous extension of commerce involved in the discoveries of sea-routes must have involved an increase in commercial traffic within Europe. As for the particular forms of trade that were responsible for taking men away from their homes, within the limits of Europe, it would probably be found, if statistics were possible, that dried fish came first, with wine and corn bracketed second. The Roman Catholic fast-days had produced a habit of eating dried fish which was not to be shaken off, in the strictest Protestant quarters, directly; and it was largely used for provisioning armies.

The second class of mediæval traveller, the pilgrim, is often in evidence about 1600, usually indirect evidence; the pilgrim who is nothing but pilgrim leaves practically no detailed record of himself except when he goes to Jerusalem. Yet Evelyn was told at Rome that during the year of Jubilee, 1600, twenty-five thousand five hundred women visitors were registered at the pilgrims' hospice of the Holy Trinity there, and four hundred and forty thousand men. Also, one who was at Montserrat in 1599, was told that six hundred pilgrims dined there every day, and at high festivals between three thousand and four thousand; while another (1619) learnt that whereas the monks' income from their thirty-seven estates stood at nine thousand scudi (say, thirteen thousand pounds at to-day's values) annually, they spent seven times that amount, the balance being derived from the sale of sanctified articles or from gifts.[3] On the whole, however, a decrease must be presupposed during this period on account of the cessation of pilgrimage among the Protestant half of Europe. Moreover, the kind of journeying which is specially characteristic of this period incidentally tended to further Protestant ideas and discredit pilgrimage. For pilgrimage was, of course, towards some relic. Now relics which mutually excluded each other's genuineness, such as two heads of one saint, were not likely to be met with on the same pilgrim route: the establishment of one such on a given route would hinder the establishment of a second for financial, as well as devotional, reasons. But when a believer travelled for diplomatic or educational purposes, his direction was quite as likely to lead across pilgrim routes, as along them. In which case he would be morally certain to come across these mutually exclusive relics, on one and the same journey, and the doubts thus started might be cumulative in their results.[4] On the other hand the very fact of opposition stimulated pilgrim zeal among the orthodox, as, *e. g.*, to the still flourishing shrine of Notre Dame des Ardilliers near Saumur, as a result of Saumur itself becoming a headquarters of the "Reformed" creed. There abided of course the permanent features of life which make pilgrimage as deep-rooted as the love of children, and one of the epidemics of pilgrimage that occur periodically burst out in France about 1585, so Busbecq writes. Whole villages of people clothed themselves in white linen, took crosses and went off to some shrine two or three days' journey away. The special cause of this epidemic may perhaps be sought in the pilgrimage to Our Lady of Chartres by their queen, in 1582, to beg for relief from her barrenness. One incident of this journey ought not to be left buried in the Calendar of Foreign State Papers, the only place where it has hitherto been printed. On being told why the queen was going thither, a countrywoman said, "Alas! Madame is too late; the good priest who used to make the children has just died."

An example of the pilgrim we have already met in Della Valle. Bartholomew Sastrow in his autobiography reveals a man travelling in search of work, a very unpleasant man, perhaps, but so strikingly true a picture of the every-day life and every-day thought of a lower middle-class man of the sixteenth century as not to be surpassed for any other century, past, present, or future, not even among autobiographies.

But for the man who is trying to avoid work, the third of the mediæval types, the vagabond, it would be out of place to select an individual to stand for the class in Renascence days, seeing that it became a stock literary type; vagabondage in general being epitomized for the time in the Spanish picaro. The picaro was one who saw much of the seamy side of life and remembered it with pleasure — it was all life and the true picaro was in love with life. The only enemy he had permanently was civilisation; yet he and it became reconciled in his old age: a picaro who grew old ceased to be a picaro. Meanwhile he was always forgiving civilisation, and being forgiven; both had equal need of forgiveness. Yet there is one picaro characteristic hard to overlook — his passion for being dull at great length when he drops into print: Lazarillo de Tormes and Gil Blas being the only ones of whom it may be said that from a reader's standpoint they were all that they should have been and nothing that they should not. The rest, when met between the covers of a book, resemble the parson whom one of themselves, Quevedo's Pablos, caught up on the way to Madrid and whom he hardly prevented from reciting his verses on St. Ursula and her eleven thousand virgins, fifty octavetts to each virgin; even then he could not escape a comedy containing more scenes than there were days in a Jerusalem pilgrimage, besides five quires concerning Noah's Ark. This same Pablos explains incidentally what his kind talked about to chance companions on the road, for meeting another making for Segovia they fell into "la conversacion propia de picaros." Whether the Turk was on the downhill and how strong was the king: how the Holy Land might be reconquered, and likewise Algiers: party politics were then discussed and afterwards the management of the rebellious Low Countries. There were, too, picaros of high degree, but these were all men of war, whereas nothing but hunger made an ordinary picaro fight. High and low, however, had this in common, that they preferred living at others' expense to working, and consequently shifted their lodgings as often as any other class of tourist, in deference to local opinion.

Of the fourth mediæval type, the knight-errant, it is hard to say whether it was extinct or not: all depends on the extent to which the knight-errant is idealised. It is certainly true in this degree, that contemporary fiction must be reckoned as a cause of travel. Don Quixote is not to be ignored as a traveller and he was not alone. The first Earl of Cork's eldest son was so affected by the romances that the "roving wildness of his thoughts" which they brought about was only partially cured by continual extraction of square and cube roots. But perhaps the knight-errant of this date is better identified with the picaro of high degree, and as such the class may be exemplified by Don Alonzo de Guzman, the first chapter of whose autobiography gives a better insight into the psychology, and life on the road, of the picaro than the whole flood of nineteenth-century comment on the subject. At the age of eighteen he found himself with no father, no money, and a mother pious but talkative; after having provided for his needs for a while by marriage, he left home with a horse, a mule, a bed, and sixty ducats. And though what follows belongs more to the history of lying than the history of the world, it throws side-lights. And at any rate, any excuse is good enough to turn to it, for Don Alonzo has much in common with Benvenuto Cellini.

Now we have passed beyond the mediæval types and come to such as are somewhat more prominent in this, than in the previous, centuries. Exiles, for instance. The economic changes that took place during the sixteenth century made it increasingly difficult for the equivalents for Chancellors of the Exchequer to meet the yearly deficits. The legal authorities were therefore called upon to assist, and a working arrangement was established in practically all European countries whereby the political ferment of the time was taken advantage of for the betterment of the finances. Instead of the slow process and meagre results of waiting for death-duties, a man of wealth suffered premature civil death, or was harried into civil suicide. He was exiled, or fled: he had become a tourist.

Inseparable from political is religious self-exile. What happened very often in England was this. A youngster is seized with that belief in the likelihood of an ideal life elsewhere and that desire for a change, which are characteristic of the age of twenty. The theological cast of the age gives the former a religious bias. He escapes. After a time it seems to him that human characteristics have the upper hand of the apostolic, even in Roman Catholics, to a greater extent than he once believed, and that he would like to go home. He lands, is questioned by the Mayor, reported on to the Privy Council, in which report his experiences are to be found summarised.

One class of men, however, which might be expected to provide many examples, is for the most part absent, — missionaries, — occupied at home converting each other at this date, or re-converting themselves. The chief, in fact, the Jesuits, were confined each one to his nation by order, and only in respect of their early training days do they appear as foreigners abroad. Acknowledgements are due, on the other hand, for information received, to captives set free, soldiers, artists, herbalists, antiquaries, and even to those who, so far as we know, only looked on, like Shakespeare; and

to many others led abroad by special reasons, such
as the Italian Marquis who felt it necessary for him
to have a long holiday after the privations of Lent.

But with all these varieties of tourist, we still
have not come to the Average Tourist. The type
is extinct, killed by reference-books, telegraphy,
and democracy. For the Average Tourist left his
fatherland to get information which he could not
get at home, and he wanted this information because he was a junior member of the aristocracy,
at that time the governing class more exclusively
than at present. In feudal days isolation was,
comparatively, taken for granted, and the fact of
that voluntary isolation implied many hindrances
to touring. The need of acquiring information of
every kind that affected political action had been
therefore less realised and the difficulty of acquiring it greater. These years near 1600 are the
years of transition, transition to a custom for
travellers to

> . . . seek their place through storms,
> In passing many seas for many forms
> Of foreign government, endure the pain
> Of many faces seeing, and the gain
> That strangers make of their strange-loving humours:
> Learn tongues; keep note-books; all to feed the tumours
> Of vain discourse at home, or serve the course
> Of state employment . . . [5]

Herein lies the unity of subject of this book; not
in its concern with a given class of experiences

during a given period. Roughly speaking, in the two half-centuries preceding and succeeding the year 1600, the practice of the upper classes of sending sons abroad as part of their education became successively an experiment, a custom, and, finally, a system. By the middle of the seventeenth century this system had become a thoroughly set system, and the "Grand Tour" a topic for hack-writers. Of the latter, James Howell was the first. His "Instructions for Foreign Travel" (1642) may serve to date the beginning of "Grand Touring" in the modern sense of the phrase, while the publication of Andrew Boorde's "Introduction of Knowledge" a century earlier, does the same for this preceding period, that of the development of travel as a means of education.

Delimiting the movement by means of English books suggests that it was a merely English movement, but it was in fact European, though true of the different countries in varying degrees. The increase of diplomatic journeys,[6] already mentioned, the core of this development and its chief instrument, was common to all divisions of Europe in proportion to the degree of the civilisation attained. In the Empire and Poland the custom grew up less suddenly; it had begun earlier. In Italy, it began later, since it was not till later that there was much for an Italian to learn that he could not learn better at home. Sir Henry Wotton[7] noted in 1603 that travelling was coming into fashion among the young nobles of Venice. In France, an early beginning was broken off by the civil wars, not to start afresh till Henry IV's sovereignty was established. As for Spaniards and Portuguese, they alone had dominions over-sea to attend to.

In England, on the other hand, political reversals being at once frequent, thorough, and peaceable, migrations were very common and usually short. That touring would result from migration was certain, because it familiarised English people with the attractions and the affairs of the continent and with the uses of that familiarity, and established communications. Other special causes existed, too, truisms concerning which are so plentiful that there is no need to repeat them here.

But the certainty of the change did not prevent it being slow. Andrew Boorde, who knew Europe thoroughly, found hardly any of his countrymen abroad except students and merchants, and for the following half century it is the tendency rather than the fact that may be noted, as indicated, for example, by Sir Philip Sidney, who started in 1572, writing later to his brother that "a great number of us never thought in ourselves why we went, but a certain tickling humour to do as other men had done." In 1578 Florio could still write in one of his Italian-English dialogues published in London: [8] " 'Englishmen, go they through the world?' 'Yea some, but few.'" Yet in 1592 and

again in 1595 the Pope complained about the
number of English heretics allowed at Venice, [9]
and in 1615 an Englishman, George Sandys, leaves
out of his travel-book everything relating to
places north of Venice, such being, he says, "daily
surveyed and exactly related." Three years earlier James I's Ambassador at Venice writes [10] to the
Doge that there are more than seventy English in
Venice whereas "formerly" there had been four or
five; and when he adds that there are not more
than ten in the rest of Italy it must be remembered that he is making out a case and even
then refers to Protestants only: between 1579 and
1603, three hundred and fifty Englishmen had
been received into the English College at Rome. [11]

The development, then, of the English tourist
may be synchronised with the rise of the English
Drama and the expansion of English Commerce.
In other words, the preparation for it came before
the failure of the Spanish Armada; the actuality
directly afterwards. But it could not have followed the course it did except in conjunction with
wider causes, which emphasise its place as but
part of a European movement. These may be
sought in (1) the slight, but definite, advance in
civilisation which made people more accessible to
the ideas which peace fosters; (2) the greater area
over which peace prevailed round about the year
1600: (3) the increase in centralisation in government, which decreased the obstacles in the way of

the traveller, and increased the attractiveness of particular points, *i. e.*, where the courts were held.

At the same time the increase in touring which really took place would be greatly over-estimated if one considered the evidence of bibliography as all-sufficient. Almost all that the latter proves is an increase in writing about it, due to the greatly increased demand for the written word which was the outcome of printing. Morelli, in his essay [12] on little-known Venetian travellers, quotes Giosaffate Barbaro as writing in 1487, "I have experienced and seen much that would probably be accounted rubbish by those who have, so to speak, never been outside Venice, by reason that such things are not customary there. And this has been the chief reason for my never having cared to write of what I have seen, nor even to speak much thereof." Yet by 1600 there were probably few countries in Europe in which recent accounts of the regions visited by Barbaro could not be read in the vernacular, accounts out of which some one expected to see a profit. Indications, on the contrary, of enormous numbers leaving home may be found in this one fact; that the names are known of twelve hundred Germans who passed beyond the limits of civilised Christendom during the sixteenth century.[13] What must then be the number of Europeans, ascertainable and otherwise, who were going about Europe then?

As regards the Average Tourist, however, we

are not left to our imagination. He is often to be
found in person, young, rich, abroad to learn. Yet
— why should he, rather than his contemporaries
of the lower classes, need teaching? The answer
will come of its own accord if we stop to consider
the similarities and divergences existent between
the Jesuits and the Salvation Army. Both are the
outcome of the same form of human energy, that
of Christianity militant against present-day evils;
it is circumstances that have caused the diver-
gence. The Jesuits were as keen at first for social
reform as the Salvation Army have become; the
Salvation Army used to be as much preoccupied
with theology as the Jesuits. In details the resemblance is more picturesque without being any
more accidental. The Salvation Army describe
themselves after the fashion of the Papal title of
"servus servorum Dei," as the "servants of all";
and the first thing that Loyola did when his associates insisted on his adopting the same title that
"General" Booth has assumed, was to go downstairs and do the cooking. The two societies with
one and the same root-idea essentially, have been
drawn into ministering to the lower class in the
nineteenth century and the upper class three hundred years earlier: the identity of spirit consisting
in the class that was ministered to being that
which possessed the greatest potentialities and the
greatest needs.[14] And in all the prescribed occupations of the Average Tourist we shall find this

implied, that the future of his country depended on the use he made of his tour.

Let us take two specimens; one in the rough, the other in the finished, state: No. 1 shall be John Lauder of Fountainhall; No. 2, the Duc de Rohan. The former's diary is not to be equalled for the insight it gives into the development of the mind of the fledgling-dignitary abroad; not a pleasant picture always, not the evolution of a mother's treasure into an omniscient angel, but of a male Scot of nineteen into the early stages of a man of this wicked world; but — it happened. We note his language becoming decidedly coarser and an introduction to Rabelais' works not improving matters. Still, the former would have happened at home, only in a narrower circle; and for Rabelais, who that has read him does not know the other side? Then, he did not always work as a good boy should: he was studying law at Poictiers, and a German who was there twenty years earlier tells us that at Poictiers there were so many students that those who wanted to work retired to the neighbouring St. Jean d'Angely. Lauder stopped at Poictiers and writes, "I was beginning to make many acquaintances at Poictiers, to go in and drink with them, as," — then follow several names, then a note by the editor that twenty-seven lines have been erased in the MS. It continues: "I was beginning to fall very idle." Later on: "I took up to drink with me M. de la

Porte, de Gruché, de Gey, de Gaule, Baranton's brother, etc."; [twenty-two lines erased] "on my wakening in the morning I found my head sore with the wine I had drunk." Even if one was wrong-headed enough to agree with what the minister at Fountainhall would feel obliged to remark about such occurrences, nothing could counterbalance the advantage to a Scot of learning that the Scottish opinion of Scots was not universally accepted. Lauder is surprised, genuinely humiliated, to find his countrymen despised abroad for the iconoclasm that accompanied their "conversion."

Lauder wrote a diary: the Duc de Rohan a "letter" to his mother, summarising the valuable information acquired in a virtuous perambulation through Italy, Hungary, Bohemia, Germany, the Low Countries, England, including a flying visit to Scotland; an harangue of flat mediocrity, imitative in character, thoughtful only in so far as, and in the way, he had been taught to be thoughtful. But, read between the lines, it is most interesting; better representing the Average Tourist in his nominal every-day state of mind than any other book. He embodies the sayings and doings of hundreds of others whose only memorials are on tombstones or in genealogies; he endures the inns in silence; never ate nor drank nor saw a coin or a poor man, for aught he says; passed the country in haste, ignoring the scenery except where "clas-

sical" authors had praised it, considered the
Alps a nuisance, and democratic governments a
degraded, albeit successful, eccentricity; and hastened past the Lago di Garda, in spite of the
new fortress in building there, to Brescia, the latter being "better worth seeing." It was just 1600
when he travelled, and the ideas of the year are
reflected in his opening lines with an exactitude
possible only to one who has the mind of his contemporaries and none of his own. "Peace having
been made, I saw I could not be any use in France."
So he employed his idleness in attempting to
learn something, in noting the differences in countries and peoples. Yet he would not be the Average Tourist made perfect that he is if there was not
some idea of the future hovering in him — he is
the only traveller, except Sir Henry Blount, the
philosopher, who notes, or even seems to note,
that the chief factor of differences between human
being and human being is geography.

Yet underneath all the special characteristics
which distinguish every one of these tourists from
every other, there remains one that all share with
each other and with us, that expressed with the
crude controversial Elizabethan vigour in some
lines which Thomas Nashe wrote towards the
close of the sixteenth century — "'Countryman,
tell me what is the occasion of thy straying so
far . . . to visit this strange nation?' . . . 'That
which was the Israelites' curse we . . . count our

chief blessedness: he is nobody that hath not travelled'"—the sense of the inexhaustible pleasure of travel. Had it been otherwise they would not have cared to write down their experiences; nor we to read them. And if at times it is hard to find a reflection of their pleasure in what they have written, it is certainly there, if only between the lines, manifesting how this continual variety of human beings is brought into touch, even if unconsciously, with the infinite change and range of the ideas and efforts of millions of persons over millions upon millions of acres, each person and each acre with its own history, life, fate, and influence. If, too, in the course of summarising what they experienced, the more trivial details seem to occupy a larger proportion of the space than is their due, it may be suggested that that is the proportion in which they appear in the tourists' reminiscences.

The permanent undercurrent I have tried to suggest where circumstances bring it to the surface in some one of its more definite forms.

CHAPTER II

GUIDE-BOOKS AND GUIDES

Now resteth in my memory but this point, which indeed is the chief to you of all others; which is, the choice of what men you are to direct yourself to; for it is certain no vessel can leave a worse taste in the liquor it contains, than a wrong teacher infects an unskilful hearer with that which will hardly ever out.

Sir Philip Sidney's advice to his brother
(about 1578).

FROM what has been said already, two conclusions may be drawn: first, that the Average Tourist was given much advice; secondly, that he did not take it. Let us too, then, see the theory for one chapter only; and, in all chapters after, the practice.

It must have amused many a youngster to hear the down-trodden old gentleman, whom his father had hired, setting forth how the said youngster must behave in wicked Italy if he was to grow up in favour with God and man; all the more so if the old gentleman, whose name, perhaps, was the local equivalent for John Smith, published his advice in Latin under a Latin pseudonym, say, Gruberus or Plotius. Gruberus and Plotius suggest themselves because they are the very guidiest of guide-book writers. They, like all the orthodox of their kind, begin by a solemn argument for and against travelling. They bring up to support them a most miscellaneous host: the Prophets, the Apostles, Daedalus, Ulysses, the Queen of Sheba, Theseus, Anacharsis, the "Church of Christ," Pythagoras, Plato, Abraham, Aristotle, Apollonius of Tyana, Euclid, Zamolxis, Lycurgus, Naomi, Cicero, Galen, Dioscorides, him who travelled from farthest Spain to see Livy ("and immediately," as some one most unkindly says, "immediately he saw him, went away"); Solon also and St. Paul, and Mithridates, the Roman Decemviri, Diodorus Siculus, Strabo, Pausanias, Cluverius, Moses, Orpheus, Draco, Minos, Rhadamanthus, Æsculapius, Hippocrates, Avicenna, the physicians of Egypt and the gods of Greece. But there is not a word about Jonah; perhaps his luck and experiences were considered abnormal; or perhaps because, as Howell says, "he travelled much, but saw little."

Then there are those who have to be refuted or explained away: Socrates, Seneca, the Lacedaemonians, Athenians, Chinese, Muscovites, Psophidius, Elianus, and Pompeius Laetus. Cain, also, the first traveller, creates a prejudice. Likewise, the argument from experience has to be met. Some return from travel, they say, using phrases without meaning, pale, lean, scabby and wormeaten, burdens on their consciences, astounding garments on their backs, with the manners of an actor and superciliously stupid. Yet is this not due to the thing itself, but to the abuse thereof;

peradventure he shall be corrupted more quickly at home than abroad, and there is less to be feared from universities and strange lands than from the indulgent mother. Moreover "non nobiliora quam mobiliora"; the heavens rejoice in motion, and transplantation yieldeth new life to plants. And shall the little sparrow travel as he pleases and man, lord of the animals, be confined to a farm or a hamlet?

Reason, erudition and emotion having thus conquered, instruction begins. The forethought necessary is as great as if he were choosing a wife. For tutors and horses, it seems, the most that can be expected from them is that they shall not imperil his soul and body respectively. First among requisites is a book of prayers and hymns effective for salvation without being so pugnacious, doctrinally, as to cause suspicion. Next, a note-book, a watch, or a pocket sun-dial; if a watch, not a striker, for that warns the wicked you have cash; a broad-brimmed hat, gaiters, boots, breeches (as if his friends would let him start without any!), gloves, shoes, shirts, handkerchiefs, "which come in useful when you perspire"; and if he cannot take many shirts, let those he takes be washed, he will find it more comfortable. Also, a linen overall, to put over his clothes when he gets into bed, in case the bed is dirty. Let him get to know something of medicine and, "like Achilles," learn to cook before he leaves home. Travel not at night, and, in daytime, be guarded by the official guards which German and Belgian towns provide; or travel in company.

Now, the aim of travelling is the acquisition of knowledge; stay, therefore, in the more famous places rather than keep on the move. Enquire, concerning the district, its names, past and present; its language; its situation; measurements; number of towns, or villages; its climate, fertility; whether maritime or not, and possessing forests, mountains, barren or wooded; wild beasts, profitable mines; animal or vegetable life peculiar to itself; navigable or fish-yielding rivers; medicinal baths; efficient fortresses. And concerning towns: the founder,"sights," free or otherwise; what the town has undergone, famines, plagues, floods, fires, sieges, revolutions, sackings; whether it has been the scene of councils, conferences, synods, assemblies, gatherings, or tournaments.

It should be mentioned that in this last paragraph I am paraphrasing Gruberus only, and presume he is confining himself to what the young tourist should discover before breakfast; otherwise he is but a superficial instructor compared to Plotius. The latter draws up a series of questions, which include enquiries about weights and ˉmeasures; about the clergy, how many and what salaries; religion, is it "reformed"? if so, what has happened to monks and nuns; how often Communion is administered; and whether strangers

are received thereat; arrangements for burial.
This last question would seem more in place at the
end, but it is only number thirty-six, and there
are one hundred and seventeen questions altogether. Then, is there a University? and, if so,
may the rector whack the students? and concerning the professors, what they teach and what they
are paid. As for local government, the enquiries
exhaust possibilities. Also, how many houses; and
what about night-watchmen; legal procedure;
"ancient lights," the right to use water, execu-
tors' duties, grounds for divorce, dress, military
training? Furthermore: are the roads clean, and
can children marry without their parents' consent?
concerning methods of cookery, and antiquity of
the town; whether the position of an officer of justice is a respected one or not; concerning notaries
public; and whether the water used in cooking
comes from river, fountain, well, or rain; how
many varieties of grain are used in bread-making;
and what means have they for dealing with fires;
their sanitary arrangements and public holidays,
with the reasons for the latter; care of paupers,
orphans, and lepers; what punishments for what
crimes.

It must not be imagined that Gruberus and
Plotius thought of all this by themselves: they
copied others, being but two among many. Where
the copying reached its most uncritical extreme
was in the origins ascribed to towns: Paris, the

guide-books say, was founded by a Gaul of that name who lived two hundred years before his namesake of Troy; Haarlem is also named after its founder "Herr (*i.e.*, Mr.) Lem"; Toulouse dated from the time of the prophetess Deborah; and so on.

But to consider the foregoing instructions, and even these three "facts," on their humorous side only, is to miss much of their interest. Two, for instance, of these etymologies are but examples of what is not only continually coming into notice in books of this date, but is especially noticeable in guide-books and tourists' notes, in which latter the habit of mind of the time is more exactly mirrored in its daily attitude than in any other class of books. They exemplify the two sources of knowledge of antiquity, the two standards of comparison, then available: classical and biblical; of more nearly equal authority than they were before or have been since; and they were the only ones. So with the objects of enquiry: they are implied by that lack of reference books from which not only the tourist, but governments also, suffered; it is clear, for example, that in 1592 much elementary information was not at hand, even in manuscript, in England.[1] The Tsar, moreover, about this time addressed a letter to the "Governor of the High Signiory of Venice," his advisers thinking that Venice was governed by a nominee of the Pope; and Rivadeneyra, who was very well-informed about affairs English, says in his "Cisma de Inglaterra," written thirty years after the reform of the English currency under Elizabeth: "The gold and silver currency is not so pure nor so fine as it was before heresy entered into the kingdom, for in the time of Henry VIII and his children Edward and Elizabeth, it has been falsified and alloyed with other metals, and so the money is worth much less than it used to be." Camden again, who wrote his Annals of Elizabeth's Reign early in the next century to correct misconceptions to which foreign scholars were liable, thought it necessary, when he mentioned Dublin, to explain that it was the chief city of Ireland; and very reasonably, too, considering that one of Henry VIII's officials in Ireland wrote home: "Because the country called Leinster and the situation thereof is unknown to the King and his Council, it is to be understood that Leinster is the fifth part of Ireland." [2] And there was a certain gentleman at the court of King James I, supposed to be an authority on things Continental, who answered, when asked for information about Venice, that he could not give much because he had ridden post through it—and it was not till the questioner got there that he became aware that Venice was surrounded by water; just as the secretary of a Spanish duke in England writes that his master took ship from "Calais, because, England being an island, it cannot be approached by land."

It may perhaps seem that the absence of knowledge which is ordinary now, indicated by the above illustrations, was extraordinary rather than ordinary even then. But the fact was that, besides the available books being practically always too much behind the times for any but antiquaries' purposes, the writers themselves had so little information at hand that it was only here and there their writings were anything but hopelessly superficial, even when obtained; and to obtain them was no easy matter. There were at least three men who published practical handbooks in English for Continental travelling later than Andrew Boorde and earlier than Howell; yet they, and Howell also, each claim that theirs is the first book of its kind in English. Whether the statement is made in good faith, or for business purposes, it proves equally well that even if a book was written, it was not easy to find.

Or again, take a book which was so often republished as to be easy to obtain, the "Viaggio da Venetia al Santo Sepolcro," for instance, the authorship of the later editions of which is ascribed to one Father Noë, a Franciscan. The first edition seems to be that of 1500, and it continued to be reprinted down to 1781; at least thirty-four editions came out before 1640, when the period under consideration ends. It was not, however, an Italian book originally, having been translated from a German source which was in existence as early

as 1465, if not earlier.[3] Since, therefore, its information was never thoroughly revised, at any
rate, not before 1640, sixteenth-century and seventeenth-century pilgrims went on buying mid-fif-
teenth-century information. They were recommended, for instance, to go by the pilgrim galley,
which ceased to run about 1586; and also to take
part in a festival held yearly on the banks of the
Jordan at Epiphany, which must have been abandoned far earlier even than that.

Still, books about what there was to notice in
given places did exist just as there were treatises
of the Gruberus and Plotius kind unfolding what
should be noticed in general, and why. Best
known of the earlier kind was Münster's gigantic
"Cosmography," which Montaigne regretted he
had not brought with him; and by the middle of
the seventeenth century several other first-rate
geographers, besides minor men, had compiled
books of the kind. But the bearing of such books
on our subject is only in so far as they reflect the
thoughts, and ministered to the needs, of the
tourist; and they may therefore be best considered in the works of those who wrote "Itineraries," which not only recorded journeys but were
meant to serve as examples of how a journey
might be made the most of. Such a book was
Hentzner's, a sort of link between Gruberus and
Fynes Moryson. Hentzner was a Silesian who
acted as guide and tutor to a young nobleman

from 1596 to 1600. They began, and ended, their journey at Breslau, and toured through Germany, France, Switzerland, Italy, and England; the "Itineraria" being based on notes made by the way. His account of England does him rather more than justice, for there is some first-hand experience there, which is just what is lacking in the rest of his book. Practically everything he says is second-hand, and the fact of his being at a place is merely a peg to hang quotations on. When he is not quoting from books he seems to be quoting from people; and half of what we expect from a guide-book is absent: means of conveyance, for instance. This is an omission, however, which can be explained: he was only concerned with the most respectable form of travelling, and that meant, on horseback. And the rest of his omissions, taken all together, throw into relief the academic character of the book, due, not to himself individually so much as to the period. His preface cannot, naturally, differ much from Plotius, nor add much, except in recommending Psalms 91, 126, 127, and 139 as suitable for use by those about to travel, forgetting, it would seem, the one beginning, "When Israel went forth out of Egypt," which Pantagruel had sung by his crew before they set out to find the "Holy Bottle"; and being a Protestant he cannot recommend the invocation of St. Joseph and St. Anthony of Padua, the patron saints of travellers; all he can do is to pray at the beginning for good angels to guard his footsteps, and, at the end, to acknowledge assistance from one, although it does not appear that he ever went to the length of Uhland's traveller: —

> Take, O boatman, thrice thy fee, —
> Take, I give it willingly;
> For, invisible to thee,
> Spirits twain have crossed with me,

and paid a fare for the good angel. On the way, having reached, say Rome, he does not, in Baedeker's merciful fashion, tell you the hotels first, in order of merit, but begins straightway: "ROME. Mistress and Queen of Cities, in times past the head of well-nigh all the world, which she had subjected to her rule by virtue of the sublime deeds of the most stout-hearted of men. Concerning the first founders thereof there are as many opinions, and as different, as there are writers. Some there are who think that Evander, in his flight from Arcadia," etc. Yet no one could write over six hundred pages about a four years' tour in sixteenth-century Europe without being valuable at times; partly in relation to ideas, partly to experiences into which those ideas led him and his pupils.

It was less than twenty years after Hentzner that another German published a record of travel which was also meant as a guide. But time had worked wonders; it was not only a personal differ-

ence between the former and Zinzerling that
accounts for the difference in their books; it was
the increase in the number of tourists. The latter
sketches out a plan by means of which all France
can be seen at the most convenient times and most
thoroughly without waste of time, with excursions to England, the Low Countries, and Spain.
Routes are his first consideration; other hints
abound. At St. Nicholas is a host who is a terror
to strangers; and remember that at Saint-Savin,
thirty leagues from Bourges, is the shanty of
"Philemon and Baucis" where you can live for
next to nothing; and that outside the gate at
Poictiers is a chemist who speaks German, and so
on. Frequently, indeed, he notes where you may
find your German understood; and also where
you should learn, and where avoid learning,
French.

Advice of this last-mentioned kind calls to
mind a third class of guide-books, intended to
assist those who, without them, would realise
how vain is the help of man when he can't understand what you say. The need for such became
more and more evident as time went on and
Latin became less and less the living and international language it had been but recently. The
use of vernaculars was everywhere coming to the
front as nationalities developed further, and in
many districts where it had been best known its
disuse in Church hastened its disuse outside.

The extent to which Latin was current about 1600 varied in almost every country. Poland and Ireland came first, Germany second, where many of all classes spoke it fluently, and less corruptly than in Poland. Yet an Englishman[4] passing through Germany in 1655 found but one inn-keeper who could speak it. The date suggests that the Thirty Years' War was responsible for the change. It is certainly true that France in the previous half century was far behind Germany in the matter of speaking Latin, as a result of the civil wars there. Possibly the characters of its rulers had something to do with this too, just as in England, where Latin was ordinarily spoken by the upper classes, according to Mory-son, with ease and correctness, the accomplishments of Queen Elizabeth as a linguist had doubtless set a fashion. This much, at least, is certain: that in 1597 when an ambassador from Poland was unexpectedly insolent in his oration, the Queen dumbfounded him by replying on the spot with as excellent Latinity as spirit, whereas at Paris once, when a Latin oration was expected from another ambassador, not only could not the King reply, but not even any one at court. With Montaigne the case was certainly different, but then his father had had him taught Latin before French, and consequently, on his travels, so soon as he reached a stopping-place, he introduced himself to the local priest, and though neither knew the other's native language, they passed their evening conversing without difficulty.

Very many were the interesting interviews that many a tourist had which he owed to a knowledge of Latin; the extent to which knowledge was acquired orally having led to its being an ordinary incident in the life of the tourist to pay a call on the learned man of the district; a duty with the Average Tourist, a pleasure for the others. And Latin was the invariable medium, part of the respectability of the occasion. At least, not quite invariable: when the historian De Thou visited the great Sigonius, they talked Italian, because the latter, in spite of a lifetime spent in becoming the chief authority on Roman Italy, spoke Latin with difficulty.

It seems curious that Latin should have been less generally understood south, than north, of the Alps, but such was the fact. Italy was, however, ahead of Spain, where even an acquaintance with Latin was rare. In the first quarter of the sixteenth century Navagero found Alcalá the only university where lectures were delivered in Latin, and, according to the best of the guidebook writers on Spain, Zeiler, the doctorate at Salamanca could be obtained, early in the seventeenth century, without any knowledge of Latin at all; while it has been shown by M. Cirot, the biographer of Mariana, that the latter's great history of Spain, published in Latin at this time, and as successful as a book of the kind ever is in its own day, was unsaleable until translated into Spanish.

Among those, too, who did know Latin there was the barrier of differing pronunciation. Lauder of Fountainhall was very much at sea to begin with, in spite of his Scotch pronunciation being much nearer to the French than an Englishman's would have been, and there is an anecdote in Vicente Espinel's "Marcos de Obregon" which is to the point here. The latter is a novel, it is true, but the tradition that it is semi-autobiographical is borne out by many of its tales reading as if they were actual experiences, of which the following is one. One day, the hero, a Spaniard, found himself in a boat on the river Po, with a German, an Italian, and a Frenchman, and to pass the time they tried to talk Latin so that all could understand each one; but they soon abandoned the plan, as the pronunciations varied too greatly.

Nevertheless, the passing of Latin out of European conversation is to be attributed rather to the growth of Italian, and later of French, as international tongues. Gaspar Ens, who wrote a series of guides to nearly every part of Europe, says in his preface to the volume on France, "At this day their language is so much used in almost every part of the world that whosoever is unskilled therein is deemed a yokel." This was in

1609, at which date, or soon after, it was as true as a general statement can be expected to be; just as much so as the assertion in the preface to an English book in 1578: "Once every one knew Latin . . . now the Italian is as widely spread." [5]

It was only in the north that French came to rival Italian during this period, for the "lingua franca," also known as "franco piccolo," the hybrid tongue in which commerce was conducted along the shores of the Mediterranean, was so largely Italian that to the average Britisher, from whom Hakluyt drew his narratives, the two were indistinguishable; but an Italian would notice, as Della Valle did, that no form of a verb but the infinitive was used. If any one was met who knew more than two languages, he would oftenest be a Jew, who usually knew Spanish and Portuguese; the latter because the tribe of Judah, from which their deliverer was to come, was supposed to be domiciled in Portugal.

Another hybrid language, as well established in its own area as the "lingua franca," was Scot-French, so constantly in use as to have an existence as a literary dialect as well as in French burlesque. These mixed languages have no place in the ordinary book-guide to languages, but were left to personal tuition; yet in the lists of the most common phrases which Andrew Boorde appends to each of his descriptions of countries may be noted a curious instance from this border-

land of philology. In both the Italian and the
Spanish lists he renders "How do you fare?"
by "Quo modo stat cum vostro corps?"

While we are on this subject we may stop to
sympathise with awkward misunderstandings like
that of the Jesuit Possevino at Moscow, when
invited to (Orthodox) Mass ("obednia") with
intent to compromise him; he went, thinking it
was dinner ("obed") to which he had been asked.
Then there are those, too, whose efforts were
hopelessly below even this standard, such as
Alonzo de Guzman, who suffered hunger in Germany because he only knew Spanish, and was
put on the road to Bologna when he wanted to get
to Cologne; or the Englishman who was trying
to find that same road and went along staggering
the peasantry with the question, "Her ist das der
raight stroze auf balnea?" the peasantry replying
by signs that he interpreted as directions, but
the road led him further than ever from Baden.
To which class belonged a certain friend of Josias
Bodley, younger brother of the founder of the
Bodleian library and author of by far the liveliest
account of a tour at this period,[6] will never be
known, but that is no reason why the tale should
not be re-told. "Not long ago I was in company
with some boon companions who were drinking
healths in usquebagh, when one was present who
wished to appear more abstemious than the rest
and would not drink with them, to whom one

of them, who could not speak Latin as well as
I do, said these words, 'Si tu es plus sapientis
quam nos sumus, tu es plus beholden to God
Almighty quam nos sumus.'" And finally there
are those who find themselves reduced to sign-
language, such as the Roman Catholics who
found a sumptuous dinner awaiting them at a
Protestant inn on a fast-day, when, to add to the
trial of refusing it, was the apparent impossibility
of making their wants understood, until one of
their number, a priest, by the way, imitated a
hen's cackle and "laid" a piece of white paper
the shape and size of an egg!

While conversation-dictionaries existed which
claimed to be useful their claim has no other
basis than that of their own prefaces; the tourists
do not own to indebtedness to them. But taking
it for granted that primary needs must be served
by persons, not books, for further acquirements
Moryson recommends the romance of "Amadis
de Gaule" which was being read by every one in
his own tongue. Probably the conversation-books
are of more use now than at the time of
their publication, from the light they occasionally
throw on customs, and, through their phonet-
icism, on pronunciation. Yet the tourists' own
evidence as to this is more valuable, as being
more authentic, when an Englishman writes
"Landtaye" for "Landtage" and "Bawre" for
"Bauer." As for sixteenth-century maps, they

seem meant for gifts rather to an enemy than to a friend. In every department, then, the tourist had recourse to persons.

The qualifications for a first-rate guide, then and now, differ in one respect only, — that a "religious test" should be applied was taken for granted on both sides. In fact, in Scotland in 1609 an edict was issued forbidding young noblemen to leave the country without a Protestant tutor: the reason being that the great danger of a tour abroad lay in a possible change in the youngster's religion, or inclinations towards tolerance developing, with the result that his political career on his return might be dangerous to his country and himself through his being more than the just one step ahead of his fellow-countrymen which is necessary to political salvation.

The prevailing state of mind may be illustrated by one or two anecdotes. The following one Lauder tells of himself is characteristic of his kind. He had entered a church where all were on their knees: "a woman observing that I neither had gone to the font for holy water, neither kneeled, in a great heat of zeal she told me 'ne venez icy pour prophaner ce sainct lieu.' I suddenly replied: 'Vous estez bien devotieuse, madame, mais peut estre vostre ignorance prophane ce sainct lieu d'avantage que ma présence.'" William Lithgow is proud to say he quarrelled with companions simply because they were

Papists, and had often seized opportunities to
tear in pieces the rich garments on images rather
than "with indifferent forbearance wink at the
wickedness of idolaters." And an Englishman
of good education and breeding and character,
says that being at Malaga cathedral during High
Mass "so long as we were bare-headed and behaved ourselves civilly and gravely, we might
walk up and down and see everything without
the least molestation." One extreme was naturally accompanied by another extreme. Sometimes the tourist's return never took place. This
was the more likely when the Papacy was in a
militant mood, at which times the Inquisition developed a taste for tutors; whose arrest served
a double purpose, a hot antagonist was secured,
unimportant enough to create no serious trouble,
and the young nobleman was left undefended
on his sectarian side, probably a vulnerable one.
One case of many is that of John Mole,[7] who died
in the prison of the Inquisition at Rome in 1638
at the age of eighty, after thirty years' imprisonment; his ward, Lord Roos, having been credited
with no particular desire to get him out.

A visit to Rome, however, and to other places,
such as St. Omer, where "seminaries" existed for
English Roman Catholics, was usually forbidden
in the licence to go abroad which every Englishman had to obtain unless he was a merchant, and
which was not granted without good reason

shown. This contained ordinarily a time limit also, one year's leave, or three; and prohibition of communication with disloyal countrymen or entry into a State at war with England: supervision of a kind which was exercised by practically every European ruler. A Roman Catholic, for instance, incurred excommunication if he passed into a country at war with the Pope.

The precautions of Protestant sovereigns were against Roman Catholicism inasmuch as there lay political dangers, but so far as religion was concerned, as much precaution might reasonably have been taken against Mohammedanism. In no European country did ability bring a man to the top so readily as in Turkey, and being a foreigner was in a man's favour; not even at Venice was there such a mixture of nations as at Constantinople; the majority of the Grand Signor's eminent subjects were renegade foreigners. Dallam might refuse the invitation; many accepted it; and a Turk considered it only humane to give an unbeliever at least one definite invitation to salvation. An occasion which many would make use of to turn Turk was during the fortnight preceding the circumcision of the Sultan's heir. One traveller saw two hundred circumcised at such a time, many of them adult, one said to be as old as fifty-three. As a particular instance of an English "Turk" there is the case of the English Consul at Cairo in 1601. He was "taking care" of

much belonging to English merchants at the time,
in the possession of which the Turks no doubt
confirmed him. At the same time there was an
exactly similar case of a Venetian, for the same purpose. But besides the causes of the chance to
rise in the world, or the attractions of others' property, there was another reason for apostacy, the
chief one — mitigating the sufferings of captivity.

But the renegades came mostly from the lower
or the commercial class, and did not come home,
so that the fact that a guide was required to be a
sectarian, in contradistinction to a Christian, is
another comment on the characteristics of the
Average Tourist. Sir Walter Ralegh, however,
did not make that a qualification, for he chose
Ben Jonson to chaperon his son. There is only
one anecdote about Ben Jonson in that capacity,
the one he told Drummond himself. "This
youth" [*i. e.*, Ralegh's son] "being knavishly
inclined, caused him to be drunken, and dead
drunk, so that he knew not where he was; thereafter laid him on a car, which he made to be
drawn through the streets, at every corner showing his governor stretched out and telling them
that was a more lively image of the Crucifix than
any they had: at which young Ralegh's mother
delighted much (saying his father when young
was so inclined), though the father abhorred it."

Another sixteenth-century guide immortalised
by another's pen is Jean Bouchet, "Traverseur

de Voies Perilleuses" as he called himself. Not
that Rabelais, to whom the pen belonged, names
him, only he applies this nickname to the guide
of Pantagruel and company, Xenomanes (*i. e.*,
"mad on foreigners"). No easy task to be an
orthodox guide with Friar John at one's elbow;
for guide-book etymologies Friar John had no
taste; only asked, "What's that to do with me?
I was n't in the country when it was baptised!"
A guide to suit Friar John would have been some
disciple of Montaigne, who while agreeing with
the others that travelling was one of the best
forms of education thought that it was not "pour
en rapporter seulement, à la mode de nostre
noblesse françoise, combien de pas a 'Santa
Rotonda,' ou la richesse des calessons de la sig-
nora Livia; ou, comme d'aultres, combien le
visage de Neron, de quelque vieille ruyne de là,
est plus long ou plus large que celuy de quelque
pareille medaille, mais pour rapporter principale-
ment les humeurs de ces nations et leur façons,
et pour frotter et limer nostre cervelle contre celle
d'aultruy."

Others, too, like Montaigne, without setting
out to write guide-books, have guidance to offer
as a result of experience of life and travel; sometimes in letters, sometimes in chance remarks.
Letters of this kind which have survived are
many, but so much alike are they as to suggest
that the fathers shrunk from explaining to the

sons how they themselves had made the most of
their time and fell back on unacknowledged quotations from a Gruberus. Of the few frank ones
the two best are by Sir Philip Sidney to his
brother, and by the ninth Earl of Northumberland to his son Algernon.[8] Although the latter
is nearly as encyclopædic as Plotius, it is so
merely in the way of suggestion, discussing only
motives and ideas and insisting on his son's freedom of choice, in general as well as in detail; with
one or two remarks added that would have scandalised the guide-book writer, but leaven the
whole of the letter. It is especially interesting
as showing how the idea of travel as a factor in
life brought out the best of a man who was a
failure at home from a day-by-day point of view.

As for chance remarks: one likens travelling
to death in so far as it means separation from
friends, letters, moreover, yielding as little satisfaction as prayers; and whereas the wise say that
death is the entrance to a happier life, there is
the opposite prospect with travel, so that it has
all the disadvantages of hell as well as of death.
And here may follow a few more remarks of
theirs, chosen as suggestive of the characteristics
of sixteenth-century travel in so far as it differs
from our own, not neglecting proverbs: —

A traveller has need of a falcon's eye, an ass's
ears, a monkey's face, a merchant's words, a
camel's back, a hog's mouth, a deer's feet. And

the traveller to Rome — the back of an ass, the belly of a hog, and a conscience as broad as the king's highway.

Line your doublet with taffetie; taffetie is lice-proof.

Never journey without something to eat in your pocket, if only to throw to dogs when attacked by them.

Carry a note-book and red crayon (*i. e.*, lead pencils were not in regular use).

When going by coach, avoid women, especially old women; they always want the best places.

At sea, remove your spurs; sailors make a point of stealing them from those who are being sea-sick. Keep your distance from them in any case; they are covered with vermin.

In an inn-bedroom which contains big pictures, look behind the latter to see they do not conceal a secret door, or a window.

Women should not travel at all and married men not much.

CHAPTER III

ON THE WATER

Chi può venire per mare non è lontano.
PAOLO SARPI, 1608.[1]

HENTZNER, in his preface, acknowledges that the troubles of a traveller are great and finds only two arguments to countervail them: that man is born unto trouble, and that Abraham had orders to travel direct from God. Abraham, however, did not have to cross the Channel. Otherwise, perhaps, the prospect of sacrificing himself as well as his only son Isaac, would have brought to light a flaw in his obedience. There was, it is true, the chance of crossing from Dover to Calais in four hours, but the experiences of Princess Cecilia, already related, were no less likely. In 1610 two Ambassadors waited at Calais fourteen days before they could make a start, and making a start by no means implied arriving — at least, not at Dover; one gentleman, after a most unhappy night, found himself at Nieuport next morning and had to wait three days before another try could be made. Yet another, who had already sailed from Boulogne after having waited six hours for the tide, accomplished two leagues, been becalmed for

nine or ten hours, returned to Boulogne by rowing-
boat, and posted to Calais, found no wind to take
him across there and had to charter another
rowing-boat at sunset on Friday, reaching Dover
on Monday between four and five A. M. It was
naturally a rare occurrence to go the whole distance by small boat, because of the risk. Lord
Herbert of Cherbury was the most noteworthy
exception; after he had made three attempts from
Brill and covered distances which varied from
just outside the harbour to half-way, arriving
at Brill again, however, each time, he went by
land to Calais, where the sea was so dangerous
that no one would venture, no one except one
old fisherman, whose boat, he himself owned,
was one of the worst in the harbour, but, on the
other hand, he did not mind whether he lived
or died.

But finishing the crossing by rowing-boat was
a very ordinary experience because of the state
of the harbours. Calais was the better of the two,
yet it sometimes happened that passengers had
to be carried ashore one hundred yards or more
because not even boats could approach. In 1576
an ambassador to France complains that Dover
harbour is in such utter ruin that he will cross
elsewhere in future; in 1580 Sir Walter Ralegh
procured reform, which was perpetually in need
of renewal. In time a stone pier was built, small,
and dry at low water, as indeed the whole harbour

was; the entrance was narrow and kept from being
choked up only by means of a gate which let out
the water with a rush at low tide. The ancient,
quicker route to Wissant, more or less the route
which "Channel-swimmers" make for now, had
begun to be abandoned when the English obtained a port of their own on the opposite coast,
and had been completely dropped by this time.
Boulogne had no cross-channel passenger traffic
worth mentioning. Dieppe, on the contrary, was
as much used as Calais, the corresponding harbour being, not Newhaven, but Rye, which was
also the objective on the rarer occasions when the
starting-place was Havre. So unusual was the
Havre-Southampton passage that among the suspicious circumstances alleged against a Genoese
who landed in 1599, one was his choice of this way
across.[2]

Going by the North Sea the usual havens were
Gravesend, and Flushing or Brill, in spite of
Brill's shallow harbour-bar, passed on one occasion with only two feet of water under the keel
when "Mr. Thatcher, a merchant of London,
who had goods therein, was so apprehensive that
he changed colours and said he was undone, 'Oh
Lord,' and such-like passionate expressions." Har-
wich was reputed so dangerous a harbour that
when Charles I's mother-in-law came to visit
her daughter in 1638 and put in there, she
found no one to receive her; it not being thought

within possibility to expect her to land there. The fact that she did was probably due to her having been seven days at sea in a storm; not that the courtier-chronicler of her voyage allows she was any the worse for it, although he owns of her ladies that "they touched the hearts of the beholders more with pity than with love." A forty-eight-hour passage was nothing to grumble at: Arthur Wilson, the historian of James I's reign, left Brill in an old twenty-five-ton mussel-boat, at the bottom of which he lay, sea-sick and expecting drowning, for three days and three nights until he came ashore at — the Hague.

Among many other experiences of the kind, that[3] of John Chamberlain, the letter-writer, may be chosen. Setting out from Rotterdam, after twenty-four hours' sailing, he had been within sight of Ostend and was back again at Rotterdam. There he stayed a fortnight, putting to sea at intervals and coming back. Then the wind came fair for Calais, but veered round rather too soon and the first haven they could reach was that of Yarmouth, after two days' running before the storm. It was low tide; they went aground while entering, and for some time it looked like being lost with all hands, but getting off again, the waves took the ship against the piles at the head of the breakwater. Some thought it worth while trying to jump ashore, three of whom the others saw drowned and one crushed to death

against the piles. But in the end the rest landed
safely in boats, and buried the dead; and Chamberlain himself, after a winter evening spent wandering about Newmarket heath in the rain and wind
through the guide losing his way, arrived in town
at 11 P. M. on the twentieth day after first leaving Rotterdam.

On this route the ownership of the vessel might
be guessed by the amount of swearing that went
on. Dutch ships had no prayers said, rarely
carried a chaplain even on the longest voyages,
but swearers were fined, even if it was no more
than naming the devil. Psalm-singing would go
on on any vessel manned by Protestants on
account of the popularity of the music written
for the Reformers, but if a vessel had a garland
of flowers hanging from its mainmast that again
would show it a Dutchman; it meant that the
captain was engaged to be married.

The passage-boats were about sixty feet long,
which then meant a tonnage of about the same
figure, and had a single deck, beneath which the
passengers might find shelter if the merchandise
left them room. The complement of passengers
may be taken as seventy. The highest total of
passengers I have found mentioned for one ship
is two thousand, of whom Della Valle was one,
but that was when he sailed from Constantinople
to Cairo, the vessels employed on official business
between those two places exclusively being the

largest in the world at that date. Apart from these, the maximum tonnage was about twelve hundred, and a 500-ton ship was reckoned a large one; an average Venetian merchantman measured about 90 feet × 20 × 16, a tonnage, that is, of about 166, according to English sixteenth-century reckoning.[4] The French traveller Villamont says the ship in which he left Venice in 1589 and which he was told cost fifty thousand crowns (say eighty-five thousand pounds of our money) to build and equip, had for its greatest length 188 feet and greatest breadth 59 feet.

As for accommodation in the larger boats, neither Dallam nor Moryson changed their clothes or slept in a bed while at sea, and there is no reason to suppose that any one else did who travelled under ordinary conditions. Cabins were to be had in the high-built sterns; even in Villamont's moderate-sized ship there were eight decks astern, the fourth from the keel, the captain's dining-room, accommodating thirty-nine persons at meal-times, all of whom, it is clear enough, slept in cabins above or below. Moryson, however, refused a cabin, preferring to sleep in a place where there was cover overhead but none at the sides.

The chief exception to ordinary conditions was the pilgrim-ship for Jerusalem in the days, which ceased during this period, when special galleys ran from Venice to Jaffa and back, in the summer. Here alone could the passenger have the upper hand, since these galleys alone were passenger-boats primarily. The captain would be willing, if asked, to bind himself in writing before the authorities at Venice, to take the pilgrim to Jaffa, wait there and bring him back, call at certain places to take in fresh water, meat, and bread, carry live hens, a barber-surgeon, and a physician, avoid unhealthy ports such as Famagosta, stay nowhere longer than three days without the consent of the pilgrim, receive no merchandise which might inconvenience or delay him, provide two hot meals a day and good wine, and guarantee the safety of any belongings he might leave in the galley during his absence at Jerusalem. No agreements, however, seem to have insured the pilgrim against starvation diet, and therefore it was prudent to store a chest with victuals, especially delicacies, and lay in wine; for, Venice once left behind, wine might be dearer or even unobtainable. Taking victuals implied buying a frying-pan, dishes, big and little, of earthenware or wood, a stew-pot, and a twig-basket to carry when he landed and went shopping. Likewise a lantern and candles and bedding, which might be purchased near St. Mark's; a feather-bed, mattress, two pillows, two pairs of sheets, a small quilt, for three ducats; and all of these will be bought back at the end of the voyage at half price. Medicines he must on no account forget. Care had to be taken, too, in choosing a position, not below deck, which is "smouldering hot and stinking," but above, where both shelter, light, and air were to be had; this, of course, for the benefit of such as were unable to secure a place in the stern-cabins.

If the passenger did not find himself in a position to get these counsels of perfection carried out, this is what he would experience: "In the galley all sorts of discomfort are met with: to each of us was allotted a space three spans broad, and so we lay one upon another, suffering greatly from the heat in summer and much troubled by vermin. Huge rats came running over our faces at nights, and a sharp eye had to be kept on the torches, for some people go about carelessly and there's no putting them out in case of fire, being, as they are, all pitch. And when it is time to go to sleep and one has great desire thereto, others near him talk or sing or yell and generally please themselves, so that one's rest is broken. Those near us who fell ill mostly died. God have mercy on them! In day-time too when we were all in our places busy eating and the galley bore down on the side to which the sail shifted, all the sailors called out 'pando,' that is, 'to the other side,' and over we must go; and if the sea was rough and the galley lurched, our heads turned all giddy and some toppled over

and the rest on top of them, falling about like
so many drunken yokels. The meals the captain
gave us were not exactly inviting; the meat had
been hanging in the sun, the bread hard as a stone
with many weevils in it, the water at times stank,
the wine warm, or hot enough for the steam to
rise, with a beastly taste to it; and at times, too,
we had to do our eating under a blazing sun. . . .[5]
Bugs, etc., crept about over everything."[6] Another,
after many similar complaints, of cold food and
warm drink, and of sailors who walked about on
top of him when he wanted to sleep, and so on,
adds a fresh one, quite unmentionable, and then
goes on that he passes over the more disgusting
features so as not to discourage intending pilgrims.

The disappearance of the pilgrim galley was
more gain than loss, but it had the advantage
of more variety in the company and the voyage,
and probably, of a bigger ship; Moryson's ship
was 900-tons and Della Valle's Gran Delfino was
a great war galleon, with forty-five cannon and five
hundred passengers, — too many, it proved; in the
end twenty or thirty fell ill every day and some
died. And the mixture that there was! Men and women, soldiers, traders, Greeks, Armenians, Turks,
Persians, Jews, Italians from almost every state,
French, Spanish, Portuguese, English, Germans,
Flemings. In Moryson's boat there were Indian
sun-worshippers as well. In another, Moors and

Muscovites. Every day in the Gran Delfino a bell was rung for prayer, when each man prayed in his own way; prayer over, the sailors, all Greeks, turned bareheaded to the East and cried three times, "Buon' Viaggio!!!" and the captain preached a non-sectarian sermon. With the Gran Delfino, moreover, the start was an impressive function; the vessel, belonging as it did to the State, being towed beyond the lagoons by thirty-three eight-oared boats, directed by a venerable signor deputed by the authorities. Once outside, however, and left to itself, it was less impressive, at the mercy of a wind so uncertain that it crossed the Adriatic from shore to shore twenty-five times.

In reckoning the length of voyages it would not be sufficient to multiply the delay by bad weather that took place in the Channel crossings by the extra mileage of a given distance; there was the additional delay due to the difficulty of obtaining a ship at all, even in the best of weathers, a difficulty proportionate to the length of the voyage. The first-mentioned difficulty must not be minimised; it was reasonable caricature for Sir John Harington, Queen Elizabeth's godson, to represent his Rabelaisian hero as returning from "Japana near China" in a "24-hours sail with some two or three odd years beside." And by way of illustration it may be added that one and the same voyage — from Messina to Smyrna

— took one man thirteen weeks and another thirty-five days; and that whereas the usual length of the pilgrim voyage from Jaffa to Venice was under five weeks, one band of pilgrims whose return journey was delayed till the winter storms caught them, were continuously at sea, or continuously trying to be at sea, from September 19th till January 25th. Yet another cause of delay, in the Mediterranean, at least, was the Italian custom of paying the sailors by the day; English ships, payment on which was at so much a voyage, were by far the quicker.

To return to difficulty number two, that of obtaining any ship, instances of it are continually occurring. Consider the complaint that one Greenhalgh writes to his friend [7] — how he wished to go by sea to Naples or elsewhere in Italy, went to the Exchange at London almost daily for a month to read the ships' bills hanging there; could find none to take him; took passage at Blackwall on one that was bound for Dunkirk, but which the wind carried along the coast of Norfolk; reached Dunkirk in four days and four nights; no ship to be found there Italy-bound; nor at Gravelines; nor at Calais; so came back: seven weeks wasted.

But it may reasonably be asked, why did n't he go by land? Well, that is a question without an answer; but for any journey where the mileage by sea was near the mileage by land, men of experience of these days reckoned it safer and quicker and consequently cheaper to go by sea. Once when Sir Henry Wotton, who exhaled sixteenth-century wisdom whenever he spoke, was at his favourite occupation of holding forth to the Venetian Signory on things in general, we find him taking it for granted that Poland and Hungary were far from Venice as compared with England and Holland; an exaggeration, no doubt; but an exaggeration that stood no chance of being believed would not have served his purpose. And it would be just plain fact to say, with regard to Danzig and Paris, and every other similar journey, the sea for choice; even from Genoa to Rome, amid all the danger of captivity for life by Barbary pirates, there was a daily service of boats in 1588 according to Villamont; it was the more usual route. Howell, indeed, leaving Paris for Spain, went to St. Malo to find a ship, but the ordinary route was to go down the Loire to Nantes, and by sea thence.

In the same way, from Rome to Barcelona was usually made a sea-trip, although the sailors coasted instead of going direct. All voyages in fact were coasting voyages whenever possible; no landsman was more scared of the open sea than the average sailor during this period, the greatest for the exploration of oceans that the world has ever seen, except, perhaps, that unknown age when the islands of the Pacific were

colonised. The fear was based on an accurate
knowledge of their own incapacity, revealed to
us by one or two travellers who were interested
in the science of navigation. A certain Frenchman embarked at Vannes for Portugal; no bear-
ings were taken, and the pilot had no chart;
trusted to his eye for his knowledge; which resulted in his coasting along Galicia under the
impression it was Asturias. So with the master
of the Venetian ship that Lithgow sailed in;
he had no compass, cast anchor at night and
guessed his whereabouts in daytime by the hills
he recognised; on his way back from Alexandria
a storm drove them out of their course and he
describes, in his doggrel verse, the sailors spending hours identifying headlands, only to find themselves mistaken. Indeed, there was no satisfactory method of ascertaining longitude at sea;
although European rulers were offering rewards
to the inventor of a method, no one was successful
in trying to solve the problem, not even Galileo.[8]
So habitual a practice was coasting that if a ship
was intent on avoiding a pirate the surest plan
was to keep to the open sea.

But for the most part they seem to have
trusted to luck with regard to piracy, knowing
pirates to be as likely to be met with as storms.
The two chief centres were Dunkirk and Algiers,
and as the Dunkirkers and Algerines met in the
Atlantic, the Baltic was the only European sea

free from them, during the latter half of this period at least. In the earlier, war was so continual as to provide employment, or pretext, for the bulk of the scoundrels and unfortunates of the continent whom the comparative peace that succeeded turned loose on commerce, and consequently on tourists.

It was bad enough in the Channel before this. In 1573 the Earl of Worcester crossed with a gold salver as a christening present for Charles IX's daughter; the ship was attacked by pirates; eleven of his suite were killed or wounded and property worth five hundred pounds stolen. In 1584, Mr. Oppenheim states, the French ambassador complained that in the two preceding years English pirates had plundered Frenchmen of merchandise to the value of two hundred thousand crowns: the answer was that the English had lost more than that through French pirates. So in 1600 we find the Mayor of Exeter writing up about the Dunkirkers, "scarce one bark in five escapeth these cormorants."[9] Repression that was exercised by the governments on both sides of the Channel had the effect of making the Mediterranean worse than it had been, for the pirates, especially English, not only followed their occupation there themselves but taught the Turks and Algerines far more about navigation than the latter would have discovered by themselves. Which, by the way, had a further result adverse to English tourists, for the Italian states that had previously been favourably inclined to England, Venice and Tuscany, both of European importance, grew unfriendly; Tuscany becoming definitely hostile.

But the state of the Mediterranean for men of all nationalities was such that it would probably be difficult to find a detailed account of a voyage during the first half of the seventeenth century which does not mention meeting an enemy. What might happen then is best illustrated in the experience of a Russian monk of rather earlier date: "half-way, a ship full of pirates attacked us. When their cannon had shattered our boat, they leapt on board like savage beasts and cut the ship's master to pieces and threw him into the sea, and took all they found. As for me, they gave me a blow in the stomach with the butt-end of a lance, saying 'Monk, give us a ducat or a gold piece.' I swore by the living God, by God Almighty, that I had none such. They bereft me of my all, leaving me nought but my frock and took to running all about the ship like wild beasts waving glittering lances, swords and axes. . . ."

Storms also were accompanied by incidents out of a present-day tourist's experience, to a greater extent than would readily be imagined; and this especially in the Mediterranean, where a large proportion of the sailors were Greeks with

vivid superstitions, and courage but one day a
year, that of St. Catherine, the patroness of
sailors, when nobody ever got drowned. Other
days it required very little danger to make them
abandon themselves to despair and to all the
signs of it which were most likely to distract and
demoralise the more level-headed; one by one
their relics would go overboard in attempted
propitiation, and the tourist was in danger of
following in person if he was suspected of being
no good Christian and therefore the probable
cause of the storm. Such is the recorded experience of more than one; and a priest who had been
in the habit of reading a Bible was threatened
with ejection as a sorcerer, and his books with
him; fortunately the storm abated when the sailors had reached that point.

It may safely be said that control of the weather
by sorcerers was altogether disbelieved in by very
few persons then, but if the belief was held more
strongly along one coast-line than another, it was
round the Baltic rather than elsewhere. As late
as 1670[10] a traveller tells us how being becalmed
off Finland, the captain sent ashore to buy a wind
from a wizard; the fee was ten kroner (say thirty-
six shillings) and a pound of tobacco. The wizard
tied a woollen rag to the mast, with three knots
in it. Untying the first knot produces just the
wind they want; S. W.; that slackening, untying
knot number two revives it for a time; but knot

number three brings up a fearful northeaster
which nearly sank them. "Qui nescit orare, dis-
cat navigare" was a much-quoted phrase; truly
enough of one traveller, it would appear, seeing
he is reported to have prayed during a storm; "O
Lord, I am no common beggar; I do not trouble
thee every day; for I never prayed to thee before;
and if it please thee to deliver me this once, I
will never pray to thee again as long as I live."

Shipwreck had an additional danger when it
happened to a galley rowed by forced labour.
Cardinal De Retz gives a vivid picture of what
happened when the one he was in ran aground.
The whole bank of galley-slaves rose; in fear, or
to escape by swimming, or to master the vessel
amidst the confusion. The commander and other
officers took double-edged swords and struck
down all whom they found standing. Even a
mere landing was not without risk, for the custom
in force almost universally of asking every new-
comer officially his business, home, destination,
was still more the rule at the coast; this same
cardinal, when a fugitive landing in shabby
clothes at St. Sebastian, was told by the soldiers
he would probably be hanged in the morning,
inasmuch as the ship's captain had mislaid his
"charte-partie," in the absence of which every
one in the ship could legally be hanged without
trial.

And if they had their special sea-troubles of

pirates and Greek sailors and small boats in high
seas, how much more certain was sea-sickness and
the length of its enduring. Lauder remembered
leaving Dover at 2 A. M. — "What a distressed
broker I was upon the sea needs not here be told
since it's not to be feared that I'll forget it, yet
I cannot but tell how Mr. John Kincead and I
had a bucket betwixt us and strove who should
have the bucket first, both equally ready; and
how at every vomit and gasp he gave he cried
'God's mercy' as if he had been about to expire
immediately." For preventives nobody has anything to suggest except, appropriately enough,
one Father Noah, a Franciscan, who prescribes
pomegranates and mint; and Rabelais, who says
that Pantagruel and company departed with full
stomachs and for that reason were not sea-sick;
a better precaution, he goes on, than drinking
water some days beforehand, salt or fresh, with
wine or meat, or than taking pulp of quinces, or
lemon-peel, or pomegranate juice; or fasting pre-
viously, or covering their |stomachs with paper.

Yet Panurge, who was always full or filling,
became sea-sick when the storm came. As a
picture of sea-sickness, Rabelais' account of
Panurge sea-sick is probably unsurpassed. "He
remained all of a heap on Deck, utterly cast down
and metagrobolised. 'What ho, Steward, my
Friend, my Father, my Uncle; . . . O, three and
four times happy are those who plant Cabbages

. . . they have always one Foot on Land and the other is not far from it. . . . This Wave will sweep us away, blessed Saviour. O my Friend, a little Vinegar; I sweat again with sheer Agony. . . . I am drowning, I am drowning, I am dying. Good people, I drown. . . . Ah, my Father, my Uncle, my All, the water has got into my Shoes, by my Shirt-collar. Bous, bous, bous; paisch; hu, hu, hu, ha, ha, ha, I drown . . . eighteen hundred thousand Crowns a year to the man who will put me ashore. . . . Holos, good People, I drown, I die. Consummatum est; it is all over with me. . . . My good man, could n't you throw me ashore?'" [11]

Sea-sickness was probably more common then than now because the discomforts were so much farther from being minimised. Moryson recommends passengers to take rose leaves, lemons or oranges, or the roots or the leaves of angelica, cloves, or rosemary, to counteract the evil smells of the boat; he might have added, of the company too, more particularly with reference to river traffic, because there the company was specially liable to be mixed by reason of the cheapness of that way of travelling as compared with horseback; and because the contact with each other was close.

It is not without signification that practically all district-maps of this date mark the courses of rivers, but not of roads. Probably few records

could be found of any touring of this period worth
calling a tour which was not partly conducted by
river. One advantage of river travel was that that
way was more regularly practicable than the
roads, which bad weather soon rendered barely
passable. Moreover, it was the pleasantest mode
of journeying, especially if the boat was towed;
for travelling in a sixteenth-century waggon produced something like sea-sickness in those unaccustomed to it. On the other hand, to get the
benefit of the cheapness of river travelling, as
compared with riding, one had to wait, at times,
for fellow-travellers to fill the boat; also, the
choice of route was, of course, more limited; and
on the swifter rivers it was not usual, or worth
while, to attempt an up-stream journey.

On the Loire, for instance, at Roanne, where it
began to be navigable, boats were all built for
sale, not for hire, as they were not expected to
come back; and the same practice was in use
elsewhere. But this must be taken as a rule with
many exceptions. On the lower Loire towing was
in regular use and Lady Fanshawe, who tried it,
right from Nantes to Orleans, says, "of all my
travels none were, for travel sake, as I may call
it, so pleasant as this." They went on shore to
sleep, but kept to the boat all daytime, for it
possessed a "hearth," a charcoal fire on which they
did the cooking. Where towing was most frequently used was probably Russia, all by hand;

sometimes as many as three hundred men were being employed at once by Charles II's ambassador for the six barges and one boat between Archangel and Vologda.

When rowing was to be done, the tourist found himself expected, practically compelled, to take his share on the Elbe and the Rhine, and often on other rivers too. The diarist Evelyn reckoned that he rowed twenty leagues of the distance between Roanne and Orleans, and no doubt Edmund Waller, the poet, did the same, as he was one of the party. If any exemptions were made, it was the boatman who exempted himself.

Another poet, or, at least, verse-writer, was deserted altogether by his boatman. This was John Taylor, on his way back from Prague. He had taken to the river at Leitmeritz, with his two companions and some one else's widow and her four small children, they having jointly bought a boat forty-eight feet by three. It was at the Saxony boundary that the man ran away, whence there were six hundred miles to cover, past one thousand "shelves and sands," eight hundred islands, and numberless tree-stumps and rocks, two hundred and forty of the islands having a mill on one side, but which side was not visible beforehand. His figures, however, need not be taken too literally as he went "gathering," to use his own words, "like a busy bee, all these honied observations; some by sight, some by hearing, some by both, some by neither, and some by bare supposition."

Equally exciting was Busbecq's passage down the Danube in a boat roped to a 24-oar pinnace. He was behind time, so they rowed night and day, pulling hard against a violent wind. The bed of the river was uncared for, and collisions with tree-stumps were frequent; once it was with the bank, so hard that a few planks came away. But the ambassador got no further answer to his re-monstrances than "God will help" from the Turkish rowers. The Danube was mainly a Turk-ish river then.

On the lakes there were, of course, storms to contend with, two of which nearly drowned two of the most gifted men of the century, De Thou the historian, and the artist Cellini. It is fairly clear, too, that their almost identical experiences took place on the same lake; that of Wallenstadt, although neither of them gives the name. The boat De Thou crossed in was made of fir-trunks, neither sound, nor tarred, nor nailed; a German was in it, too, with his horse, which fell about; the helmsman left his post, called out to all to save themselves if they could; nothing was to be seen but rain and lake and perpendicular rock, until a cave was sighted towards which all joined in an effort to row. A way up the rock was found, at the top, an inn, just where Cellini had found one nearly half a century earlier.

On the rivers themselves there were two further disadvantages to meet; delay through running aground and danger in shooting the bridges.
The latter was very great: the bridge which gave
its name to Pont-St.-Esprit on the Rhone was as
notorious a place for shipwrecks as any headland,
and no doubt it happened then, as it used to
happen later, at Beaugency, on the Loire, that
all card-playing and talking ceased from the moment the boatmen began to prepare for the passage underneath till the passage was safely over.
As for running aground, it did not happen so often
as might have been expected, to judge by what
is left unsaid by the travellers: one must not
strike any average from Peter Mundy's feat of
doing it forty times in two days.

Both these drawbacks were present, nevertheless, to a serious extent, and for the same reason;
the total absence of regulation of the flow of
water. Locks, or "sluices" as they were termed
then, were being introduced exceedingly slowly;
how slowly is evident from a Frenchman explaining [12] the working in detail in his journal (without the use of any specialised terms) of one on
the Reno, between Bologna and Ferrara. Considering that he must have had much experience
of France and had by that time traversed all the
waterways generally used for passenger traffic
in Italy, it may be concluded that locks were at
least very rare in both countries. Some such de-

duction may also be made for England and France from an Englishman doing the same when at Montargis on the Loire, nearly seventy years later.[13] Even in Holland, the nursery of the lock-system, its development was slow. In 1605 a Venetian ambassador mentions that the lock-gates between Brussels and Antwerp were only opened once a week, when the weekly trade-barge went along; at other times every one had to change boats at every lock; just as was done on the series of canals formed out of the marshes between the Reno and the Po, according to the Frenchman just quoted. In the middle of the seventeenth century, the same arrangement was in force between Antwerp and Brussels, so Evelyn says, whereas, he implies that between Bologna and Ferrara a lock system was fully in use.

In canals, the great achievement of the period was the cutting of one for nine miles between Amsterdam and Haarlem in six months at a cost of £20,000, finished not long before Sir W. Brereton passed through it in 1634; the previous route had been by a canal in the direction of Haarlem Meer, the boat having to be lugged by hand past the dam which separated the canal from the Meer. Here, in Holland, too, was by far the best passenger service in Europe; in many cases boats were towed, or sailed, between town and town every hour with fares fixed by the local authorities, and the only complaint that is to be heard concerns the drunkenness of the boatmen, who frequently landed the passengers in the water. But there is an isolated complaint, by an Italian chaplain, which shows what the others accepted as no more than reasonable. Nearing Amsterdam, he and his passed the night in the open barge, unable to sit up, much less stand, because of the lowness of the bridges, but forced to lie, in pouring rain, on foul straw, as if they were "gentlemen from Reggio," a phrase that is still used in Venice as a synonym for pigs.

Practicability, comfort, cheapness, and speed — for all these qualities the water could more than hold its own against the land under even conditions; and a traveller from Italy to Munich finishes his journey by raft down the Iser and reckons himself a gainer in time by using that means in preference to horseback.

It is in France, however, that the importance of waterways reaches its maximum. Almost every tourist's way from Paris, except that by Picardy, lay along a line which a river traversed; the windings of the Seine did not prevent it being quite as convenient as the road; while the Loire and the Rhone were far more so; and for approaching Paris, the Garonne was very frequently part of one route, even up to its mouth; the upper Loire of another. An even clearer idea of the importance and amount of usage of riverways in France is gained by considering how

Lyons has maintained a high and steady degree of prosperity before, during, and since the rise and fall of Venice and of Amsterdam, and how at this period the only neglected parts of France were those which lay between the chief rivers, which have, in fact, so far dictated the course to be followed by the main road routes that the neglected parts of France are the same now as then. To Lyons the Rhone gave access to Italy, Spain, and Africa; twelve leagues away the Loire becomes navigable, and from Gien on the Loire was one day's journey to a tributary of the Seine, the Loing: which three rivers put Lyons in touch with North Spain, most of France and all northern Europe. Neither was Lyons very far from the Rhine and the Danube.

In Spain alone were the rivers unused by the traveller. In southern Italy they were less used than in Roman times, when passenger traffic was customary on the Tiber and smaller rivers,[14] which certainly was not the case three hundred years ago; the disuse of the lower reaches of the Tiber is accounted for by the fear of the Turks, to prevent an attack on Rome by whom the mouth of the river was closed. In North Italy on the other hand, the Adige, Brenta, and Po are frequently mentioned; the Po, indeed, from Turin must have been as constantly in use as any river in Europe in proportion to its length. From Mantua to Ferrara in 1574[15] a boat sailed every night as a matter of course; between Mantua and Venice communication by water was regular in 1591, and even from Milan to Venice it was quite an ordinary thing to travel by the Po, finishing the journey along the Adige to Chioggia by means of a canal which linked up the two rivers. As for the Brenta, it had its own proverb, that the passenger boat (between Padua and Venice) would sink when it contained neither monk, student, nor courtesan, which is as much as to say that the tourist would always find company, as well as a boat, ready.

It is in connection with the waterways of North Italy that one of the debated questions of Shakespeare's life has arisen: as to how much, or how little, he knew of Italy first hand. But hitherto the commentators have been contented with so little evidence that his references to them have been misinterpreted and the accuracy of the impression that they give, and would give still more distinctly had his editors done him justice, has been denied. A recent writer [16] has set out the facts and some evidence so clearly that there is no need to add to the latter further than has already been done by the few instances just mentioned: a few out of an almost indefinite number which are to be found in the writings of these tourists contemporary with Shakespeare, who are surely the most satisfactory witnesses in a case like this, wholly concerned with what he, if a tourist, would have seen. What they show is that in practically every North Italian town passenger traffic by water formed part of the daily life, and that is the impression clearly shared by Shakespeare. When he represents the passenger traffic in an Italian river being dependent on the tide, it must be remembered that he lived near old London Bridge, where the tidal rush was tremendous; and that for his purpose in writing accuracy did not matter in the very least. Neither is any mistake of his over routes to be compared with one of the careful Villamont, who asserts that he reached Este from Padua by the Brenta and that the Brenta is navigable no farther than Este. Now Este is southwest of Padua and the Brenta reaches the latter from northwest and never gets within seventeen miles of Este; but what is more particularly to be noted is that Villamont's "Voyages" was the book of European travel most frequently reprinted in Shakespeare's lifetime and that the error was never corrected. At the same time, it is, perhaps, worth while laying stress on the fact that no deduction can be made from all this as to whether Shakespeare ever left England or the reverse, because his capacity for using second-hand knowledge was so unique that it may be said of him as can be said of probably no other writer, that it is impossible to make a reasonable guess as to when his knowledge is first-hand and when it is not.

Another subject which needs to be treated here, although at first sight it also seems out of place, is that of the characteristics of the islands of Europe as seen by foreigners; for among the advantages of choosing the sea must be reckoned acquaintance with those places which one would never get a glimpse of without a voyage; that is, those which ships touched at but which did not form parts of the tourist's objective. Far and away the chief of these were the islands of the Levant. The opinion that the tourists have of them is probably rose-coloured by the fact that these broke the monotony of a longer voyage than they had need of otherwise; but the fact remains that all agree in depicting them as the spots where human life was at its pleasantest. Of Chios, in particular, might be used the childlike phrase which the Italians used to express the height of happiness, — it was like touching heaven with one's fingers. Nowhere was there greater freedom or greater pleasure. Such was Della Valle's opinion, who calls it "the pleasure-place of the Archipelago and the garden of Greece"; nothing but singing, dancing, and talking with the ladies of the isle, not only in daytime but up to four or five in the morning. Their costume was the only thing in Chios that could have been improved and this seems to refer to the style only, for Lithgow says that they were so sumptuously apparelled that workmen's wives went in satin and taffety,

and cloth of gold, and silver, with jewelled rings
and bracelets; and when he goes on to say that
they were the most beautiful women he ever saw,
it is worth remembering that he not only covered
more ground in Europe, but visited a greater
number of the islands of the Mediterranean
than any of the others. Besides, there are so
many to confirm it; and although three hundred
years ago there was little of what we call appreciation of nature, or rather, of the modern custom
of definitely expressing such appreciation, there
was no lack of appreciation, and expression of
appreciation, of nature when taking a human
and feminine form. Singing, too, seems to have
been part of living hereabouts: in Crete, for instance, the men, women, and children of a household would usually sing together for an hour after
dinner. When there was a seamy side to their
life it was associated with politics; in this same
Crete Lithgow stayed for fifty-eight days and never
saw a Greek leave his house unarmed: generally
it was with a steel cap, a long sword, a bow, dag-
ger, and target-shield. In Zante, too, labourers
went to the fields armed; but then it must be
taken into account that the men of Zante were
peculiarly murderous; if a merchant refused to
buy from them his life would be in danger: and
also, it was under Venetian rule, a double evil;
first, because it had no other object than that of
benefitting Venetians, and secondly, it implied

opposition to the Turks, which was worse, much
worse, than the rule of the Turks. Chios was
under Turkish rule; so was Coos, the next hap-
piest place, very rarely visited, but well worth it,
partly for what Della Valle calls the "Amore-
volezza" of that generation, partly because there
were still to be seen the houses of Hippocrates,
Hercules, and Peleus, Achilles' father. At Corfu
was the house of Judas; also his descendants,
however much the latter denied their ancestry;
and near Lesbos, the islet called Monte Sancto
because it was thither that the Devil had borne
Christ to show him all the kingdoms of the earth.
Then there were all the natural curiosities which
the tourist might see in the Levant and nowhere
else; asbestos at Cyprus, likewise ladanum "gene-
rated by the dew," and at Lemnos the "terra
sigillata" famed throughout Europe for its healing properties, an interesting example of an ancient superstition taken over by Christianity; for
the priestess of Artemis who had the charge of
the sacred earth in Pliny's time had been succeeded by the Christian priest whom the Turkish
officials watched at work without interfering, in
case there might be some rite which they did not
know of and on the use of which the efficacy of
the earth depended.

So also, with volcanoes; it was only he who
went by sea who saw any other than Vesuvius;

and in addition to their scientific, they had also
a theological, attraction, being generally considered
as mouths of hell, Stromboli, in particular, more
continually active than the rest. Concerning
Stromboli there is a curious tale which is worth
borrowing from Sandys, how one Gresham, a
London merchant, ascended the volcano one day,
at noon, when the flames were wont to slacken,
and heard a voice call out that the rich Antonio
was coming. On returning to Palermo where there
was a rich Antonio, well known, he learnt that
the latter had died at the hour the voice had been
heard, and the fact and hour were confirmed by
the sailors who had accompanied Gresham, to
Henry VIII, who questioned them. Gresham
himself retired from business and gave away his
property.

Another Levant incident, characteristic, mys-
terious, and one of Sandys' telling, moreover,
is this. He was at Malta one day, alone on the
seashore, and what he saw seemed like a part
of a masque. A boat arrived; in it, two old women.
Out they stepped with grotesque gestures, and
spread a Turkey carpet, on that a table-cloth, and
on that victuals of the best. Then came another
boat which set "a Gallant ashore with his two
Amorosaes, attired like nymphs, with Lutes in
their hands." But the "gallant" turned out to
be a French captain and the nymphs far from
spiritual.

Or again; once, on the way to Constantinople,
they were near land and he made a day's excursion. Returning at evening, he found the captain
lying dripping wet, struggling, it seemed, with
death. The crew were all quarrelling, some on
board, some on shore. "Amongst the rest there
was a blind man who had married a young wife
that would not let him lie with her and thereupon
had undertaken this journey to complain unto the
Patriarch. He, hearing his brother cry out at the
receipt of a blow, guided to the place by the noise
and thinking with his staff to have struck the
striker, laid it on with such force that, meeting
with nothing but air, he fell into the sea, and was
with difficulty preserved from drowning. The
clamour increased; and anon the captain, starting up as if of a sudden restored to life, like a mad-
man skips into the boat, and drawing a Turkish
scimitar, beginneth to lay about him (thinking
that his vessel had been surprised by pirates):
whereupon they all leaped into the sea, and diving
under the water ascended outside the reach of his
fury. Leaping ashore, he pursues my Greek guide,
whom fear made too nimble for him, mounting
a steep cliff which at another time he could have
hardly ascended. Then turning upon me (who
was only armed with stones) as God would have
it, he stumbled, and there lay like a stone for
two hours, that which had made them so quarrel-
some being now the peace-maker. For it being

proclaimed death to bring wine into Constantinople and they loath to pour such good liquor into the sea, had made their bellies their overcharged vessels."

But it would be doing the Levant injustice to let the last word on it be an explained miracle, and therefore you may be informed on the testimony of John Newberie, citizen and merchant of London, who, "being desirous to see the world," has become enrolled in the band of Purchas, His Pilgrims, that there was a small isle near Melos, to wit, the Isola de' Diavoli, uninhabited but by devils; and if any vessels are moored thereto, as may be done, the water being deep by the shore, the ropes loose their hold unless the sailors make a cross with every two cables. And once upon a time, when a Florentine galley was moored there without a cross, a loud voice was heard warning the sailors to row away.

And lastly, this is what happened when a funeral had to take place at sea; an inventory of the deceased's goods was made, the ship's bell was rung twice, a fire-brand thrown into the sea, and the announcement made: "Gentlemen mariners, pray for the soul of poor —— whereby, through God's mercy, he may rest with the souls of the faithful." But it is pleasant to say that on the only occasion this form of burial is recorded the deceased was alive, if not kicking; he was at his post, the "look out," curled up asleep, as he had been for forty-eight hours previously, sleeping off the effects of Greek wine.

The amount of attention given to the other islands of the Mediterranean, Sicily, which may be considered part of Italy, excepted, might well be represented by saying nothing about them, but Cardinal de Retz's remark about Port Mahon, Minorca, is too characteristic of his age to be passed over; he praises it as the most beautiful haven of the Mediterranean, so beautiful that its scenery surpassed even that employed at Paris for the opera!

CHAPTER IV

CHRISTIAN EUROPE

PART I

EUROPEAN EUROPE

From the report of divers curious and experienced persons I had been assured there was little more to be seen in the rest of the civil world after Italy, France and the Low Countries, but plain and prodigious barbarism.

EVELYN, *Diary* (1645).

THE route of the Average Tourist being determined by the considerations above-mentioned, he was naturally directed to those countries whose situation enabled them to influence the course of events in his fatherland, whose development and conditions contained the most pertinent lessons for him as a man and as a statesman, and whose climate, accessibility, and inhabitants were such as hindered travellers least. These countries were: Italy, France, the United Provinces (*i. e.*, Holland), the Empire, the Spanish Netherlands (corresponding to Belgium), England, Poland. This order is that in which they would probably have appeared to arrange themselves according to their importance for the purposes under consideration. The omission of England in the chapter heading is due, of course, to Evelyn having started thence; of the

Empire and Poland, to the date at which he is
writing, near the close of the Thirty Years' War; a
date which, while within the period with which
this book has to deal, is later by nearly half a
century than the central date, 1600, to which all its
undated statements should be taken as referring.

Whatever criticism might have been passed on
this order of importance by this or that adviser,
not one would have been found to dispute the
preëminence of Italy. Whereas now there is no
form of human effort in which the inhabitants of
Italy have not been equalled or surpassed, it
seemed then as if there had never been any in
which they had been surpassed and very few in
which they had been equalled. So far as Art and
antiquities go, there will be no need to persuade
anybody of the likelihood of that; nor probably,
with regard to venerableness of religion or romance
of history. But the very easiness of imagining
the supremacy which would have been conceded
Italy on these points tends to close the enquiry
into the causes of its hold on men in times gone
by, and consequently to obscure the fact that
Italy then not only stood for all that Italy stands
for now, but also in the place, or rather, places,
now occupied by the most advanced States in
their most advanced aspects; for everything, in
fact, that made for progress on the lines considered
most feasible or probable at the moment; for
progress, not only in culture, but in commerce

and commercial methods, in politics, in the science of war, in up-to-date handicraft, and, especially, in worldly wisdom. Even a baby-food was assured of greater respect if made from an Italian recipe, such as the paste made of bread-crumbs, wheat-meal, and olive-oil, of which De Thou nearly died. In short, if the value of Italy as the colonizer of Europe in regard to mental development belonged by this time to the past rather than to the present, its reputation as such must not be ante-dated, as is generally done, and ascribed to the age when it most thoroughly deserved that reputation. Here, on the contrary, as usually, merit and credit are not contemporary.

And there was plenty to deceive those who did not look far below the surface. In discussing politics the newest set-phrases would be those brought into use by Italian writers; "balance of power," "reason of state," etc.; the word "status" itself, as a substitute for "Respublica," was both a sign of the times and of Italian influence.[1] So with commercial terms, we find, for instance, the word "provvisione" (commission) being used as late as 1648,[2] by an Englishman who had never been to Italy, while the control of Italy over one of the later forms of the Renascence, that of the art of gardening, is indicated by the introduction of the word "florist" from the Italian during the seventeenth century. The only modern author, moreover, whose acquaintance a Eu-

ropean schoolboy was certain to make, was the
Italian versifier whom Shakespeare calls "good
old Mantuan," and even if we look at things from
to-day's standpoint the most remarkable profes-
sorship of the period would surely be accounted
that of Galileo at Padua, 1592–1610. In another
respect, too, connected with education, the relative maturity and crudeness of civilisation south
and north of the Alps is even more apparent to-
day than it was then. The "Trans-alpine" shared
more or less Erasmus' belief in the power of words
as a means of education, whereas in Italy, and
in Italy alone, was it insisted that the influence of
environment, personal and physical, is the factor
compared to which all else is of but little account.
The first theory is abandoned now by all who can
afford to do so, the second is that of the best
effort of to-day.[3]

As for the technique of war, more than half-
way through the seventeenth century, when
Louis XIV wanted the very best available talent
to design the completion of the Louvre, it was to
Rome that he sent, and the artist, Bernini, is
recorded [4] as saying, to allay jealousy, that there
was no need for Frenchmen to be ashamed of an
Italian being called in for this purpose, seeing
that in the kind of knowledge in which they excelled all Europe, that of war, their teachers were
still Italians. And the modernity of the latter's
reputation for supremacy in military knowledge

is thrown into relief by a remark of Bertrandon de la Brocquière, writing in 1433, taken in conjunction with the above. The latter was a clear-headed Fleming of wide experience who, when drawing up a plan for the right composition of an army which should suffice to drive the Turks back, only mentions French, English, and German soldiers.

As regards applied science, again, we find Evelyn writing of the harbour-works at Genoa, "of all the wonders of Italy, for the art and nature of the design, nothing parallels this." Now Evelyn was certainly not a man to underrate the rest of the wonders of Italy. As for comparisons outside of Italy, all Europe had by his time settled down to compete in the application of science to every-day life. And as to the products of the soil, is it not probable that if, nowadays, Europeans left the soil to take care of itself, and the day-labourer to take care of the seed and the preparation of the product, Italy would regain the first place as a producer of luxuries?

Such points as these, just a few that have chanced to suggest themselves in the course of reading for other purposes, are merely put forward as typical of the relations existing between Italy and the rest of Europe; the Italians themselves admitted their own superiority by the slightly contemptuous meaning that attached itself to their word "Transalpini," and very rare

is it to find one of these "Transalpini" taking the
view that Sir Philip Sidney and Fynes Moryson
did, that the first characteristic of Italy was pre-
tentiousness. On the contrary, it was assumed
that little but experience could be so easily, or
so satisfactorily, acquired elsewhere. Diverse
forms of government, at least, could not be met
with elsewhere in the same variety within such
narrow limits. The south was what they termed
a "province," *i. e.*, a dependency held down by
force, belonging to Spain; so, too, was Milan,
with its surroundings. In the centre was a monarch, the Pope, who was both elected and "absolute," a term which had a specialised meaning,
that of power unlimited except by the extent to
which the holder made himself disliked. Further
north were free cities, Lucca, Genoa; six hereditary
principalities, Tuscany, Mantua, Urbino, Savoy,
Modena, Parma; and lastly, the Republic of
Venice with its miniature empire in Lombardy.
And concerning Venice, there is this to be noted,
that it was exhibiting solidity combined with
elasticity to a degree all the more astonishing in
"an impossible city in an impossible place";
which gave it a position not unlike that of England to-day, namely, that peculiarities of its
"constitution" received an even greater degree
of respect than they were entitled to and tended
to be imitated by constitution-formulators of the
period who expected to reproduce what had been

achieved by geography and a national temperament, by means of reproducing some of the formu-
las that the latter had adopted. All of which was
of great interest to the Average Tourist; and in
consequence, if you happen to be reading one of
his accounts of a tour, at the first mention of
the word "Doge," skip twelve pages.

What remains to be seen concerning Italy is
— what were the details that mainly occupied
the foreigner as student there. In which connection the chief fact to be noted is that his stopping-
places were invariably towns; and this not in
Italy only, but throughout Europe. As regards
the Average Tourist, this is fully accounted for
by the objects he set before himself, but it is
equally true of all. Bathing-places excepted, the
only holiday resorts lay in the very last places
where we should think of looking for them — in
the suburbs. The Riviera, for instance, was no
spot to delay in when Mohammedan pirates were
forever coasting along in search of Christian
slaves; and so on. But the essential explanation
is to be sought in a census of Europe. The population of London exceeds that of most sixteenth-
century States, and there are London suburbs
which house more than any but the biggest sixteenth-century cities. Many villages consisted
of no more than three or four houses; and even
near Paris, of six or seven or eight; in Spain one
might journey eight leagues without seeing a

house at all. Whereas, therefore, the difficulty, and the pleasure, of a modern tour consists in escaping from people, the difficulty, and the safety, of all tourists in 1600 lay in reaching them.

Crossing the Alps, then, and making for the towns, one came, say, upon Turin; not a town that would detain one, but a point of the parting of the ways. Hence to Rome, the direct way lay through Genoa; a second viâ Milan and Bologna, a day's journey longer but yielding the advantage of seeing those two cities; while the third way, the longest but most comfortable and no more expensive, lay down the Po to Ferrara, thence to Venice, thence by sea to Ancona, by land to Loreto, and so to Rome. The two former routes converged at Florence. Of these two the longer would be chosen either going or returning. Milan must no more be missed than Rome. It was the city of all Europe on which the question of peace and war permanently depended; being the key to the most debateable district. And as such, it may be imagined what the castle was then from what it is even in its present state as a sort of museum of military architecture. Then it was alive with the finest soldiers of the age, Spaniards; a small town, complete in itself, with rows of shops and five market-places. And the city itself was recognised as unsurpassed as a school both for the accomplishments that befitted a gentleman and for craftsmanship; for everything, in fact, that made life possible or pleasant. Yet Bologna had the advantage of it in one respect, in possessing a University; to matriculate in an Italian university continued an inexpressible honour to the "Transalpini," evident though it was that the merest smattering of book-knowledge was sufficient to pass; and even though the Italian said openly, "We take the fees, and send back an ass in a doctor's gown." Florence again, had its own supremacy; the most attractive town in the district where the best Italian was supposed to be spoken. Siena was preferred by purists for language, but the slight distinction was outweighed by just those charms which have not been impaired by age. One more has indeed been added that might be expected to have existed then, but did not; what Ben Jonson wrote in "Volpone" in summing up the qualities of the poets of Italy and eulogising Guarini.

> Dante is hard and few can understand him

was but an echo of the Italians' own opinion. "Like Dante's 'Inferno' which no man understandeth" was a Venetian Senator's description of Henry IV's policy in 1606.[5]

Assuming the third route to be the one chosen, there was Ferrara to pass, but not to stay at when Venice was almost in sight — Venice in 1600! to have been a witness of that would make it well worth while to have been dead for the past three hundred years. The essence of the change is best expressed in the words of Mr. L. P. Smith in his "Life and Letters of Sir Henry Wotton," when he speaks of it as "a shell on the shores of the Adriatic deserted by the wonderful organism that once inhabited it." Outward and visible signs of the vividness and breadth of its life were two in particular; the infinite variety and number of persons and nationalities that filled its streets with colour and contrast and a sense of new worlds and of mystery in the midst of commerce; and secondly, the Arsenal. In all Europe there was not such another organisation as the Arsenal; not one so completely prepared with everything that went to the fitting out of a fleet, and very few so well able to fit out an army. Villamont was shown twenty-five great galleasses and eighty-five galleys, all of them so new that they had not been out to sea. Probably, also, its managers were the greatest direct employers of labour in Christendom; 2880 is one of the more moderate estimates of those permanently at work, including the 200 old women always mending sails, a number increased to 700 at times; and all these employees were assured of a pension from the State when past work, an otherwise unheard-of custom then, in practice, at least. It had its place, too, in the tourist's mythology; one after another repeating the tale how when Henry III of France visited Venice, a galley was built and three cannon turned out while he was at dinner.

Yet Montaigne has something to say about Venice that cancels all the intervening years and changes, and brings him into touch with us. He went his way towards it with the highest expectations, explored it eagerly, recollected it with the keenest pleasure: yet at the end of his second day there his feeling was one of disappointment. It may be taken as characteristic that he alone should experience then what seems more appropriate to the present; more probably, other visitors shared it but were too much subject to convention to say so; or, perhaps, re-writing their experiences later at home, as they generally did, they record their later thought only, whereas Montaigne left his unrevised and unashamed. This explanation seems the more reasonable inasmuch as the causes of the feeling had already come into being. On the surface the sight rested satisfied, while the imagination remained as hungry as ever. In a country, France, for instance, the tourist always had a consciousness of towns and districts unseen, all of which had contributed to the past, for evidence of the existence of which the imagination looks, however unconsciously; but after two days in Venice, all that is important and visible may seem to have been seen; no suggestion of anything beyond, not even the ruins of a half-buried city, as at Rome. It is true it was clear then that the word "Venice" meant an Empire as well as a city, though by the time the

tourist had reached the city, he had passed through
the conquests, barring an island or two in the Levant which the Turks were in course of subtracting.
Yet the third meaning of the name was as dim to
him as both the second and the third are to most
of us, that of the source of an Empire, the whole
collection of islands in the lagoons, whose larger
life had already been drained away into the central settlement, but where Venice and its history
were equally discoverable — but not in two days.

Another similarity between Venice of old and
of to-day lies in the fact that the gondoliers knew
much better than the visitors whither the latter
wanted to go and took them there, with, or
against, orders; only with this difference, that
then it was always to the house of the courtesan
in whose pay he was.

When the tourist had released himself and was
proceeding on his way to Rome there were the
beacons dotted along the coast for him to notice,
beacons for signalling the sighting of a Turk or
corsair vessel from south to north in a few hours.
Ravenna received little notice, Rimini less, but
Ancona was kept in the memory by one of those
rhymes characteristic of the contemporary guide-
book.

Unus Deus, Una Roma,
Unus turris, in Cremona,
Una portus, in Ancona.

And then Loreto. Here it must be remembered,

first of all, that it was unpardonable to ask for a meal before visiting the "Santa Casa." The town was little more than one long street, well fortified by reason of the treasure that the offerings represented. Bassompierre relates in his memoirs how he was invited to be one of the witnesses at the quarterly offering of the poor-box one Christmas; the contents amounted to 6000 crowns (in our money about £7500); this for one quarter only. Many men, and towns too, were represented by models of themselves in solid silver. As to which votive offerings Montaigne makes an assertion, unconfirmed by any one else but with this in its favour, that no tourist but himself gives any details concerning a valuable offering from himself made at Loreto. He says that the craftsmen refuse to take any payment for such articles beyond the cost of the materials. It seems incredible that a town which had been the resort of pilgrims for more than two centuries should not have become demoralised, but Montaigne adds that the officials refused tips, or received them unwillingly; and certainly no one complains of extortion.

If the tourist was lucky enough to see a ship-load of pilgrims arriving from the farther coast of the Adriatic, it would be worth while to stay and watch, for as soon as Loreto came in sight they rose and cried out without ceasing from that moment until they reached the "Santa Casa," beseeching the Madonna to return to Fiume, where, once upon a time, so the tale ran, her house had stood. Leaving Loreto, not forgetting, of course, to wear the pilgrim's badge peculiar to the shrine — a leaden image of Our Lady surmounted by three porcupine quills fastened together with a silk thread, a tiny flag on each quill — leaving Loreto, then, a détour was often made to visit Assisi, joining the main road again at Spoleto. And so to Rome, where the new arrival, if a Roman Catholic, should first make his way to the Scale Sante to return thanks for his preservation during the past journey; where, too, at his departure, he should pray for assistance on the one to come.

It made considerable difference to his recollections of Rome what date it was within this period that he arrived. If at the beginning, he would have found St. Peter's half-finished and the interior in a state better suited to a pig-sty; and the rest of the city to match; the most confident Protestant would be gratified to find himself scandalised beyond expectation. By 1601 St. Peter's was practically in all its glory, the city unsurpassed in its care for the needy and sick, and of average morality. In the interval, too, the catacombs had been discovered, and though Bosio, the explorer of them, did not publish the results of his explorations till 1632 they became more accessible meanwhile; continuing, however, to be regarded as isolated "crypts." It was his

book "Roma Sotterranea" that first caused them
to be considered collectively; and it was under
that name that Evelyn paid his visit to them
in 1645, the first of these tourists to make
anything that can be called an excursion among
them. He entered through a burrow in a corn-
field two miles from the city, so small that he had
to crawl on his stomach for the first twenty paces.
But the main feature of the Rome of 1600 was
still its power. Not simply influence in the present as a result of power in the past, but the
strength of age, middle-age, and youth existing in
unison. To begin with, their reverence for Ancient
Rome was greater than ours; an effect partly of
their theory of history, partly of the narrower limits of their acquaintance with the materials of history. For the former cause, it was bound to be
an axiom of history as long as the Bible remained
authoritative as a statement of historical fact,
that mankind had proceeded from good to bad,
and from bad to worse, as time had advanced.
And whatever, in the thought of the age, tended
to shake this view, was held in check by the discoveries, in different, previously unexplored, parts
of the world, of communities which seemed to be
possessed at once of a higher morality and also
of a more primitive civilisation, than the European. It is probably impossible for us to realise
the alteration that the theory of evolution has introduced into current ideas about history.

For the second cause, the greatness of the Roman Empire appeared the greater for their having so little with which to compare it. The empire of the Ottomans had, it is true, by now eclipsed it; but Spain's was a vague wilderness, inhabited by savages; the Persian of old they only knew through the doctored accounts of the Latin writers; and of the overwhelming antiquity and extent of the Chinese they had no real knowledge at all. All, the Turkish excepted, that were not shadowy to them, were what Rome had obliterated, the moral effect of which, associated, as it must needs be, with the name of the city, endured as the chief asset of the Papal power. If any one then had taken Gibbon's view, that the remains of the Roman Empire were approaching dissolution, it would only have been because he thought that the end of the world was equally near. And this unbroken continuity of power did not merely exist, but was alive with fresh life. Nothing had replaced Rome; there was nothing to replace it; there was no need to replace it, since there was nothing effete nor slack about it, however much corruption was patent to the "Reformed."

The relations between visitors who were "Reformed" and Rome is another interesting feature of the tourist-life of the time when both were militant and a large proportion of tourists anti-Catholic. Much depended on the reigning Pope.

In the time of Sixtus V (1585–90) Protestants
came in fear, lived in disguise, and sought protection; Englishmen from Cardinal Allen, who
readily granted it for a few days, to enable them
to see the antiquities. Clement VIII (1592–1605)
was much more lenient, yet Moryson thought it
advisable even then to pass for a Frenchman,
and to safeguard himself through Cardinal Allen,
as well; also to leave before Easter, when there
was a house-to-house visitation to enquire if all
were communicants. Precautions, on the other
hand, might be overdone. It was all very well to
make a practice, as one did, of going through a
church on the way to his morning drink, in case
spies were about, but to tell one's host, as a certain German did, on returning home from an
afternoon walk, that he had just been to mass,
when all the masses were said in the morning,
was going too far! And conforming to custom
had its own dangers, too, when it formed a habit,
as Moryson found, who, on entering a church at
Geneva, reached out his hand towards the poor-
box in mistake for the holy-water stoop to which
he had accustomed himself; all the more embarrassing a mistake for his being in the company
of Theodore Beza.

Gregory XV (1621–3) — to return to the Popes
— forbade even the other princes of Italy to ad-
mit any but Roman Catholics to their dominions;
and there were, besides, the already-mentioned

prohibitions from the authorities at home. The
state of affairs in general may be taken as that
suggested by the localisation of Shakespeare's
plays. Two-thirds of his scenes are laid abroad,
in Italy more frequently than elsewhere outside
England: yet his contemporary Italy is practically
always the North, the South being reserved for
the "classical" period. Nevertheless, it may safely
be assumed that the danger was not quite so
great as the fear, and that where the former was
incurred, the sufferer had only himself to blame.
Whether or no the high officials at Rome were
faulty in dogma or in virtue, they were usually
both men of the world and gentlemen. Montaigne's belongings, for example, provided the
searchers with plenty of material for a charge of
heresy, but a short conversation overcame all
difficulties. And one William Davis, an English
sailor[6] who fell ill at Rome in 1598, found by experience that a Protestant who was civil would be
cared for in a hospital free and given food and
money on leaving. The more usual kind of behaviour has already been illustrated; only it must
not be imagined that the incautiousness and incivility which turned the Protestant into a martyr
were less conspicuous among other sects. By the
law of Geneva a three-days stay was permitted
to travellers of every creed. The poet-philosopher,
Giordano Bruno, and the Jesuit missionary, Parsons, both rested there; their zeal prescribed the

extremes of controversial outrage in return for
tolerance and courtesy.

But Rome and its associations have had more
than their share of attention. Imagine, then, the
traveller started on the invariable excursion to
Naples, the equal of Milan as a finishing school,
and one of the few cities with underground drainage. Some, but not many, might go on to Sicily;
to Syracuse for the feast of Santa Lucia, for choice.
But what with robbers and corsair-raids, there
was no travelling there without a strong guard,
and the towns were so unsafe that Messina seems
to have been the first of European towns to evolve
a combined bank and safe-deposit under municipal guarantee; established by 1611, when Sandys
noticed it. Those who did reach Sicily usually
visited Malta as well; small boats with five rowers
left about two hours before sunset, and if no Turkish sail was sighted, went on, reaching Malta
about dawn.

But the foregoing presupposes the Mont-Cenis
route into Italy, and leaves out three towns which
must be included: Padua, Verona, and Bergamo.
Padua had its university, the most-visited in Europe; Verona, its relics of Roman times, which commanded an attention that they now have to share
with the romantic aspects of mediæval history,
romance that sixteenth-century people were not
inclined to be attracted by, having too first-
hand an acquaintance with feuds to look at their

picturesque side. Moreover, the visible remains
of these feuds, here and in every Italian city,
showed a ludicrous side, for in so far as they did
not take the form of assassination by the foulest
means, they consisted in the two parties of re-
tainers parading the town, armed with an absurd
completeness, each one confining itself to certain
quarters of the town by tacit agreement in order
to render collisions impossible. The habits drama-
tised in the first scene of "Romeo and Juliet"
are those of Londoners, in so far as they are at all
contemporary. The third town, Bergamo, thousands pass by now, year by year, within a few
miles, never knowing what they miss by not stopping, but then it lay on the north-and-south road
as much as any town in Italy, and not even the
Frankfort fair surpassed that of Bergamo, August 25 and the following week, when lucky was
he who could find sleeping-room in a stable.

Yet however complete was the outfit obtainable across the Alps, there remained other countries which were factors in politics; and which
possessed, moreover, histories, courts, universities, and men of learning; fewer temptations, possibly, and more "true religion." Of these France
was the one the most easily accessible to a greater
number. As to its boundaries, they were somewhat narrower in almost every direction than at
present; especially southeastwards; Lyons was

a frontier-town. Its attractions lay principally in Paris, the only city north of the Alps comparable to Milan as a centre for the training of a man for a courtly, or an international, life; and in the government, which, in its extreme centralisation and in its idealisation of monarchy, corresponded most closely with the more practicable ideals of the day.

In planning a route through France it was advisable to go straight to Paris, if only for a few days, since to have been in Paris gave one a position in the provinces. As a place to stay at, Orleans was really far more frequently chosen by foreigners than Paris. Its university was as international as any in Europe, and ahead of any other in maintaining a circulating library for students, which lent any book on a receipt being given for it; "an extraordinary custom" says Evelyn. Here, too, began the district reputed best for spoken French, which brought strangers to stay at Blois and Tours and Saumur as well; to Saumur, perhaps, more than to the other two, by reason of the number and quality of its teachers on all subjects; it was a centre for Protestantism and learning in combination. Poictiers for law, Montpellier for medicine; and there is an end of the towns that the student-tourist abided in. For the country in general it should be added that just here, where centralisation and autocracy were developing most rapidly and thoroughly, was reckoned as the most decidedly free region of Europe, "liberty," according to sixteenth-century standards, depending not on administration being either lenient or constitutional, but on the extent to which the individual was not interfered with by social conventions. Political tyranny was not regarded as objectionable on principle, except by authors.

The United Provinces differed in no noteworthy respect from Holland of to-day, so far as territory goes, and during the earlier part of this period attracted but little attention; but as time went on and from imminent destruction they escaped into independence, they drew the tourist, first out of curiosity and subsequently as a State which compelled the study of every one who needed to observe the present and foresee the future. Many minor interests, too, brought individuals thither, as a result of Dutch enterprise. We find, for example, Sir William Brereton surveying the country in order to understand their methods of decoying wild-fowl; and Sir Richard Weston, who introduced locks into English rivers and the rotation of crops into English agriculture, learning both these novelties there. And though no one as yet went abroad to study the possibilities of practical philanthropy, there were many who noted, with an admiration that doubtless bore fruit, their charitable institutions of all kinds, unequalled then outside Rome. In one respect

they were ahead of Italy: the suddenness of their
prosperity resulted in the latest improvements
in laying out towns — wider streets and greater
regularity being more in evidence there than
elsewhere. So uniform was the appearance of
the houses, says one, that they seemed to have
been all built by the same workmen at the same
time; whereas the Italian towns, even in re-build-
ing, made no such experiments, because the old
narrow streets formed the best safeguard against
the surprise-attack of which they lived in constant dread, especially from the Turks' corsairs.
No one town could claim precedence, though
Amsterdam, even as early as 1600, struck De
Rohan as equalled by few in Europe for wealth
and beauty; it was rather the excellence and frequency of the towns that occasioned remark —
twenty-nine fine ones within sixty leagues of
boundary; together with the number of storks
which the municipalities cherished, as animals
known to harbour a preference for places where
representative government flourished.

As for the Empire, it meant many different
things to different visitors. The variety of territory and government was absolutely bewilder-
ing, yet certain marked cross-divisions presented
themselves, such as the triple division of it into
upper Germany, Hansa League (with Saxony),
and frontier; the frontier being those districts
which were forever either meeting, or fearing, a

Turkish invasion. Then there was division according to politics, Catholic, Reformed, Protestant, to be studied by the Average Tourist for purposes of alliance, and a third classification according to form of government, the imperial authority, venerable and increasingly vague; princes; "free" towns. The first system of division has, however, most in common with the greater number of foreigners' interests, and of its three subdivisions upper Germany was paid the greatest attention, partly because it lay across so many routes, partly because there was so much to see. It gives the dominant note to references to German-speaking countries in the travel-literature of the day, a note of peaceful energy and hopeful prosperity. While not recommended to these travellers' notice by a well-known past such as the greater coherence of France and Italy had enabled historians to evolve for them, those who lingered there, as most did, saw that its possessions, human and non-human, gave it a present interest and a promise not surpassed elsewhere. The Germany of the last fifty years of the sixteenth century is practically ignored by modern English historians: the story of its continual activity and of its continuous relations with England contain none of those sensational hindrances to the advance of civilisation with which historians concern themselves, but the frequent references to those relations by the contemporary historian of Queen Elizabeth's reign, William Camden, bear witness to the current opinion and knowledge which found expression in the number of visitors from all quarters and the attention they devote to it in relation to that accorded to other countries.

Among the towns of the Empire Augsburg was easily first; its finest street was the finest street in Europe, with roofs of copper; Nuremburg ran it close in many ways but had nothing to show in comparison with that one street. The cause of Augsburg's preëminence was its being the home of the Fuggers, the greatest financiers of Europe, but with their decline one function of the town that meant much in the way of attracting wayfarers, that of being the General-Post-Office for correspondence between Italy and Central Europe, passed to Frankfurt. The frequency of the use of stone as house-building material in these towns of Upper Germany and the show of burnished pewter and brass that was the pride of each inhabitant of standing, who let his huge hall-door lie open all day to exhibit it, were details which the Average Tourist would not overlook if he was observing as he ought where the wealth and security prevailed that were valuable in an ally. Thus did Strassburg fix itself in De Rohan's recollections. Democracy, to him, was a barely credible superstition; yet nowhere was he more courteously treated, nowhere did he see completer prepa-

rations against a long siege, nor any better arsenal,
a model of cleanliness, orderliness, and efficiency.
Neither was it lost on him that amongst all their
collection of cannon there was not one for siege
purposes; their aim was defence, not offence. As
little to be ignored as the others was Ulm. A
feature of the age was the development of the
methods of water-supply in towns; Ulm was the
centre for this industry; even Augsburg's water-
supply had been planned there. And it was equally
the leader in woodwork.

Similar characteristics would be found repeated on a somewhat less striking scale among
the Hansa towns, with Lübeck ranking first
in pleasantness by general consent. A specially
charming feature lay in the number of swans
swimming in the moats, though no Englishman so
much as mentions them; doubtless because the one
town that excelled it in this respect was London.
Going east, the various capitals would provide
each its own object-lesson, and, collectively,
would illustrate the absence of avarice among
German rulers as contrasted with the princes of
Italy. Saxony formed the only exception and
Dresden showed it. In spite of it being the last
big town that Hentzner visited, its armoury
aroused more enthusiasm in him than anything
except the gardens of Naples and the all-sufficiency
of Milan; and Moryson confirms this, adding also
that the stable was the finest he had seen, with

its 136 horses, all foreigners (the German horses had another stable to themselves), each with a glazed window and a green curtain in front of his nose, a red cloth, an iron rack, a copper manger, a brass shower-bath, and a separate cupboard for his trappings.

No Protestant who reached Dresden would miss Wittenberg, but the contrast must have been painful; poor and very dirty; the dwellers therein mainly students, prostitutes, and pigs, recalling the verses in use concerning Angers —

> Basse ville, hauts clochers,
> Riches putaines, pauvres escoliers.

Leipzig was in favour for the purity of its German and Munich for pleasure, but Prague was another disappointment in spite of the Emperor living there; few stone houses and the wooden ones rough, and so filthy that the saying ran that the Turks would never take it despite the feebleness of its fortifications, because it was so well-guarded by its stenches; much as a Frenchman remarked at this time of Massa, between Genoa and Pisa, that it had a castle, but its chief defence was its fleas. Vienna was likewise far too well defended to attract visitors; a frontier-town against the Turks, always garrisoned by mercenaries and its streets unsafe in consequence.

To go on to the Spanish Netherlands, they were bound to be passed and re-passed in the course of the work of Europe, for geographical reasons,

but still more so as a storm-centre of European
politics. Nevertheless, the tourist, however serious, did not stay there long. The viceroy's business
was generalship, and consequently there was no
settled court: little to note, in fact, but the Spanish infantry at work and the effects of that; towns
in ruins, dwindling trade. Yet the localisation
of the war was intermittent enough not to inter-
fere with the travellers from Upper Germany
making a practice of reaching France through
this district, according to Zinzerling, rather than
direct, a habit resulting not only from the attractions that remained to Flemish towns, but still
more from the direct route through Burgundy having become a highway of German mercenaries into
France.

Moreover, no one who knew his business as a
sight-seer omitted Antwerp. Trade and political
importance had for some time been deserting it
until it suggested to Howell in 1619 "a disconso-
late Widow, or a superannuated Virgin that hath
lost her Lover," but in 1600 it had not passed a
state of mellowness without stagnation, with
traces of its greatness fresh. Every visitor repeats the same idea — "the most beautiful town
in Europe"; and not in the same formula, as
would result from the idea being a guide's commonplace, but in words drawn from his own experience: "as seen from the cathedral tower the
most beautiful town after Constantinople," says

one; or Lithgow, extolling Damascus, "the most beautiful city in Asia," compares it, for every respect save style of architecture, to "that match-less pattern and mirror of beauty, Antwerp." It would seem to have been the first town to turn its fortifications into promenades, laid out in walks and planted with trees.[7] The citadel, too, was the finest out of Italy, on the word of a Venetian ambassador.

Elizabethan England, on the other hand, was rendered still more remarkable by possessing no fortresses at all. Two exceptions, Berwick and the Tower of London, served but to call attention to the rule, the Tower in particular, whose out-of-date character in the matter of defences greatly amused connoisseurs. One Venetian ambassador, indeed, with this fact in his mind, together with the miscellaneous character of its contents, describes it as not so much a fortress as a "sicuro deposito" — a safe-deposit.[8] The peacefulness which brought about this state of things is still borne witness to by the large glazed windows on the ground floors of Elizabethan country-houses, but no foreigner remarks on that in the presence of the other more striking points that testified to it then. Foscarini, the successor of the ambassador just referred to, had occasion to traverse the length of England in 1613. Writing home [9] he remarks on five facts concerning the country he passes through which seemed particularly noteworthy: (1) No unfruitful land throughout; (2) Every eight or ten miles a town comparable to a good Italian town (this was on the post-road to Scotland); (3) Number of navigable rivers; (4) and of beautiful churches; (5) No mercenary soldiers.

To make it clear why the visitor should be so specially struck by these features, it is necessary to recall how differently matters stood abroad.

During this period two thirty-year civil wars broke out in Europe, one in each half of the period, the first in France while the Empire was at peace, the second in the Empire while France was at peace. Between these two came twenty years of comparative quiet, but never a year when war was not to be seen in progress, or its effects still horribly new, in the course of a Continental tour. Incidentally, it may be pointed out that this peculiarly even distribution of peace and war gives the writings of travellers in Europe at this time striking value in relation to the effects of war and peace, not only in themselves but also as to their special characteristics in the sixteenth and seventeenth centuries. No tourist came into contact with both wars; almost every tourist saw something of one district under the influence of war or of peace, while some other is seeing another district in an opposite state. There remains, therefore, in their writings, a continuous comment on each other; so continuous and so unconscious as to leave no room for this or that man's bias to influence the general impression.

Yet striking as the peacefulness of England was, it probably lessened rather than heightened what degree of attraction England possessed; since with war so normal a condition, war and its incidentals became a primary object of study even to those who did not profess soldiership. Neither did any but the Dutch need to learn the language of the country, which was what induced so many to make a lengthy stay in Tuscany and in Touraine. Neither was England a thoroughfare. Nor, even, were the recent achievements of Englishmen more than a minor cause of the considerable influx of visitors; not, at least, apart from the idea which is best expressed, perhaps, in the private letter of an Englishman writing from Aleppo: "Your last letter made me exceeding sorrowful, for therein you acquainted me with the death of blessed Queen Elizabeth, at the hearing whereof not only I and our English nation [*i. e.*, the residents] mourned, but many other Christians who were never in Christendom, but born and brought up in heathen countries, wept to hear of her death, and said that she was the most famous queen that ever they heard or read of since the world began."[10]

For the "Virgin Queen" was a far greater marvel to contemporaries than to posterity. Except for her namesake of Spain, a century earlier,

who throughout her political life had been the ally
and wife of one of the cleverest statesmen of the
age, there was no instance since the mistiest past
of a queen-regnant a leader of men. At her accession civil war or conquest seemed inevitable and
insolvency was a fact: yet before her death the
bond of London "is," writes one of the chief financiers of the time,[11] "the first to-day [1595] in
Europe," and she had added victory abroad to
peace at home. To say "she had added" suggests
nowadays the phraseology of the lady's paper, but
it does really express not only the convention
which the tourist may be taken as accepting but
also the belief of reasonable men of the time.

It is true that many denied her right to the
title of "Queen," or, indeed, to that of "Virgin";
but no one had the opportunity of doubting that
both claims belonged to that secondary order of
facts known as "historical." And just as her position as sovereign, and a strikingly successful
one, was more wonderful then than it seems to-
day, so too did her celibacy assure her of more
reverence than we should instinctively concede.
The mediæval idealisation of virginity, one of the
most beneficial, perhaps, of all the ideas of the
past that the Reformation killed, ensured a place
in the life of the world, and the self-respect con-
tingent on that, for all the unmarried women
whose counterparts since have had no assistance
socially from any convention, from nothing but

their own individuality. But this idea, though dying, was not dead; and, as is the way with ideas, challenged attention all the more definitely for ceasing to be taken for granted.

These two facts, then, glorified Elizabeth in the eyes of foreigners; first, that she was a queen and a great ruler when effective queenship was half a myth; secondly, that she remained unmarried when virginity, considered as a virtue, was, so to speak, due to have its last flicker before finally dying down. The reign of James I was a sort of after-glow, except in so far as he had a reputation as a philosopher-king.

These ideas have a marked effect on the visitor's itinerary. He hurried, as a rule, to London, and thence, if the court was away, to that one of the palaces which was in use for the time being. The other country palaces, none far from London, would receive a visit, at any rate Windsor and Hampton Court; Oxford probably, Cambridge possibly, and there an end. Of Scotland and Wales it can only be said that the former was practically ignored except by a few Frenchmen, as a result of the ancient alliance; while to Wales they paid as little attention as the semi-Welsh queen did — none at all.

Among the foreigners who have given us their impressions of England are several who have much that is of interest to say and yet who seem to have been entirely overlooked. Nevertheless, these pages are already more numerous than the relative importance of England warrants. Let us therefore take but one, and that one the briefest; the more so since he is the likeliest to continue to be overlooked, writing as he did in Polish, from which hitherto no translation seems to have been made, not even in paraphrase.

Jakób Sobieski, the only man who was ever four times Marshal of the Polish Diet, travelled all over Europe in his youth. Henry IV of France made a personal friend of him, and it was at Paris that he spent more time than elsewhere, where, eventually, he witnessed the assassination of the king and was nearly lynched himself on the spot by the mob who took it into their heads to regard him as the murderer. However, he not only escaped, but after justice had been done on Ravaillac by his being torn asunder by horses, Sobieski had an invitation to dinner from a bootmaker who had collected certain pieces of Ravaillac and was arranging a loyal dinner-party at which they were to form the chief dish.

It was in the previous year (1609) that he visited England in the train of Myszkowski, the Marshal, negotiations being then in progress for the marriage of James I's daughter Elizabeth to Wladislas, son of the King of Poland. Sobieski, very young and very Catholic, was easily enough taken in by appearances to speak of James I as a model king, and to accept without question the declaration of the English Catholics that things had improved greatly since the death of the "severe and overbearing Queen Elizabeth." But it must be borne in mind that the King had not yet come to the bottom of the Treasury. One of Sobieski's remarks—that the Palace at Westminster is finer inside than outside — is an interesting comment on the impoverishment of the Crown that set in, if taken in conjunction with the remark of Gölnitz of Danzig, less than ten years later, who says exactly the opposite. In comparing the palaces around Paris with those of the English king, he says that the former are fine externally, but contain many rooms in which a respectable German would not care to receive an acquaintance; cobwebs, unpolished woodwork, walls in disrepair. One thing that scandalised Sobieski greatly was that in St. Paul's he found buying and selling going on, a statement confirmed by a Venetian ambassador here in 1607, who says that London possesses many fine churches but that these are mostly used for nothing but driving bargains in.[12]

Sobieski's business, however, lay at the court, and the court was out of town: the King at one palace, the Queen at another, Princess Elizabeth at a third. On paying their respects to the last-named a curiously characteristic thing happened; her chamberlain met them and asked in what language they would speak with the Princess,

French, Italian, or Latin; she was equally at home
in all three. Myszkowski chose Italian. The occasion, of course, was not a decisive one, but the
conversation turned on Wladislas, the most
anxious enquirer being an elderly lady-in-waiting
who wanted to know if he was tall; the Princess,
she would have them know, was tall, really tall,
not made so artificially, with high heels, etc.,
to prove which she raised her mistress's skirt until
they saw not merely blue stockings, but also saf-
fron garters and white lace.

The last country of "European Europe" is
Sobieski's own country, but only the last because,
like England, it led nowhere. If omitted from a
tour it was omitted with regret and consciousness
of loss, being the largest monarchy in Christendom, 600 miles by 800, with a frontier reaching
to within 150 miles of Moscow and 100 of the
Black Sea; always on the verge of war, moreover,
and a paradise of aristocracy, three good reasons
for claiming the Average Tourist's attention, especially as among this aristocracy was always to
be found a welcome and as high an average of
attainments and qualities as anywhere north of
the Alps. The statement, too, that it was not a
thoroughfare must not be taken as absolute. Negotiations between the Tsars and the Papacy were
frequent and these of course implied journeys
through Poland by the friars whom the Papacy

was wont to use as emissaries for long distances,
as being more accustomed to endure privation
and fatigue than bishops.

Besides, from southeast to northwest stretched
the high road from the Black Sea through Kamie-
nietz to Danzig, which one of these travellers as-
sures us was the most thickly-populated highroad in Europe.[13] Danzig itself was one of the
great centres of world-commerce; so great that
its citizens were well justified in one detail of their
daily life that Moryson records, that of taking off
their hats as they passed the town hall. The commerce was very varied, but its main export seems
to have been grain and its main import, Scotchmen. Of these latter there were certainly thousands;[14] in fact, from some date in the reign of
Stephen Bathory (1575–86) till 1697, perhaps
later, a "brotherhood" of Scots existed, recognised officially; and boys of fifteen to seventeen
came over in such quantities and so often with
such disastrous results, that in 1625 an edict was
issued in Scotland prohibiting skippers taking
over any who had not been sent for or had not
500 marks. But these can hardly be reckoned as
tourists, travelling, as they did, Scot-fashion, on
the "ubi panis, ibi patria" principle, with the
object of sharing the retail-trade with Jews, so
successfully that there has long lingered in Eastern Prussia the proverb, "Warte bis der Schotte
kommt," alluding to the annual visits of these

pedlars. Many, too, can be traced as becoming burgesses of Danzig, or of Posen.

Of visitors of the type with which this chapter is more specially concerned, the reign of the Henry who afterwards became Henry III of France marks a starting-point, judging partly from the evidence available before and after that date, partly from the statement in the report of the first resident Venetian ambassador there, Girolamo Lippomano, who came in that reign, that Poland was at that time an unknown land to Venetians.

So much for the Average Tourist at work. Let us now see how he spent his spare time. It goes without saying that the degree to which the foreigner enjoyed himself was more or less dependent on the behaviour of natives. Let us see, first, then, what reception he might expect. Small boys, of course, are the same yesterday, to-day and forever, but they were, if possible, somewhat more outspoken then. An ambassador's wife went to the Hague once, never again, "by reason of the boys and wenches who much wondered at her huge farthingales and fine gowns, and saluted her at every turn of the street with their usual caresses of 'Hoore! hoore!'" Concealing herself from view was impossible, no cart would hold her farthingale. And although with all the detail that is poured forth concerning the Venetian constitution, the feature in it which,

though informal, has outlasted all the others, that
of the limited despotism of the small boys, is ignored, yet in practice it was felt; Sastrow, for one,
did not forget being pursued with "Tu sei tedesco,
perciò Luterano."

As regards the adults, Frenchmen, or any one
dressed in French fashions, had to beware of the
Italian towns where the French had been masters for a time, and although Strassburg had a gate
on the west, any one coming from the French side
had to enter by the east gate. Commercial quarrels
were even more bitter than political. When, for
instance, the English removed their "staple"
from Hamburg to Stade, nearer the mouth of the
Elbe, it was not safe for an Englishman to be seen
at Hamburg after the citizens had reached their
mid-day stage of drunkenness. As for theological
enmity, a Roman Catholic was saying his prayers
one evening in Frisia with the windows open; an
old woman marked it and came across the street
to spit at his inn; the next morning she came
again, to spit at him, and he had to put up with
it for fear of worse happening.

With such exceptions as these there was not
much to be feared from the upper classes; nor
even, on the main routes, from the lower; in
Dauphiné, for instance, all classes were pleasant
enough, whereas at Rochelle strangers were
liable to be pulled off their horses if they did not
remove their hats when passing the guard at the

gates. The two worst towns for brutality towards foreigners were, by general consent, London and Toulouse. In the former, according to Giordano Bruno, whose account only differs from every one else's in being more picturesque, the shop-people and artizans, on seeing a stranger, make faces, grin, laugh, hoot, call him dog, traitor, foreigner, the last name being the rudest they can think of, qualifying him for any other insult. Should he take the offensive, or put his hand to his weapon, an army of ruffians seems to spring out of the ground, flourishing a forest of sticks, poles, halberds, and partizans. In a more playful humour, one will pretend to run away behind a booth and come out charging on the stranger like an angry bull; if an arm gets broken, as happened to one Italian, the bystanders shout with laughter and the magistrate sees nothing reprehensible in the affair.[15] Oxford was a change for the better, for there it was only the students who behaved like brigands; as they did at Carcassonne, too, where the law-students insisted on tribute from visitors, — they called it a "bienvenu," — or if it was not forthcoming, the contents of the visitor's trunks were shaken out. Yet among those of Oxford, Zinzerling makes an exception in the case of Queen's College, where as soon as a foreigner is recognised as such, he is brought an ox-horn full of beer.

Such presents were customary on a very large scale on the continent; in France they generally consisted of wine and were presented to persons of high rank only, but in Germany every gentleman received gifts of drink and food which usually cost more than their value in tips and dinners. The higher the rank of the visitor, the greater the quantity; the Infanta Clara Eugenia writes home that at the stopping-places in her passage through Switzerland the gifts require thirty or forty men to carry them, who lay them at her feet until she is surrounded by barrels and has the greatest difficulty in preserving her gravity. At Lucerne she received barley as well as wine, and two oxen, both too fat to move. Many other local customs had to be submitted to which have died out since; such as ceremonies of initiation into the freedom of Hansa League towns, which were accompanied by practical joking; the obligation on Protestants staying at Geneva to attend service at 7 A. M. whenever there was a sermon; and so on.

Among these exceptional customs and regulations should be mentioned those concerning weapons in Italy. At Lucca no knife might be carried unless blunted at the point; in the Papal States, a sword was allowed, but no short, easily hidden, weapon; in Venetian territory fire-arms only were forbidden; elsewhere a license from the local authorities had ordinarily to be obtained for wearing a sword, and in Florence the license only referred to day-time. This is Moryson's account of the regulations; before his time the regulations were laxer, and later they became stricter, which gave a great impetus to the poisoning trade; in fact, the bakers in Lombardy were mostly Germans, and those of Rome, Jews, the Italians being unwilling to trust their fellow countrymen.

Such subjects naturally suggest executions, which formed one of the commonest and principal "sights" throughout Europe. Lithgow landed at the Piazzetta at Venice just when a friar was being burnt alive there for getting fifteen nuns with child in a year. It was in Venice, too, that Moryson saw two young senators' sons, who had had too uproarious a night, have their hands cut off at the places where they had done the mischief, their tongues cut out where they had sung blasphemous songs, and finally beheaded by a sort of guillotine in the Piazza. And when he was staying at Leipzig, where, as was the custom in Germany, adultery was punishable by death, a case had recently occurred of a girl giving birth to an illegitimate child in a church, during service. It was under consideration when he left whether an ancient precedent should not be revived to meet her case, that she should be tied up in a sack with a cat, a cock, a snake, and a dog, all alive, and so drowned. To quote one more as a sample of many, there is the detailed description of a man being broken on the wheel at Hamburg, by

Taylor the "water-poet." The place of execution was on a mound, so that the enormous crowd could see well; moated, to keep the people at a distance, and approached by a drawbridge which was raised during the execution; the criminal was drunk, according to custom. In Germany exceptional criminals were on view for some days before execution, nailed by the ears to posts. Torture accompanying execution was common, and branding and mutilation things that no traveller could well avoid seeing. But none seemed to want to avoid them: Evelyn went to the Châtelet prison at Paris to look on while a prisoner underwent legal torture. The only occasions that seem to have struck them as too horrible was when the headsman bungled matters: a Dutchman at Paris saw one try sixteen times and then have to be assisted. And as in the towns, so by the wayside. Gallows and wheels bearing the bodies of men and sometimes of women, dying, dead, or decaying, were continually to be seen: Taylor says he counted seven score between Hamburg and Prague, and Moryson mentions a criminal hanging in chains near Lindau, starving to death, with a mastiff at each heel, in order that he might be partially eaten before death.

No less awful a sight, and no less frequent in certain places, such as Marseilles, was the galley-slave, naked except for a pair of breeches, shaven, dragging behind him when ashore the chain fixed to his feet, treated worse than a beast, and yet not necessarily criminal: at Leghorn was a tent, at Naples a certain stone, where a man might stake his liberty against a few shillings on a throw of the dice. Among the few who obtained their release by being bought out were those who, on that condition, acted as deputies in the processions of flagellants which tourists often mention: Montaigne witnessed one at Rome with five hundred persons in it. He, like others, was astonished to note their unconcern; the scourging was genuine: their backs were raw and bloody, the thongs of the scourges adhering to each other with the blood; yet so far from showing signs of pain, they marched along, careless and talkative, in an every-day mood.

Other forms of slavery were ordinarily met with: at Naples an open slave-market was held; at Lisbon, too, where men and monkeys were sold side by side. And here and there one might come across settlements of those who could not claim all the benefits of the law. Zinzerling picked up a cagot servant near Toulouse, a young man, well-informed, who told him how his brother-outcasts had just petitioned for permission to marry whom they chose, offering to have their blood tested to prove it no different from other men's. Those who did not act as servants, lived by handicraft, carpentering mostly; they were forced to dwell in the suburbs, and nothing they owned was heritable except furniture, which was looked on as sharing their taint.

But he does not mention the goose-foot badge which distinguished them from "clean" persons. The badge of the Jew, on the other hand, often seen, is often mentioned, varying according to the extent they had acquired influence and used it. In Poland, thanks to the Jewish mistress of one of their kings, they had almost equal rights with Christians. Elsewhere, except in those places, such as England, which they were nominally forbidden to enter, a badge was compulsory; lightest in Mantua, merely a bit of yellow lace tacked on inside their cloaks, but generally a red hat for the men and a red garment for the women: red as betokening their guiltiness of Christ's blood. An alternative colour was yellow, as in Rome, where a short-sighted cardinal once mistook a red-hatted Jew for a brother cardinal and obtained a change of colour in order to safeguard himself against being so polite again.

But the tourist's leisure, so far, has been too much occupied with blood and social damnation; let us look for a lighter mood: let us see him at the Zoo. Florence seems to have been the best stocked. Rabelais saw two Zoos there, and this was not an optical illusion of a credible kind, for he localises them differently; one at the Palazzo Strozzi with porcupines and ostriches as the "stars"; one near the Belfry, boasting lions and tigers. Moryson mentions one only, the Duke's, containing five lions, five wolves, three eagles, three tigers, one wild cat, bears, leopards, an Indian mouse which could kill a cat, and wild boars. After another fifty-year interval comes Evelyn, who looks down upon all the animals housed together in a deep court, a pleasanter confinement, he thinks, than the narrow cages of the Tower at London. But I have forgotten Audebert, who should have come between (1576) Rabelais and Moryson, and who found a Zoo near the "Annunziata," possessing fourteen lions, a tiger, an eagle, and a vulture therein. In 1592 at Prague there were twelve camels in the Emperor's Zoo, very probably the sons and daughters of those whom Busbecq brought back from Constantinople in the hope of naturalising them in Europe as beasts of burden, — not the only attempt of the kind, for Sir Wm. Brereton saw some so used in Holland, and a German others near Aranjuez. The leopards, moreover, in this same Imperial Zoo, were taken to assist in hunting.

Experiments and novelties such as these, of course, provided a larger part of the interest of a journey then than is the case now, when such news is communicated immediately through the newspapers. We find Tommaso Contarini, ambassador to Flanders, greatly struck by the value of peat as fuel, and bringing back some to Venice to as-

sist him in ascertaining if anything of the kind is
obtainable near. Then there was "Der Einlasse,"
the complicated night-entrance to Augsburg,
worked by mechanism which allowed a person
to be admitted without seeing any one, — such a
mystery that many allowed themselves to be
locked out on purpose to see it work, and Queen
Elizabeth sent a special agent to acquire the
secret; in vain. But in Augsburg front doors were
habitually opened by pulleys from some room,
and shut automatically; it was at Augsburg, too,
that a coach was to be seen "driven by engines"
within it by the occupant so that it seemed to
go of itself; it had been driven about the city.[16]
This occurs in the year 1655; three years later
fountain pens[17] were on sale at Paris for ten francs
each, twelve to those whom the inventor knew to
be eager to have one; that is, £5 to £6 in our money.
Even an Italian might learn: like the Florentine
who discovered in England what garden-rollers
were, in their early solid-stone-cylinder form.
But Tasso had the chance to learn something important and not only passed it by but places it
first among the three customs in France which he
strongly condemns. It is that in some districts
the people nourished the children with cow's milk.
How, he asks, can any good come of feeding in-
fants with the produce of an animal that is a beast
of burden and has to endure blows daily? An Englishman in Italy noted the method of stripping

hemp with wooden instruments instead of with the fingers, the laborious English way; and fans, forks, and umbrellas would be new to every one who crossed the Alps; but a learned physician warned Moryson against using the last-mentioned, "things like a little canopy," as concentrating the heat of the sun on the head.

In Flanders, again, every one might learn what kind of a thing a door-mat was, and a Dutch barber had only to cross the Channel to find that he was behind the times in using dregs of beer as a lather. And if it was possible for a twentieth-century Englishwoman to cross into sixteenth-century Germany she would find out what a convenience it was for an invalid to have a towel attached to a wheel running along the head of the bed, to assist him or her in changing position. Where, too, except from travel, his own or some one else's, did Sir John Harington get his ideas concerning the introduction of real water-closets, with gold-fish visible swimming about in the cisterns, just as they are to be seen at railway stations to-day?

A greater discovery than all these put together lay in the differences in the position of women in the above countries. Take the United Provinces and Italy, as the two where the contrast was greatest. In the former, girls of good birth and looks might not only settle down in the common-room of an inn instead of hiring a private room for meals, but would sit round the fire and share the after-dinner drink of the men as a matter of course. All-night skating-parties were so common that the liberty was not misused; whereas in Italy the strictness was as extreme as the Dutch freedom, and its result, too; only, in Italy, the result was the demoralisation of both sexes. Chioggia was an exception, where Villamont was surprised to see the women and girls sitting at their doors, needle-working; and where French influence had made itself felt some relaxation had taken place, especially at Genoa, where one foreigner even notes that the women walked with a longer stride than most Italian women. But the unmixed Italian convention gave most girls no choice between becoming either prisoners or prostitutes, that is, of course, like everything else in this book, from the foreigner's point of view. Of the former class the tourist saw next to nothing; the men of the household did even the marketing themselves; while the latter formed one of the best-known features of Italian life. The numbers may seem at first sight incredible — 30,000 is the figure always quoted for Naples; but there was some check on such statements inasmuch as every government licensed each one for a fixed sum and therefore could reckon the total. Moreover, Sir Henry Wotton writes in 1592 that a census just taken in Rome counted 40,000, and he had it on good authority; and in 1617, that the Es-

pousal of the Sea at Venice had been spoilt as a
sight because the courtesans, offended at an edict
directed at them, had abstained from taking part
in it. Those at the head of the profession lived
"like princesses," not only so far as expenditure
went, but also in their command of marks of
respect in public, except that every now and then
some sumptuary edict would create, and perhaps enforce, some distinction between those who
populated and those who depopulated Italy. It
is pleasanter to turn back to Holland again, to
the homely arrangements of Thursday in Delft
fair week, when the women who had had enough
of waiting for husbands sat in the church and
the men who had waited long enough for wives
came to look at them. A few questions, a pot
of beer, a few details to be settled; and then the
wedding.

There were plenty of these fairs, Lyons had
four a year, so had Rouen; but the attraction they
possessed for the sixteenth-century human being
lay rather in the amount of wholesale and finan-
cier's business done than in homely picturesque-
ness; sentimentality is the last vice he can be
charged with. Who, for instance, nowadays, would
dare to say he saw nothing charming in a Breton
festival? but Brittany was left to itself in those
days, and a travelling doctor who chanced on one
leaves it with the remark that the Breton girls
singing their folk-songs reminded him of "the

croaking of frogs when they are in love." Yet St. John's Eve was a festival that gave plenty of pleasure to lookers-on as well as those who took part in it; at Paris, in particular, where there was hardly a citizen named after the saint who did not light a fire at his door that night. And it is perhaps worth mentioning how they kept that feast at Naples, according to Audebert, in 1577; how the custom was to bathe in the sea previous to paying one's devotions at "S. Giovan' a' Mare," seeing that he adds that the custom was dying out, the younger people scorning it as a pagan survival.

A larger proportion of the public pleasures of Europe were bound up with religious ceremony than is the case at present; and as regards pilgrimage, the reference above to the subject in general needs to be supplemented by some details concerning the relics, since there is no room for doubt as to whether or not they held their ground as "sights," the more so inasmuch as a sceptical attitude did not become a conventional habit of mind until, to judge by tourists' books, about the third quarter of the seventeenth century. At the abbey of Marmoutier, near Tours, for example, was shown a vessel which had been sent from Heaven filled with oil for the healing of St. Martin's leg, a breakage of which the devil had caused by taking away the stairs. They also showed a vast barrel wherein St. Martin kept his wine; but

not till 1675 does any one remark that that was
probably the fiend who stole away the stairs.
Disbelief finds expression in plenty, it is true,
but it is always that of the Protestant who dis-
believes, not because his reason tells him the tale
must be false, but because Roman Catholicism
affirms it to be true. When there was no suspicion of a friar at the back of the story, there
was nothing they would not swallow: even Evelyn accepts Mettius Curtius and his chasm as if
all four evangelists had guaranteed both; or, to
take a still better example, that of the monument
near Leyden to the lady who had 365 children at
one birth — (she had laughed at a poor woman's
tale that the latter's two babies were twins, and
the woman had expressed a hope that the lady
might give birth to as many children at one confinement as there were days in the year) — Münster, the great Protestant geographer, repeats the
story without throwing doubt, and consequently
one tourist after another has no hesitation about
it.

So happy a frame of mind must have increased
the interest of many a resting-place. Breaking
one's journey at Angers, for instance, there was
a porphyry vase to be seen, one of those used at
the wedding feast at Cana in Galilee; others were
preserved at Famagosta, Magdeburg, and the
Charterhouse at Florence. At Angers, also, at
St. Julian's, was a copy of the portrait of Our Lady

which St. Luke had painted; at Arras, manna which had fallen in the days of St. Jerome, looking like white wool; at Milan, the brazen serpent which Moses set up in the wilderness; at Vienna, one of the stones wherewith St. Stephen had been stoned, another at Toulouse; and at the monastery of the Celestines at Louvain, one of the thirty silver pennies for which Christ had been sold, bearing the head of Tiberius on one side, a lily on the other. It is well known how Mary Magdalen came to Provence to live after the Crucifixion, but less known that at Maximilien near Marseilles the tip of her nose used to be on view: no more than that because she had been cremated, but the tip of her nose remained imperishable because there Christ had kissed her. Pontius Pilate also ended his life in Europe: in exile at Vienne, where the tower in which he had been imprisoned was pointed out to the visitor, likewise the lake wherein he had committed suicide, although it was on the shores of another lake, one in the territory of Lucerne, that he was to be seen walking once a year in his official robes. But this every one was content to take on hearsay, since he who saw him then died within the year.

The monastery of St. Nicholas at Catania, in Sicily, had an excellent collection: a nail from the Cross, one of St. Sebastian's arrows, and pieces of St. George's coat of mail, of St. Peter's beard, and of the beard of Zachary, father of John the Bap-

tist. This, and the places previously mentioned,
serve to show what treasures would surely be met
with on the road; great relic-centres like Venice
and Rome would require pages to catalogue their
wealth; even a secondary centre like Trier held
as many bodies of saints as there are days in the
year, besides the well by which Athanasius sat
when he composed the "Quicunque Vult" and
the knife wherewith St. Peter cut off Malchus'
ear.

As for their belief in relics, it is only fair to
point out what may not occur to every reader,
that they had the same reason, neither more nor
less, for believing so, as we for believing that the
earth moves round the sun: it is common knowledge. 'Common knowledge'—is not all of it,
whether scientific or theological, equally an act
of faith? and is it more reasonable for us to quote
Baedeker to ourselves than for pilgrim Nicholas
to put his trust in friar John? "Howbeit (if we
will truly consider it), more worthy is it to believe,
than to know as we now know"—that is not a
quotation from a theologian but from Bacon's
"Advancement of Learning." Of two things we
may be sure, that the true history of a relic would
probably be far stranger than its legend, and that
whatever marvels the southerner saw or heard,
he came across nothing more novel or more miraculous than the ebb and flow of the northern
tides.

In speaking of relics, the secular ones must be remembered, too: foremost among them the original Ephesus statue of Diana, which Hentzner saw at Fontainebleau and Evelyn at the Louvre. Most frequently mentioned is the buck's head at Amboise. It bore antlers of enormous size, and for that reason had enjoyed Francis I's special protection while alive. By Sir John Reresby's time (1654) it had been ascertained that the buck was of English birth, having reached France by swimming the Channel; while thirty-three years later it had been dead for three hundred years and at the date of its death was nine hundred years old. These details need no explanation; any caretaker can equal them under pressure. The writer once asked the sextoness of the church where Spinoza lies buried how he came to be laid there considering he was not exactly orthodox: the answer was, without hesitation, that he became a Protestant before he died!

These secular relics cannot possibly be left without a digression concerning unicorn's horns, which were more prized than any other kind of exhibit. St. Mark's Treasury at Venice seems to have been the only museum that possessed more than one; it contained three. Dresden owned one, which hung by a golden chain; that at Fontainebleau, three yards high, was valued at one hundred thousand crowns. It was, however, a wise unicorn that knew its own horn: the Danish sailors kept their secrets quiet and prices high, the more easily since, owing to disasters, there were temporary cessations in the Greenland whale-fishery, of which unicorns' horns were a by-product, thus rendering the supply small and fluctuating. It was an open secret by this time that sea-unicorns existed, but the heraldic animal had the overwhelming advantage of support from Pliny, Aristotle, and the Bible and therefore fought for the "crowns" so to speak, with every success. It was not till this time, in 1603, that the unicorn was introduced into the arms of the King of England; and its horn was in the greater request because of its supposed quality of an antidote to poison. To the lore of this part of the subject Zinzerling makes an addition. At Tours lived a lawyer who had travelled in Spain and India, and had brought back three great rarities: "Rolandi gladium, Librum in pergameno Geographiæ et Hydrographiæ, membrum masculum Monocerotis majoris contra toxica efficaciæ quam cornu."

He did not see these personally, but mentions them because it would be a pity for any one to miss them for lack of a word or two from him. For himself, he could not find the lawyer, a kind of trouble from which these tourists ordinarily suffered, for it was part of their experience to make acquaintance with private collections. Not that there were any public ones to the extent we are accustomed to, except the churches, which, as picture galleries, had this advantage, that the pictures were seen in the setting for which they were designed. Practically all the official "treasuries" were only public to the extent that a remarkable country house like Compton Winyates is so now; yet on the other hand, and for that very reason, it was somewhat more customary for private collections to be accessible to strangers than is the case, probably, at present. What attracted the greatest number of visitors, however, was water-mechanisms.

Up till the beginning of the seventeenth century these were found at their best only in Italy; and of the Italian, those at Pratolino ranked first, belonging to the Duke of Florence, who was reputed to spend more on his water than on his wine. The invariable custom of secret devices for soaking the visitor as he sat down or walked about was there carried further, and with greater variety, than elsewhere. Besides, there was Fame blowing a trumpet; a peasant offering a drink to a tiger who swallows it and then looks all round; Syrinx beckons to Pan to pipe, whereupon Pan gets up from his seat, puts it aside, pipes, pulls his seat towards him and sits down again with a melancholy look because Syrinx has not rewarded him with a kiss. And so on, with a multitude of devices for making music and attracting attention, only equalled by those at the Villa d' Este at Tivoli.

It is noteworthy how long it took to introduce them into France, where everything Italian was fashionable. Marguerite de Valois speaks of those she saw in Flanders in 1577 in a way that implies no previous acquaintance with anything of the kind, but when peace was restored, we find St. Germain-en-Laye stocked with a poet who plays on a lyre, and with various animals which gather round him, and trees which bend down, as he plays; and the king passes by with his suite. On the other side of the Rhine ingenuity seems to have been devoted rather to clock-work. The clock at Strassburg, one of the chief marvels of Europe, was outdone by one in a private house at Augsburg: for besides displaying all the clever puerilities which the seventeenth century rejoiced in, it reproduced the movements and stations of the planets and the advent and effect of eclipses, all in their due time. Somewhat later, at Lübeck, the striking of the hour by the town clock was accompanied by the Virgin kissing her Baby, and St. Peter dropping his key and picking it up again, while at Hamburg could be seen a marvellous Annunciation, with a most gorgeous Gabriel and five attendant cherubim who flapped gilded wings, and a Blessed Virgin dressed in the French fashion who was discovered reading a book and ended by dropping a curtsey.

Of amusements which required people to take part in them, card games were rarely seen in

Germany, and in Italy were banned as much by public opinion as by law, whereas in England they were an occupation rather than an amusement. So also with hawking and hunting. In six years abroad Moryson saw hawking but twice, once in Bohemia and once in Poland, and implies that in England it was common; while of hunting he definitely says, "England lacks not Actæons, eaten up by their own dogs." The same contrast he observes with regard to itinerant musicians and plays, of which latter he is sure that more are performed in London than in all the other parts of the world that he had visited put together. A variety of angling, on the other hand, he notes as peculiar to Italy: that with bait and hooks fastened to corks and held out of window for birds; while golf was only played in Scotland, Holland, and Naples; and the most frequently played game in Europe, pallone, was as unknown in Britain then as now. The piazza S. Stefano at Venice was reserved for pallone every Sunday evening, and in the disused papal palace at Avignon one room was given up to pallone and another to tennis, which came next in popularity, the chief centre being Paris. In 1577 it was credited with 1800 courts, but the Dutch ambassador resident there eighty years later had them counted and only discovered 118.

And so the list might go on and on and on — in all its seeming irrelevancy! And yet, when it is

borne in mind that every detail is one that some
tourist or other noticed, to the point of thinking it
worth recording, a certain, at least symbolic, rele-
vancy comes into view, even though it be nothing
more vital than that of a 16th-century variety of
subjective imbecility under the stimulus of a jog-
trot. On the other hand, all this comes under the
heading of
> . . . things
> Which cannot in their huge and proper life
> Be here presented.

So the scenery must be shifted.

PART II

THE UNVISITED NORTH

" . . . a few days earlier I had read certain News-Sheets
printed here in Venice by these good fathers [the Jesuits], relating
their progress in Muscovy, the conversion of a King in Africa,
and so on. I said to myself, all right about Muscovy, it's a cold
Country, far away, few go there — and few return. . . ."
>   SIR HENRY WOTTON,[1] 1606.

ANDREW BOORDE has something to say about
Iceland in his guide to Europe. He puts into the
mouth of a native the words, —

> "I am an Icelander, as brute as a beast,
> When I eat candle ends, I am at a feast.

And that is all they knew about Iceland. As a
country with a political history and a literature

it was no more present in their minds than as a
holiday resort. Nor were any of the countries
that bordered the Baltic, except on the South.
But Danzig alone was enough to keep the Baltic a busy sea, and consequently Denmark was
not as much ignored as would otherwise have
happened; for both sides of the entrance to the
Baltic belonged to the King of Denmark, whose
extortions in the way of tolls kept his name before the public.

Norway was thus practically isolated from Europe. Sweden, however, during the Thirty Years'
War, attracted some attention, partly on account
of its share in the war, partly on account of the
development of its silver mines. There is an interesting account of a visit to those at "Sylf-
bergen," twenty leagues from Stockholm, in 1667,
which may serve as an indication of experiences
that might have been met with at an earlier date.
The visitor, a Frenchman,[2] descended, half-naked,
in half a cask, which was attached to a cable by
three iron chains, accompanied by two workers
whose grimness, flavour, and unpleasant personalities, gave him an attack of nerves. Among
the miners he found French, Germans, English,
Italians and Russians, all, as he says, digging their
own graves, for the conditions of mining in those
days was terrible. A traveller through Hungary
in 1615 [3] notes that the miners there could not
work more than four hours at a stretch, and that

few reached middle age, what with the number of casualties and the conditions of the mines. One result of this was that they usually married at fifteen. Yet weekly wages, after making allowance for the cheapness of living in Hungary, were equivalent to no more than twelve to fourteen shillings at present values. It was a most natural question at the time to ask whether, working as they did in the bowels of the earth, they ever came across demons. To which question a miner answered that sometimes they did, and on those occasions they appeared in the shape of little black boys, chattering, but doing no harm beyond blowing the lamps out.

Returning northwards and continuing the journey to the other side of the Baltic, the dominions of the Grand Duke of Muscovy would not be reached immediately. Riga, the port most usually aimed at, belonged to Poland; the alternative harbour of Revel to Sweden. The choice of Riga is another instance of the contemporary preference for travelling by water rather than by land. However far out of the straight line between Danzig and Moscow, it was both the nearest coast town to the latter and also at the mouth of the river, the Dwina, which is navigable for the longest distance west of Moscow. One other route remains, discovered by the English, left wholly to them and to the Dutch, and only used by them because of commercial quarrels with the rulers of the Baltic. This was the sea-voyage of about two months from London to Archangel, then up the Dwina and Suchona to Vologda, and thence by land to Moscow.

Moscow then possessed about forty thousand houses. It may be doubted if any town in Europe surpassed that number. Yet it was not size that caused going to Muscovy to be practically identical with going to Moscow, but the fact that the latter was the residence of a ruler whose despotism was so unlimited that every other settlement became insignificant compared with that where he dwelt. This is typified by the prominence given by all foreigners to the banquet they generally attended as the guests of the Tsar, a display of barbaric magnificence that must evidently have been one of the most striking sights of Europe. Unfortunately the magnificence was apt to stop short at the door of the banquet-hall. One Italian[4] in particular could not forget leaving after three hours, picking his way through the outer rooms, pitch dark and strewn with courtiers in the weeping-stage of drunkenness, down the stairs. About twenty yards away from the foot of the stairs a crowd of servants were waiting with horses to take their masters home. Towards these they had to wade, knee-deep in mud, still in pitch-darkness, and so continue a good part of the way home, since no one was allowed to ride till he had passed out of the palace precincts.

Nowhere was this despotism more felt than in relation to travel: every foreigner was half a prisoner from the day he entered the kingdom to the day he left, even though he were an ambassador. The very Jesuits sent by the Pope, in 1581, at the Tsar's own request, to negotiate a peace between himself and the King of Poland were under surveillance to such an extent that they were not allowed to water their own horses. Neither was any subject allowed to leave the land: the penalty for unlicensed travel being death. It is clear that leave must have been more freely granted than one might imagine from the general statements of visitors, since Russian pilgrims and merchants are by no means uncommon, and indeed, at this period, Peter Mogila, Metropolitan of Kiev, and Boris Godunov, ruler at Moscow, endeavoured to encourage travel by Russians as a means of education.

Godunov's efforts, in fact, beginning as they did with his accession in 1586, synchronised with the growth of the same idea in England. But his efforts failed through being too far ahead of public opinion; those whom he sent stayed away permanently, those who stayed at home remained unconverted.[5] Two instances of public opinion as regards foreigners may be quoted, both occurring on the direct road to Moscow at the very end of this period, during the whole of which the number of visitors goes on increasing. The first is the experience of some Dutchmen who came by invitation of the Tsar and consequently had a house commandeered for them. The wife of the owner, seeing no help was to be had from the local authorities, rushed to St. Nicholas and would, she believed, have obtained a miraculous expulsion of the visitors had not her husband tired of the length of her prayer and stopped it by force. The second is that of a Danish gentleman who, with his companions, was prevented from entering a village by bees which the peasants had irritated for that purpose.

So, too, with the Muscovites and travel on their own account. Whereas other Europeans only thought of dying when they travelled, the Muscovite only thought of travelling when he died. Then his friends shod him with a new pair of shoes for the long journey that he had to go, and put a letter in his hand to St. Nicholas, by way of passport, testifying that the bearer died a Russian of the Russians in the one true faith.

The distinctive characteristics of the people as seen by strangers were drunkenness, endurance of heat, cold, and torture, and slavish obedience to the Tsar. Drunkenness in particular. As the English verse-writer, Turberville, who went there, puts it, —

Drink is their whole desire, the pot is all their pride,
The soberest head doth once a day stand needful of a
    guide.

The habit went the farther since it was encouraged by the government, for the recent taking-over of the drink-traffic by the State was but a reversion to the state of affairs in 1600, though then it was an offence against the State to urge a man to leave one of the State-owned taverns, even though he was pledging the clothes off his back: a common custom. At every season of public rejoicing in winter two or three hundred died in the streets of Moscow as they lay there naked and dead-drunk, and the stranger might see the bodies brought home by tens and twelves, half-eaten by dogs. One traveller tells a tale of a Muscovite whom he saw come out of a tavern in shirt and breeches only, meet a friend, return, and come out again with no shirt. The traveller, who knew Russian, expressed sympathy with him as if he had been robbed, but was answered, "No, it's the man at the bar and his wine that have brought me to this, but as my shirt's there my breeches may as well keep it company." And accordingly, a few minutes afterwards, he came out once more with nothing to cover him but a handful of flowers picked at the tavern-door!

There had been a Tsar who tried to repress drunkenness, but he became a dead failure in every sense of the phrase shortly before the above incident happened, and even during his lifetime achieved nothing more than preventing people going about the streets naked. Neither was it

just the average man who could not endure life
sober, but the priest frequently needed a lay-
helper on either side of him in order to get through
the marriage service, a result of the festivities
preceding the wedding. And the women were no
better than the men. When a Russian lady enter-
tained her friends, it was etiquette to send round
afterwards to know if they all got home safely.
Yet one traveller unconsciously gives the Muscovite's own point of view: there was a quarter of
Moscow known as the "drunken" quarter: that
was where the foreign soldiers lodged.

The excessive misuse of tobacco was also bound
to be noticed, considering that smoking became
general more quickly there than anywhere else
outside England and Turkey. But the Tsar who
failed to check drunkenness succeeded against
smoking, which he prohibited, under penalty of
slitting the nostrils, in 1634, on the ground of it
being a frequent cause of fires among the houses,
all wooden ones, and of the unholy state of the
Muscovite's breath when he addressed the saints.

Along with other accusations which the travellers have to lodge, such as that of a grossness of
indecency without parallel in their experience,
is hardly to be found one note of pleasure, except
with regard to the charm of the Russian spring.
It may be doubted if foreigners' opinions underwent much change until such writers as Turgenev
compelled attention to the point of creating sym-

pathy. But yet, if their tales be few and their enjoyment scanty, their records possess all the greater comparative value from the very fact of their fewness. That the pre-Christian Slav religion still remained in memory, if not in use, at Pskov as late as 1590 would probably never even have been guessed but for the remark of one Johann David Wunderer, who was there at that date, that he saw two stone statues there, one holding a cross, the other standing on a snake with a sword in one hand and fire in the other, idols, he was told, who were still known as "Ussladt" and "Corsa."[6]

PART III

THE MISUNDERSTOOD WEST

Et si pur effecti quasi miraculosi vi trovasse, come ja vi sono, V. S. non l'imputi al scriptore, ma a la variatione et deità de la natura.

ANTONIO DA BEATIS, 1518.

IT will have been noticed that the tourist was nothing if not unsympathetic. Yet nowhere does this stand out so sharply as in regard to the two countries farthest west. So far as the Spanish peninsula was concerned, a reason may be sought in the route usually chosen, a route which treated the peninsula as part of "European Europe" and implied seeing a little of it, seeing that little in a one-sided way, and mistaking it for an epitome of the whole.

Starting from the southwest corner of France, the most direct way was taken for the Escorial and Madrid, whence the return journey led past Barcelona to Montserrat and so over the Pyrenees again to the southeast corner of France. The objective, of course, was the capital and the court. And it was taken for granted, here as elsewhere, that the other chief objects of interest were the towns, which claimed an even greater proportion of attention than in other countries, inasmuch as the hardships of travel in Spain were more trying to a foreigner than those experienced elsewhere, and his mental energies were often, in consequence, the less free for observation in Spain as long as he kept on the move. Now it unfortunately happened that the seamy side of Spanish life thrust itself to the front in undue proportion in the towns. Moreover, the French districts which lay nearest to Spain were those whose characteristics contrasted most favourably as against those of the Spanish districts that lay nearest to France. The liveliness and gaiety of the Bayonnais, playing bowls all day on the carefully levelled, sanded court between his house and the street, was thrown into relief by the sternness of the Pyrenees and the poverty and gloom of the Vizcaino.

The injustice done by these first impressions was deepened by almost all that caught the attention on a journey like that just outlined, whatever the momentary point of view, whether historical, geographical, social, superficial, or political, — especially political.

The Spanish king was looked on as the most powerful Christian monarch of the time, in prestige, in financial resources, and as the head of an empire whose limits were the more impressive for being mathematicians' lines imagined in the midst of the Unexplored. It was natural, then, to consider his capital the centre of each, as well as of all, of his dominions, and as the Holy of Holies of European kingship; and this, too, at a date when monarchical ideals were so strong that a highly respectable middle-class man like William Camden could allude to Simon de Montfort, who figures in modern school-books as the ever-glorious founder of "representative" government, as — "our Catiline." [1] In addition, the annexation of Portugal in 1580, and its revolt in 1640, accentuate such ideas more in this period than in any other as the only one during which the whole peninsula was under one king.

Neither was this illusion of solidarity merely a traveller's mirage which those on the spot would rectify. Philip II's people loved to have it so; witness one of Sancho Panza's favourite proverbs: "Un rey, Una fe, Una ley"; and how was the tourist to know that the Spaniard did not appreciate his differentiation between ideals and facts? The voice of Sancho Panza is, of course, the voice of Castile, but then Castile has always the monopoly of forming foreign, and leading Spanish, opinion on things Spanish.

The choice of route, then, predetermined by the usual considerations, applicable only to other countries, failed to do justice to Spain. Yet it was accompanied by these special assumptions, as regards political supremacy, at the back of the tourist's mind, no evidence in favour of which was forthcoming; at least, no evidence of a kind which he came prepared to recognise as such. On the contrary, he could not avoid being struck by the insignificance of Spanish buildings, especially, curiously enough, at Madrid itself, where the houses were mostly of one story; a result of it being necessary to obtain a license from the King for anything higher, the conditions imposed by which license, such as that of housing ambassadors in the second story, would prove too burdensome. This particular impression was deepened in the latter half of the period by the linen windowpanes, which made the interiors seem gloomy at a date when the use of glass in windows was spreading in the countries which the visitor had come from and had passed through. And so with many other matters, until one Dutchman who had travelled viâ Italy, after being taken to see a water-mill as something quite out of the common, makes the general deduction: "What is very common elsewhere, here often passes for miraculous."

Furthermore, as has been said, there were the historical illusions, too, which would be shaken. What Montaigne experienced at Venice took place on a larger scale in the minds of all who visited Spain. The deeper the previous study, the deeper the disappointment; but the latter was felt nevertheless by him in whom it was unconscious; and in both cases the recovery was slower than at Venice where all that was visible was so near. In fact, it is clear enough that with most a recovery never happened.

The histories they depended on were a variety of heroic fiction whose theory of causation consisted of immediate causes and God. National limitations only appeared, therefore, in so far as they had contributed to national achievements. But to the tourist these limitations, and even the qualities which were simply strange to him, stood out as defects, and the necessary minutiæ of daily life as the unworthy preoccupations of degenerate descendants; while the people, accordingly, whose ancestors were represented as having done nothing but conquer for centuries, showed up as ordinary human beings, muddling along in the way customary among one's own countrymen. Yet successes of Spanish diplomacy were so recent, and the supremacy of Spanish infantry so terribly obvious, that strangers could not account for all this disillusion by assuming degeneration to be the sole reason; while it was likewise too sudden for them to see in it nothing but an example of the falsification of proportions inherent in all knowledge drawn from books or other second-hand sources. Their attitude to Spain when they revised their journals was thus mystification rather than contempt or disgust, though both the latter are usually present.

This same unpreparedness to take a totally fresh point of view is even more marked in relation to religion. However greatly at odds the matter-of-fact foreigner and the matter-of-faith Castilian might be over details, both were equally unwilling to accept the illusions of to-morrow on that subject in place of the illusions of yesterday. The tendency to accept the face values of things theological was then as strong as to-day it is weak; but, with the possible exception of seventeenth-century Ireland, it was nowhere so strong as in Spain. The latter's place in Europe was bound up with leadership of the cause of Roman Catholicism; foreigners took this for granted, and the Spaniards unconsciously set a value on their creed apart from its relation to theological logic or religious experience — it had so long been the only rallying cry which could bring about a sinking of differences and achieve the temporary unity which was essential to success in war. But to the contemporary stranger, the varnish of the water of baptism was opaque, and the Celt, the Moor, the Pre-historic, the Outrageous-Pagan, and the all-pervading Jew, seemed all one thing, ultra-Holy-Roman. Another source of mystification — except to the Protestant, who knew exactly what it all meant and so went further astray than the rest, in the same direction.

Socially, the unintelligible contradictoriness was as great. Witness one whom a Burgos gentleman invited to dinner. The dining-room was that in which the hostess lay ill in bed with a fever; and he remembered afterwards that he had behaved with grossly bad manners inasmuch as he had taken off his hat at meal-time.

To go on to the means whereby geography also contributed to strain the sixteenth-century tourist's easily ruptured sympathy, there was the climate. The majority started in fear of the heat and suffered only from cold, expecting to find an Andalusian spring perpetually reigning at, say Burgos, instead of its "ten months of winter and two of hell" (or, to retain the pun, "diez mezes de invierno y dos de infierno"); whereas the visit to the South which was so rarely paid would have restored beliefs which had foundation enough. Besides, through this fear of the heat they traversed what they did traverse at the seasons when what fascination it possessed was least in evidence.

Among other conditions, the economic seem to have scandalised observers most. Perhaps the student will have noticed that whatever year during the last three hundred he may chance to be reading about in the history of Spain, the country will always at that moment have reached the last stage of economic exhaustion. Another quarter of a century or so, and, curiously enough, a lower stage will have been reached; yet another twenty-five years and one still lower; and so on until one would think the most hypothetical zero of bankruptcy must belong to a happier past and the population can consist of no more than a few emaciated grandees licking the rocks for sustenance. The natural attempt will be to go farther and farther back to trace the steps of the decline; and in time one will come upon these whose accounts are under consideration; but it will be without satisfaction. There is nothing for it but to go right back to the golden age. But in Guicciardini (1513) there is just the same tale, scarcity of inhabitants; poverty; mean aspects of daily life; stagnation in commerce owing entirely to Spanish aversion from work; industries under foreign control. It suggests that possibly the same phenomena have been in existence early and late, and that what earlier writers describe as an undeveloped country is the same as the "exhausted" one of later days; the difference, if this is the case, lying not in the conditions seen but in the extent of the stranger's expectations, moderate when the power of Spain had just become of international account; too high, later, when it was assumed that political power of long standing could not have grown up except in association with economic strength of equal greatness. To travellers of this period any unsoundness or "exhaustion" seemed the more incomprehensible in that Spain was by far the chief importer of bullion, the universal value of which they were accustomed to overrate.

Guicciardini, however, says nothing about the misbehaviour of Spanish women by which the next three or four generations of travellers are invariably shocked, with one exception, that of Lady Fanshawe, who saw much to admire in them and nothing to condemn, and had she seen what the men saw there is no doubt whatever her scorn would have been very pronounced. According to the men, neither the Italian fashion of the men restraining the women, nor the trans-alpine fashion of the women restraining themselves, was used in Spain. But it must be remembered that the male tourist tends to see the women-folk of the country he visits nearer their worst than their best.

Too warm a welcome was not a fault into which the males fell. In Madrid a Protestant might feel safe, and in centres of international trade, such as Medina del Campo, free from insult; at Burgos there was even courtesy, and at Barcelona civility, although it went hand in hand with robbery. But for the most part, it was needful to be

both callous and plucky. In particular, the traveller must take care to get his hair cut short at
Vittoria at the latest. French and many Germans
as well as English wore their hair long, and nothing
laid them open to insult, and even injury, so
much as that; if they were clean-shaven as well,
it was taken as certain that they carried effemi-
nacy to extremes; neither were they the last to
hear of it. "Rogue" and "thief" were ordinary
terms, even after a hair-cut, and when the queen
was a German, one of her countrymen, a man
who could be trusted not to give offence, had to
buy a new hat at Toledo because the one he was
wearing bore too many traces of cow-dung; at
Seville he was stoned.

Yet considering the average elsewhere, the
individual Spaniard stood to gain by comparison;
one of the most prejudiced and illiterate of the
tourists admits being treated with great courtesy,
and there is a general agreement that the standard of honesty was remarkably high. It is amusing, too, to notice what disconcerting answers
were sometimes received by the gentlemen from
abroad who thought that the peasantry of a Roman Catholic and poverty-stricken country only
needed to be questioned in order that the pitiable
state of their mind should become apparent, even
to themselves.

To one question, why extreme severity should
be reserved for heretics, the reply was that heresy

was the only crime which had not the excuse of
giving pleasure; while another who was asked why
a saint's day should be honoured so highly and
Sunday practically ignored, pointed out that the
saint's day came but once a year and Sunday
every week. So, too, it came as a surprise to the
Protestant to find Spanish nuns neither neurotic,
depressed, nor prim, but bright and attractive,
and their education "infinitely beyond all our
English schools."[2]

Nevertheless, what with the above experiences,
together with others which will be more in place
farther on, it is not surprising if Spain was considered a country of especial danger and difficulties, where there was nothing to be learnt that
had not better remain unlearnt, nor anything
worth seeing.

The best guide, in answering this last objection,
urges that the court at Madrid and the church of
San Lorenzo at the Escorial are alone worth the
journey, and names fifty-eight towns to complete
the answer. It would be superfluous to enter into
details; it is more difficult for us to doubt it than
for them to believe it. But Seville must not be
passed over altogether, the Seville of Cervantes'
"Novelas Ejemplares," the Seville which was
what Madrid pretended to be, the Spanish capital of Spanish Spain. Half the buildings that the
modern visitor goes to see there were new in 1600,
but the great sight, as great a sight as any in Eu-

rope both in itself and for its associations, was the arrival of the silver fleet from the "Indies."

Of the two chief places of pilgrimage, Montserrat, being on a main road from France and not far from Barcelona, is very frequently mentioned, but an account of a journey to Compostella is far rarer. Concerning the former, one account contains a particular of which there is perhaps no other record. The occupant of the highest of the almost inaccessible hermitages around the monastery, that of St. Jerome, in 1599, could bring the wild birds flocking round him when he called them, in such numbers that the writer, who had been throughout the peninsula, mentions the sight as the most wonderful in all Spain. Two ravens lived with the hermit in his cell.[3] As for Compostella, Andrew Boorde tells how he met nine men leaving Orleans on the way thither, and how he tried to dissuade them, saying he would rather go from England to Rome five times than once to Compostella, and that the government might well set in the stocks persons who proposed going thither without special leave, as being a waste of valuable lives. They persisted, and he accompanied them. Not one of the ten survived the journey except himself; and he was a doctor. Only one account preserves much detail of a stay at Compostella, that of a German soldier,[4] in 1581, who confessed to an Italian priest, nicknamed Linguarius for knowing Italian, Spanish, French, German,

Latin and other languages; and saw all that a good pilgrim should see, including the two great bells whose sound was so terrific as to frighten lady pilgrims into miscarriages. At Santo Domingo de la Calzada on the road, according to a Pole,[5] there remained a curious survival of divination by birds. In the church porch white capons were reared in a copper-wire cage, to which the pilgrim used to offer bread on the end of his staff; if the bird refused the bread, it was held an omen that the pilgrim would die on the journey.

Among the other things that Spain had in common with "European Europe" may be mentioned the royal Zoos: one at Madrid, where a crocodile was to be seen, also the first rhinoceros that had been brought to Europe; the other at Valladolid, containing four lions, an eagle, four seals, and canary-birds. In water-works Aranjuez could hold its own against Italy, with its brazen statue of Priapus, casting forth water from every extremity, a cave with two dragons and many birds, the birds being made to sing by the movements of the water; with satyrs and savages, and artificial cypresses and white roses which soaked the visitor who touched them. Neither were the horribles kept out of sight: at Seville some one speaks of seeing a thief shot to death with arrows, and two other criminals beheaded with swords, the bodies being laid up against a church-wall to attract alms to pay for their burial.

The coupling of Ireland with Spain does not result from the mere chance of westernmost position, nor even from the political needs that they shared, or from the supposed kinship of the peoples. While other countries aroused curiosity and then gratified it, these two occasioned, successively, illusion, disillusion, mystification. Which often led to abuse, but not so often, as regards Ireland, by Englishmen, as is represented by experienced controversialists who well know the effect of sixteenth-century phrases torn from their context and set up on a background of journalese, where the flavour of the original spelling fixes their seeming harshness in the memory of those controversialists cater for.

There can be no more effective counterblast to this than a study of the books of the time recording journeys from everywhere to everywhere, for from these it will be evident that what the Englishmen say of Ireland and the Irish is more favourable than what contemporary foreigners usually say of the countries and nations that they visit; and also that where the English are unfavourable they are borne out by other foreigners. All adverse comment may be included under the charge of barbarism. Now Captain Cuellar, as unprejudiced a witness as could be required, being a Spaniard wrecked there from the Armada and a man who took everything as it came, invariably speaks of each Irishman as "el selvaje," which cannot be translated as anything but "the savage."

But here lies the fact which supplies the contrast between Spaniards and Irish, a contrast within the similarity which classed the two together, as countries seen by foreigners. The latter's disillusion was produced by the barbarism interwoven with the civilisation of Spain, but, in Ireland, by the civilisation co-existent with the known barbarism. It was a perpetual surprise to all visitors to find many of the individuals of a society that persisted in the crudest and rudest way of living, showing a force of intelligence and character, and in certain ways a refinement and a degree of education, which seemed to presuppose all the advantages that the best of European surroundings and training had to give.

Most are content just to note these and other contrasts; the sum of their opinion as regarded the people being: "If they be bad you shall nowhere meet with worse; if they be good you shall hardly find better." [6] Of experience of this, Captain Cuellar's narrative stands out as a quintessential example. It is equally handy for those who wish to prove the Irish the most charming, or the most abominable, nation that ever existed. He found them equally ready to strip him and to feed him, to wound and to heal, to betray and to shelter, to make him at home and to make him work. Compare with this the conclusions of an impartial Italian[7] seventy years earlier. The women he found very beautiful and white, but dirty; the people generally, very religious, yet do not consider stealing a sin. He was given to understand that Irish people looked down on such as were averse to share and share alike as regards the blessings of fortune, and certainly came across many on the road anxious to give effect to communistic theories; these he terms robbers.

Aliens of a philosophic turn of mind, after passing through the state of surprise, not so much, even, at their being this or that, as at their being content or able to continue to be both at once, turned to looking for reasons. The foreigner who brought to bear on this question as great an amount of knowledge, experience, and fair-mindedness as any was Sir John Davies, who, in his "Discovery," after referring to the Irishman's "contempt and scorn of all things necessary for the civil life of man," goes on, "for though the Irishry be a nation of great antiquity and wanted neither art nor valour and . . . were lovers of music and poetry, and all kinds of learning, and possessed a land abounding with all things necessary; yet . . . I dare say boldly that never any person did build any stone or brick house for his private habitation, but such as have lately obtained estates according to the course of the law of England. Neither did any of them in all this time plant any gardens or orchards, enclose or improve their lands, live together in settled villages or towns, nor make any provision for posterity; which being against all common sense and reason, must needs be imputed to those unreasonable customs which made their estates so uncertain and transitory in their possessions."

If Sir John Davies thought thus, it is not surprising that hastier foreigners who had less knowledge of the ancient Irish civilisation, thought so too. We have just seen how, with regard to Spain, a history made up of the imaginary glories of an imaginary past helped to give the foreigner so high an idea of the individuals of the nation that the reality came as a shock. Here in Ireland, in this matter as in others, was a similarity with a difference. However true it may be that the Irish suffered from a radical lack of adaptability to modern conditions, the defects of it were undoubtedly heightened in the eyes of strangers by the latter's ignorance of the conditions that the Irish could accept, the Brehon laws, for instance, and all that they imply, especially the check on their misuse by means of public opinion.

Two features, however, were almost invariably commended: Irish harping and Irish girls. And the latter were at no disadvantage among the foreigners, since even in the far west which Captain Cuellar visited, they spoke Latin fluently, although content with one garment, often with less. The only fault that could be found with them was that of growing older as years went on, for to see an old Irishwoman before breakfast was, says Moryson, enough to turn a man's stomach. The country, too, received unlimited praise, with one abatement here also: in respect of its wetness; greater then than now, it may be said with some certainty.[8] Lithgow, in particular, when he visited "this sequestrate and most auspicuous monarchy," in 1619, discovered there "more Rivers, Lakes, Brooks, Strands, Quagmires, Bogs, and Marshes than in all Christendom besides." In five months he ruined six horses and was himself more tired than any of them.

Great, however, were the fetiches, and they prevailed. The essentials of life, as they appeared to the Irishman, and as they appeared to most Europeans, differed so utterly, and the reasons underlying the differences were so unrealisable to each other, that Ireland remained comparatively unvisited on account of its lack of the kind of interest for which travellers felt themselves bound to look. So, at least, the balance of the evidence seems to show, but the evidence is as conflicting here as in relation to everything else to do with Ireland. While the Bollandist fathers affirm that fifteen hundred foreigners made the pilgrimage to St. Patrick's Purgatory during the "Counter-Reformation,"[9] the native contemporary Catholic, Phillip O'Sullivan, living at Madrid, had to go back beyond the memory of living man for the written account of such a pilgrimage with which he wished to preface his history of the struggle against England. Or again, the excellent knowledge the Irish leaders in this struggle received of foreign affairs presupposes a great deal of going to and fro; yet De Thou, in a letter dated 1605,[10] by which date he had been working at his history of his own times for many years and was well known as a man worth helping to correspondents all over Europe, writes that he has not hitherto come across any one who has personal knowledge of Ireland nor even any one who has talked with some one who has been there.

Neither are there nearly so many casual references to visitors as one chances on with regard to other countries. Two exceptions which suggest the likelihood of others are, however, to be found mentioned in the correspondence between the English Privy Council and the Deputy at Dublin.[11] In 1572 the latter announces the arrival of three German earls with one Mr. Rogers, their guide, adding, to Lord Burghley, "according to your directions, they shall travel as little way into the country as I can manage." This is explained by the second reference, seven years later, when three more Germans come across with letters of introduction from the Privy Council, who half suspect them, young though they are, of being spies. But after the close of this period, in 1666, we find a Frenchman [12] noting that the Provost of Trinity College "seemed astonished that out of mere curiosity I should come to see Ireland, which is a country so retired and almost unknown to foreign travellers."

CHAPTER V

MOHAMMEDAN EUROPE

PART I

THE GRAND SIGNOR

"He who would behold these Times in their greatest glory, could not find a better scene than Turkey."

Sir Henry Blount, 1635.

FROM an historical point of view, a continent consists not only of land but also of the seas from which attacks on the land can be made at short notice. For this reason Mohammedan Europe used to be far wider in extent than the Turkish territory, although the latter, indeed, bordered the Adriatic and stopped but a few miles short of Vienna. The Mediterranean was under Mohammedan, rather than Christian, control. Independent, too, in varying degrees, as were the rulers of North Africa, a bond of union existed among them owing to the peoples of the opposite coasts professing a creed different from theirs; a bond which was not interfered with by jealousies, inasmuch as the Sultan, or as he was usually termed then, the "Grand Signor" (or the "Grand Turk"), was so infinitely superior that there was never any question as to who should take the lead. His fleet, in fact, resembled that

of Queen Elizabeth, being made up of crews who
pursued the same course of life in peace and in
war — that of attacking wherever attacks seem
likely to pay — with no more difference than this,
that their behaviour was official in the second case
and unofficial in the first. These corsairs, then,
were all part of Mohammedan Europe, carrying
out the foreign policy of the "Grand Signor"
whether they had been previously adopted or
were subsequently to be disowned.

For the tourist, it has already become evident
that he was almost certain to be confronted with
the subjects, or the agents, of the Ottoman Empire, sooner or later; and then was to be made
aware that, if one of the two existed on sufferance,
that one was himself. Here is the beginning of
a prayer introduced into the English liturgy in
1565;[1] — "O Almighty and Everlasting God, our
Heavenly Father, we thy disobedient and rebellious children, now by thy just judgment sore
afflicted, and in great danger to be oppressed,
by thine and our sworn and most deadly enemies,
the Turks . . ." Historians agree that it was in
the third quarter of the sixteenth century that the
Turks' power reached its height. Rarely, later
than that, are they mentioned otherwise than incidentally in the books from which modern Christendom draws its information, and their earlier
appearances are rather on account of sensational
events and minor indirect influence than as one

of the Powers of Europe. Yet throughout this period, that is, for three-quarters of a century after decline, according to historians, had begun, the Turks were not only one of the Powers, but the chief one, equal with any in diplomacy, superior to any by land and by sea.

At a date when our text-books represent England as wresting the supremacy on the water from Spain, contemporary opinion regarded Turkey as the first naval power. The chief of the sensational events just referred to, the battle of Lepanto, is made to stand out, as that of Agincourt in English history, not because it typifies the course of events, but because it is a bright spot for the Christian pupil's eye to rest on. Within one year afterwards the Turks were ready to meet the Christians again: within two years they had the biggest fleet in the world: within three the Venetians agreed to pay 300,000 ducats (worth now about £500,000) as indemnity; and the fifth year afterwards the Venetian Lippomano takes it for granted, in speaking before the Signory — in other words, a man representing the pick of the diplomatists of the day speaking, after full consideration, to the most critical of audiences — that without the joint help of the Muscovites and Poles Christendom can never hope really to get the upper hand of the Turks.[2]

It must be remembered, too, that the Atlantic then was what the Pacific is now, the ocean of the

future; "command of the sea" meant, to the
average sixteenth-century man, command of the
Mediterranean, from the basin of which had risen
all the civilisations of which he had any knowledge,
through which lay the most used trade-route,
and round which lay the biggest cities known to
him: Cairo, Constantinople, Aleppo, and Fez (all
Mohammedan).

But when this period of their supposed decline
had set in, the Mohammedans, for the first time,
ceased to be content with the Mediterranean
and began to practise —

> Keeping in awe the bay of Portingale
> And all the ocean by the British shore,

as Marlowe phrases it on behalf of Tamburlane.
In 1616 Sir G. Carew writes to Sir T. Roe that
the Turks are passing out of the Mediterranean
now, had just carried off all the inhabitants of
St. Marie, one of the Azores, and might be looked
for round England soon.[3] In 1630 they took six
ships near Bristol and had about forty of their
vessels in British seas.[4] In the following year
they sacked Baltimore in Ireland; but so far
was the English government from being able to
assert itself that Robert Boyle writes of his passage from Youghal to Bristol past Ilfracombe
and Minehead in 1635, that he passed safely
"though the Irish coasts were then sufficiently
infested with Turkish galleys,"[5] while in 1645

they called at Fowey and carried off into slavery two hundred and forty persons, including some ladies.[6]

Where the English were fortunate was in the raiders having made so late a start. Throughout the previous century the inhabitants of south-Europe coasts were always expecting the Turks. Philip II kept sixteen hundred coast-guardsmen always patrolling on the lookout for them: but then he was their chief enemy. More remarkable is the league [7] of the south of France maritime towns in 1585 to take steps to prevent their ruin from this cause; seeing that France had been the ally of the "Grand Turk" for half a century. In 1601 the Duke of Mantua and his sister, the Duchess of Ferrara, were captured close to the shore near Loreto by a Turkish galley.[8] As for the tourists themselves, Moryson passed a village near Genoa destroyed by Turks just before his arrival, when the belle of the district had been carried off the day after her wedding; and had Montaigne been but a few miles nearer to the coast than he actually was on a certain date we should perhaps never have had the "Essais" — thanks to the Turks. This would have been no more than a parallel case to that of Padre Jeronimo Gracián, St. Teresa's confessor, who was captured between Messina and Rome in 1592, stripped naked, and made to row on the benches of a galley. He had with him his book "Armonía mistica," which he had just finished, and had to look on while the pirates cleaned their firearms with leaves from it.[9]

Some preface of this kind is necessary to explain the view tourists habitually take of the Ottoman power, because the naval strength is less often alluded to than its achievements by land and its position as an Eastern conqueror. But even these latter call for a word or two to complete the picture.

While it is true that the phrase concerning "the empire on which the sun never sets" had been invented by this time, in reference to that of Spain, the Turkish was regarded as, to quote a traveller of 1612, "the greatest that is, or perhaps ever was from the beginning," just as the phrase "the sick man of Europe" had also been employed, but in reference not to Turkey, but to England (in 1558).[10] To these words may be added those of another level-headed, well-educated Englishman, Sir Henry Blount, "the only modern people great in action and whose empire hath so suddenly invaded the world and fixed itself on such firm foundations as no other ever did." Whereas, late as Blount's visit to Constantinople was, he found the wiser Turks considering the Christians not so strong as they used to be; not so strong as the Persians. Busbecq, too, in his earlier days, sums up the outlook in despair, concluding that the

worst feature of it all is that the Turks are used
to conquering, the Christians to being conquered;
and confirms it later (when he was sixty-three and
had had thirty-eight years' experience of European politics, mostly official, including eight years
at Constantinople), by writing that the object of
the Turks' war (1585) with the Persians is to leave
themselves freer to extinguish Christendom, and
that, the former war over, " they will fight us for
existence and empire; and the chances are greatly
in their favour." As late as a century after this
the Turks were besieging Vienna with an army
200,000 strong.

But the test of the hold of a given idea on the
minds of ordinary men, such as these tourists
mostly were, is the frequency with which it recurs
in the works of their favourite writers. Now, badly
off indeed would the seventeenth-century novel-
ist have been without the Turkish corsair to defer
the wedding-day for a respectable number of
pages; and the echo of the convention has attained immortality in the stock quotation from
Molière, "Mais que diable allait-il dans cette
galère?" There is a passage, too, in "Othello"
which illustrates the above beliefs still better —
Othello's last words: —

<blockquote>
Set you down this —
And say besides, that in Aleppo once,
Where a malignant and a turban'd Turk
Beat a Venetian and traduced the State
</blockquote>

I took by the throat the circumcised dog
And smote him, thus —

There are an infinite number of passages in Shakespeare, whose meaning in relation to the plot
seems so obvious and so sufficient, that the further half-unconscious sub-meaning is never enquired into, and is, in fact, passed by until some
special knowledge, like that of the author of the
"Diary of Master William Silence," throws light
on it. In this case, an acqaintance with sixteenth-
century Christian travel in Mohammedan lands
compels the idea that Othello's mind turns at the
last to what he knows his hearers would unhesi-
tatingly recognise as his greatest deed, the killing
a Turk in Turkish territory; as the greatest possible claim to forgiveness and to fame. Moryson
left his sword behind him at Venice, as a thing
which it would be madness to use.

The state of mind, then, of the Christian of this
period in face of the Turks may be compared to
that of a Chinaman towards Europeans between
the fall of Pekin and the victories of Japan. As
for the reasons of the Turks' success, as noted by
tourists, they refer primarily to the army, since it
was on the army that the Turks were, and had been,
dependent for their greatness. First, in regard
to the soldiers' behaviour to their own people,
discipline was so severe that the country people
took no precautions against robbery, "whereas,"
says one (an Englishman), "we cannot raise

two or three companies but they pilfer and rifle wheresoever they pass." Teetotalism, again, was prescribed by their religion, and although the prohibition was losing its force, the infractions were secret and not practicable in camp. The benefit of this lay not merely in the freedom from disorderly behaviour but in the fact that the carriage of wine was a serious item in the expenses of a Christian army. Then besides orderliness and sobriety and the absence from the camp of gambling and women, there was personal cleanliness and sanitation. On these two last points the "Franks," as Europeans were generally known in the East, had much said to them to which there was no effective reply, even on their own showing. It was common knowledge among Europeans who stayed at home that they were despised in the East for their carelessness about drainage, and a typical case concerning cleanliness is that recorded of one Englishman. One day he fell overboard: "Now God has washed you," said the Turks.

Another characteristic that rendered the army more efficient was the extent to which autocracy was in favour among them, a principle which, applied throughout all grades, caused discipline to be a matter of course. Among European armies there was nothing that could be termed discipline, only personal influence. In this respect, both the cause and the effect, the striking resemblance, in relation to the Europeans contemporary with them, of the sixteenth-century Turk with the modern Japanese, stands out. Other respects were courtesy, frugality, cleverness in handicraft and the fine arts, and, on the other side, lower ideas about women. It was only, likewise, where the copying of the human form was concerned that the Turk technique fell below Western achievement; Della Valle, who was used to the best that Europe could produce, further notes their relative excellence in cooking, bookbinding, tailoring, gardening, and, especially, all leather work.

From our point of view the Franks had also much to learn from the Turks as to kindness to animals, but that did not even appear a superfluous virtue to the former, who only mention it as a curiosity, except Busbecq, who remarks that Turks' horses lived the longer for it, were more useful, and were companions as well as useful.

It may be noted, further, that the Turks had acquired the use of pyjamas ("linen breeches and quilted waistcoats," says Fynes Moryson), while Western Europe was in process of being converted to night-dresses. Says the contemporary playwright, Middleton, in his "Mayor of Queenborough," "Books in women's hands are as much against the hair (*i. e.* against the grain), methinks, as to see men wear stomachers, or night-rails" (*i. e.* night-shirts). Even with ladies the process was not a short one. N. Brooke, in Southern

Italy, late in the eighteenth century, discussed night-wear with a lady there; it was not the custom to wear anything, she explained, in the warmer months; for one thing, it was cooler so; and for another, *so* much easier to catch the fleas.

It would be strange if among all these visitors some were not found noting signs of demoralisation. The chief of these is Moryson, who, without explaining what means he has of comparing past and present, finds the Emperors less warlike, their whole forces not available through fear of internal rebellion, the pick of the troops not equal to the pick of times gone by; a shortage of firearms; a decrease in religious zeal; an increase in extortion and oppression. This latter Della Valle notes, too, on his return-journey, when, at Cyprus, a governor had left, and while a successor was on the way out, orders came reinstating the former; which implied bribery and outbidding.

More general are the references to the increase of wine-drinking in defiance of the prohibition of it by their religion; a habit which was bound to be noticed by the traveller, since the ambassadors' houses were used for the purpose principally, at first solely. One old gentleman in Busbecq's time tried to evade his conscience, too; he gave a great shout before each drink, to warn his soul to stow itself away in some far corner of his body lest it should be defiled by the wine he was about to enjoy and have hereafter to answer for his sin. Towards the end of the next century concealment was abandoned, and at a Greek village outside Adrianople, whither an Englishman went during plague-time, he found the population living by the sale of wine to Turks, who came in troops to get drunk: the parson did the biggest trade because he had the biggest warehouse — his church.

It was frequently noticed, moreover, that their most capable workmen were mostly foreigners, and that two inventions which attracted everyone's notice — carrier-pigeons and incubation, both practised exclusively in Turkish territory and the latter on a scale which would qualify the proprietor for knighthood to-day — were not of Turkish origin. Nevertheless, the fact remained that many of the products of civilisation existed mainly, or at their best, in Turkish dominion alone; and this, and the prestige it implies, have to be recognised and remembered as two of the main facts in sixteenth-century history. It may be added that in no way can this be so satisfactorily ascertained as through travellers' narratives.

Yet the Turks were deemed barbarians by the Frank; he and they practically never spoke each other's language, which put out of the question those casual conversations which pave the way to mutual understanding. Their faith remained to him a "filthy error"; and to the Christians, whose chief bond of unity had just been riven by the Reformation, the remaining one, that of a common literature, was all the more to be prized. No Turk, as one observer remarks, would write history because no Turk would believe it; it being unsafe to record the truth, and impracticable to ascertain it. Accordingly, the complete Livy which the Grand Signor was reputed to have inherited from the Byzantine Emperors had only its selling value to Christians for him. He had refused one offer of 5000 piastres (about £6500 now) for it, thinking that the offer proved it was worth more. But Della Valle knew better than to make offers to the Grand Signor: the way to buy his books was to bribe his librarian, and he only missed securing it for 10,000 crowns (say £12,500) through the librarian at Constantinople not being able to trace it.

Constantinople — the change from Byzantine Emperors' days was striking. But the gloriousness of the position was unchangeable, and the sight of it from the sea was more glorious than ever, the finest city to see, then, that earth held. With its various levels, each one descending as it was the nearer to the shore, a marvellous proportion of the roofs, and even windows, came in view; and the waywardness of the designs, and

the balconies with their lattice-work, were thrown
into relief by the brilliance and the variety of the
colouring; while the colouring itself stood out
against the white of the walls, the green of innumerable cypresses, and the darkness of the
leaden domes.

But once inside, and all was spoilt. The streets
were very narrow and ill-kept; a raised foot-path
each side took up two-thirds of the way, and the
other third was barely practicable for asses;
carcasses of animals, and even of men, were left
lying there till they rotted. The only street
which was a pleasure to pass was the long straight
one which led from the gate of Adrianople to
the Palace, and was used for all occasions of state,
such as the entrances of ambassadors. Dignity
was a thing that the Turks understood; it was
characteristic that the most impressive procession to be seen ordinarily in Europe was that
to the Grand Signor's Privy Council, more impressive even than the Cardinals going to Con-
sistory at Rome. Yet the private houses, as seen
from the streets, were no more attractive than the
streets themselves: of wood mostly, or wood and
mud. Some fine houses remained from pre-
Mohammedan days, but besides those, only the
mosques, and some other public buildings, were
other than repulsive. The palace that was called
Constantine's was already in ruins, abandoned
but for one great room used as a tent-factory.

Even the baths were not in all respects superior
to those of dirty Christendom, but that was because the rich men had private ones. In Turkey
none but the poor used the public baths; in
Christendom few but Germans and the ailing
rich used any. The reason the houses were so
wretched was "that they might not be worth
taking from the child when the father died"; for
the property of a dead man was the Sultan's; the
latter's palace was free from restrictions; only,
few there were who saw it.

This happened sometimes when the court was
away and the tourist could bribe the right man.
Then, besides all that might be expected, he saw
the best Zoo in Europe; and, in the middle of a
wood, a certain pond, all lined with porphyry,
wherein it was one "Grand Signor's" diversion to
send the girls of the harem and shoot at them with
bullets that stuck to their skins without doing
harm; and he could regulate the depth of the
water till they had to keep afloat to breathe;
tiring of that, he let the water down and sent the
eunuchs in to fetch them out — if alive.

The only recognised means, however, of seeing
the inside was to accompany an ambassador on
one of the two occasions when he saw the Grand
Turk; when he came and when he left. This happened on a Sunday or a Tuesday, and could be
but hurried glimpses while going to and from the
audience chamber to kiss the robe of the great

sovereign whose position was such that the ambassador was taken off his horse at the gate and searched and led to the audience by two men, each one holding a hand. When the English ambassador, in 1647, at his first audience, did not bow low enough, the men on either side of him thrust his head down to the required level.[11] He was further obliged to be lavish with his presents and content that they should be received as tribute, and that no present should be given in return but a garment. In the estimate for the cost of the embassy which the above-mentioned French league proposed to send to Constantinople 2000 écus d'or au soleil (over £4000), one twelfth of the total cost, is allotted for presents and tips. Neither did the Grand Signor ever speak to a Christian.

The interest of life in Constantinople was largely discounted by the ways of the natives, for courteous as the Turk was as a man, as a Mohammedan things were very different. While, on the one hand, incredible as it may sound, a Turkish sailor was always civil even if you got in his way on board ship, a Christian his nation "regard no more than a dog," and if the Christian wore green, which was reserved for Mohammed's kindred, he was lucky to escape injury. One stranger with a pair of green breeches had them taken away from him in the street. In any case, there was a likelihood of ill-usage. No one dared to refuse, or even hesitate, when a Turk commanded, without regretting it, except Della Valle, who carried a passport from the Grand Turk himself, and even then, upon his refusal to pay his respects to a certain governor in the customary way, which was both undignified and costly, the whole company were so proud of him that the Greek nuns could not refrain from kissing him in public. Typical experiences were those of Moryson, whose hat struck a Turk one day as so quaint that he borrowed it for a few minutes for his own use — not as a hat — and returned it to Moryson's head; and of one Manwaring [12] in Aleppo; — "we could not walk in the streets but they would buffet us and use us very vilely: . . . one day I met with a Turk . . . saluting me in this manner: . . . took me fast by one of the ears and so did lead me up and down the street; and if I did chance to look sour upon him he would give me such a wring that I did verily think he would have pulled off my ear and this he continued with me for the space of one hour, with much company following me, some throwing stones at me, and some spitting on me; and because I would not laugh at my departure from him, gave me such a blow with a staff that did strike me to the ground."

But that is not the end of the story. Manwaring went home and complained to the Janizary who acted as guardian to his party. The latter took a stick, found the Turk, who was of high enough position to go about in cloth of gold

and crimson velvet, and thrashed him till he
could not stand.

This was a form of protection open to all. The
payment was low; the Janizary's standard of
honour and honesty very high, their power practically unlimited. Moryson was one of a band of
a hundred, who accidentally set fire to the grass
while cooking their supper. Out came a Janizary
from the local governor and compelled them to
use their clothes to quench the flames; which done,
he drove them all, priests and armed men included, before him to the governor, with no
weapon but a stick, and whoever lagged behind
he cried, "Wohowe Rooe," and hit him.

But with regard to insults, it must be remembered that certain characteristics of the Frank the
Turks never ceased to despise. They wished their
enemies "no more rest than a Christian's hat."
Four things especially puzzled them, why (1) the
latter walked about when he might sit down, (2)
wore his hair long when he might get it cut short,
(3) shaved instead of growing a beard, refusing
sometimes to do business with beardless Christians,
believing such to be under age, (4) bought material for clothes and then cut bits out; themselves
wearing their garments plain.

Barring the results of misunderstanding and
contempt, there was plenty of interest in life in
Constantinople. The Greeks, at any rate, whom
Della Valle visited, were not grievously oppressed,

considering that while among the Turks to be reputed rich was more dangerous than any crime;
he found the ladies at a wedding dressed in stuff
that cost twelve zecchini a "picco" (at least
£20 a yard) and, as their custom was, they frequently retired to change their dresses, of which
they brought eight or ten. There were the market
places to see, which were used as a promenade,
especially by the ladies, who in this respect had a
decidedly better opportunity to make acquaintances than was generally supposed; their veils did
not prevent them making themselves recognised,
and the press of people was sufficiently great to
allow of an "unintentional" dig in the ribs as a
means of introduction to an attractive foreigner.
Tommasetto, Della Valle's servant, was even
more favoured because he conformed to Turkish
standards by growing a beard, and accordingly,
in passing the streets, the ladies frequently
touched his cheeks, saying always the same word,
which he found meant "handsome man!" If,
in the market or elsewhere, a Christian wanted
to buy food, there was no such thing for him as a
fixed price or a bargain; he gave the Turk money
and the Turk gave what he chose to give. Every
Friday was a slave market, where the tourist
might see his countrywomen for sale; a virgin
would fetch about £25, and an average widow £9,
as money is now, and if the tourist was not careful of his company, he would find himself şold as

he walked through the streets; Fynes Moryson, when very ill, was told by the Janizary who was his guide that an old woman had just offered 100 aspers (thirty shillings) for him.

For the population of Constantinople and what the population consisted of, nothing more can be stated than the beliefs on the subject, of which this one may be mentioned, that in less than three months in 1615 there died of plague 120,000 Turks, 2000 Jews, and 18,000 Christians. Plague was always present in Constantinople; no precautions were taken against it; when a man died from plague, his clothes were put up for auction immediately, and bought, and worn. But the fatalism which decided the Turks' attitude towards plague did not manifest itself in all directions; their behaviour in danger at sea was the reverse of what might be expected on Christian-manned ships. After they had taken Cyprus, moreover, which suffered greatly from locusts, it was prescribed that every farmer should bring a fixed quantity of locusts' eggs yearly to a stated official, who was to see the eggs ground to powder and the powder thrown into the sea. They had their medicines too, and were the only people in Europe who had hitherto managed to make medicine-taking pleasant, because they alone had sherbets and took medicines in their sherbet. Moreover, what may be said of drinks applies equally to games. For swings, they were part of every Turkish festivity; likewise roundabouts and "great wheels"; how well acquainted Christians were with all these may be judged by the fact that both an Englishman and an Italian describe them all in detail. Yet with all that we have imported, there still remains one hint to take. A Mohammedan crowd kept itself in order for the most part then; George Sandys, in nine months' stay in Constantinople, never saw a Mohammedan quarrel with one of his own creed; but to restrain the excitability that might occur in a crowd, they had policemen in leathern jackets, bearing bladders, both bladders and jackets being smeared with oil and tar, which commanded the respect of the cleanly Turks in their most youthful moments.

The relations between Turks and Christians being what they were, it is not surprising that one feature of life in the sixteenth century as seen by travellers should be more often under notice in Turkish dominion than elsewhere, at any rate to the traveller who was a Christian — examples of human misery. Many such there are scattered about the pages under notice, such and such a name comes up, probably for the only time in any writing that remains, just an incident connected with it, or a life-history in a few lines; nothing else known of the man or ever likely to be, oblivion before and oblivion after; just that one glimpse of utter misery. There is the merchant of Ragusa in Blount's caravan who was defiant towards some

Turks; beaten with axes and iron maces, two ribs broken; left behind helpless; of him it is very unlikely there was anything further to tell beyond what the wolves knew. Then there was another whom Blount came across by the side of the Danube, formerly a man and a Christian, now castrated and a Turk; enduring degradation and remorse only so as to be able to revenge himself by throwing Turkish children into the river at night; every week had its victim. One John Smith, again, became a Venetian soldier and was sent to Crete, where he borrowed forty-eight shillings (say twelve guineas) from his officer. Being unable to pay it when the five years' term of service was up, he was turned over to the officer's successor with his debt; so again at the end of the tenth year. There Lithgow found him at the end of fifteen years, no nearer release, and paid his debt and obtained a passage back for him. Then there was the sailor-traveller who was made a galley slave by the Turks and was placed beside an old Russian. Twenty-four years had the latter been there; attempts to escape had been without result beyond the loss of ears and nose, and he was under threat of burning for the next attempt; yet he was only waiting for a man who was ready to be his companion. The sailor-traveller was ready; and they succeeded, after swimming two miles with a three-headed arrow right through the old Russian's thigh.

But, indeed, these individual Turks and Christians were no more than carrying out in person the general relations that existed between the races. That the former's navy reached the Atlantic, their army to Vienna, and their shadow over all Europe, has already been illustrated; and also that they were setting an example in many of the directions which imply being ahead in civilisation, summed up in verse which Gruberus-of-the-guide-book quotes as an aid to remembering the notabilia of Turkey.

Meschita, maratium, charavansaraja, lavacra,
Fontes et pontes fluviorum, et strata viarum.

More than all these, in sixteenth-century eyes, was the fact that they possessed Constantinople, recognised as the city whose possession necessarily carried with it the political headship of the world by reason of its situation taken in conjunction with its imperial associations. They dominated Greece, also, the source of intellectual light, and Egypt, the home of science. More than all these, they ruled at Jerusalem.

PART II

JERUSALEM AND THE WAY THITHER

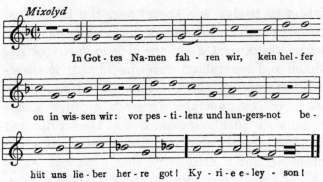

PILGRIM-SONG IN 16TH-CENTURY SETTING[1]

FROM all points of view except that of geography Jerusalem was forming part of Europe; the spot where was localised what was recognised as the prime factor in their mental and spiritual ancestry, life, and future. What it is now to a convinced Zionist, it was then to the average Christian. But the idea of securing Jerusalem as an axiom, almost an incidental axiom, of practical politics requires, perhaps, a word or two of explanation, considering how far the modern habit of weeding out theology from all politics but party-politics has gone; and this the more so since little help is to be had from histories, written, as they naturally are, to defend, attack, or explain the present rather than the past, and dealing, consequently, with the past, only in so far as it throws light, not on itself, but on things current.

History having become specialised into accounts of the political events of the past in relation to to-day and to-morrow, the interest of the sixteenth and seventeenth centuries has come to be concentrated on the development of national and centralised governments. It is therefore left out of account that the ideas at the back of the average sixteenth century man's mind were such as assumed that the world, and Europe in particular, was under theocratic government; and consequently that what seem to us independent sovereigns developing national monarchies seemed to him so many deputies of the Almighty — "many," because of the sins of the world — ruling by permission until the appointed time should come for the unification of Europe under the one true head, the completion of whose work would be a final gigantic Crusade which would pulverise the Turk and secure Jerusalem for Christianity, world without end. In fact, the conquest of Jerusalem held much the same place in international politics as "disarmament" with us; just so far ideal as to make discussion of it interesting, and sufficiently impracticable to be common ground. If these ideas seem too mediæval to be attributed to the sixteenth century, it is because their more "modern" ideas have been disproportionately insisted on since; seven-eighths of

their life was mediæval—and a large part of the
remaining eighth the majority would have wished
to disown.

Where the leaven of new ideas was showing itself was not in a cessation, but in a decrease, of
pilgrimage to Jerusalem. The state of transition
is definitely marked by the diversity of the preoccupations which men carried thither; the change
itself by the discontinuance of the pilgrim galleys.
This took place between 1581 and 1586. It had
been usual for two galleys to sail to Jaffa and back
each year specially for pilgrims, from Venice,
starting on different dates between Ascension Day
and early in July; the latter date being dictated by
the weather, the former doubtless by everybody's
desire to wait to witness the Espousal of the Sea.
In 1581 a boat [2] started on May 7 or 8 with fifty-
six on board, all told; this was wrecked in the Adriatic, thirty persons only being saved. On July 14,
another left, but the pilgrims by this had to change
into a smaller vessel at Cyprus. In 1587, however,
a guide-book writer,[3] advising on the basis of his
experiences the previous year, tells the pilgrim to
take the first boat to Tripoli in the spring, before
Easter if possible, otherwise there may be none
towards Palestine till August, since the pilgrim-
galleys have ceased sailing, although the procession is still kept up at Venice in which every intending pilgrim had the honour of walking on the
right hand of a noble, bearing a lighted wax can-

dle. That this discontinuance was sudden and recent may be assumed from the fact that a priest who was visiting the shrines of Christendom as the deputy of Philip II, who had vowed such a pilgrimage when his son was ill, hurried [4] on his way to Italy in 1587, expecting to find a pilgrim-galley ready to start. But that this discontinuance was not merely temporary is clear enough from all subsequent writers.

The complement of a pilgrim-galley may be taken as about one hundred, although in 1561 one carried four hundred. After 1581 nobody mentions finding more than twenty-three "Franks" at Jerusalem together, not even at Easter, when "indulgences" were doubled. Possibly the attack on "indulgences" which prefaced the best-known schism of the century suggested, or testifies to, an incredulity concerning them which might be felt far outside the districts which persisted in schism. If felt, this would re-act on pilgrimages, the nominal object whereof was to secure "indulgences." On the other hand, there is no reason for assuming a decline in devotion; the non-Catholic point of view is well expressed by Moryson:—"I had no thought to expiate any least sin of mine; much less did I hope to merit any grace from God — yet I confess that through the grace of God the very places struck me with a religious horror and filled my mind with holy motions." One reason for the decrease is certain, however, and sufficient to account for it alone; the increase in the dangers and the cost of the journey through the stopping-places on the route falling into the hands of the Turks, and, still more, the changed attitude of the Turks towards Western Christians as a result of these victories.

Yet this abolition of the direct and speedy route was not all loss to him who was as much tourist as pilgrim. He saw the more. There was a pleasant choice of routes, too; for, of course, thenceforth each one had to make his own arrangements. The main routes numbered three; on each of them further choice was possible. The three were viâ (1) Jaffa, (2) Damascus, (3) Cairo.

The starting-point was sometimes Marseilles, but rarely; almost invariably it would be Venice. Here, too, information was obtainable better than elsewhere. At the Franciscan monastery "Della Vigna" was a travel-bureau in charge of the "Padre Provisore di Gierusalemme" who survived the galleys: in 1609 he was a Venetian noble. The post had a semi-official character, since its holder was charged to view the permit to visit Jerusalem, the "Placet" as it was called, lacking which a Roman Catholic would incur excommunication; and also to assure himself that the pilgrim had one hundred zecchini to spend, in the absence of which the permit was cancelled. The respect in which this "Placet," which required eleven signatures, was held was immense; one soldier, even, who had touched at Tripoli and Jaffa in the course of serving Ferdinand de' Medici, came back to Leghorn to get leave before visiting Jerusalem. But the warden of the friars at Jerusalem had authority to absolve from the excommunication such as did not pass through Italy. No "Placets" were granted to women.

These preliminaries over, a start for Jaffa would be made by taking ship for one of the islands in the Levant on the chance of finding another ship thence to Jaffa itself, which extended the four–five weeks' voyage of earlier days into one of unknown duration. Arriving at Jaffa, past the rock from which St. Peter had his fishing-lesson, no city was to be seen; little but two towers.

In times gone by when the pilgrims arrived in bulk, word was sent to the warden of the monastery of San Salvatore at Jerusalem, and they did not start the land journey till he came to supervise it. But now the traveller had to arrange as best he could with Turk or Arab and reach Rama somehow or other; probably on an ass without saddle, bridle, or stirrups. At Rama he would find Sion House, built by Philip the Good on the site of the house of Nicodemus, and nominally a monastery; all the monks had gone, but it remained a lodging for pilgrims. At Rama dwelt the official Christian guide to Jerusalem, into whose charge you had no choice but to commit yourself; if any one tried to evade his control and charges, the dragoman could send word to the Arabs, and life passed the limit of barely endurable, which was the pilgrim's ordinary lot. The dragoman dwelt at Rama for the reason that the routes to Jerusalem, west, north, and south, converged there; and for that same reason we will go on to consider route No. 2, viâ Damascus.

There was at times the chance of approaching by the Damascus road, and yet going mainly by sea; that was when there was a ship bound for Acre or some port on the coast of the Holy Land other than Jaffa. But in practically all cases the Damascus route meant getting to Constantinople first, and this is equally true of route No. 3.

From Europe to Constantinople there were several main routes. Two tourists took the trade route from Danzig through Lemberg to Kamenetz, the frontier town of Poland, then down the river Pruth to Reni, a centre of the caviare trade, and so down the Danube to its mouth and by sea to Constantinople, which last part coincided with the route of the Russian pilgrims who sailed down the Dnieper or the Don and coasted along the Black Sea shore. A weird crew on a weird journey, in boats which, big or little, were used to being mounted on wheels, through country where nothing living was to be seen but wild beasts and nothing to mark distances save the

mouths of tributary streams. Then there was
Busbecq's way, who used the Danube, but not to
the mouth; leaving it soon after Belgrade had
been passed and travelling by the great road
through Sofia and Adrianople along which the
Grand Signor marched to bring war and Christian
ambassadors came to buy peace. From this road,
going westward, diverged the roads to Spalato
and to Ragusa, the two most direct ways to Venice. Yet but few tourists travelled by these two
roads. It was not that they were little used. Besides the ambassadors to Constantinople from
Ragusa itself, which meant at least two journeys
each year on account of the tribute, Della Valle
speaks of the ordinary post taking that direction
and the Venetian representative at Constantinople keeping forty Schiavonians for post work,
who travelled on foot. The mountain passes were
terrible, and the danger from wolves and dogs in
Servia considerable; also from robbers. At certain points on Mount Rhodope, for instance, men
were stationed to beat drums when the road was
supposed to be clear of them, and a feature of the
district was the "Palangha," a roughly fortified
enclosure large enough for sixty or seventy Turks
to live within and to serve as a temporary shelter
to those who lived roundabout; for the robber
bands sometimes numbered three hundred. Except at the regular stopping places few people
were seen, for the Christians established their vil-

lages off the main road for fear of the Turks, who were so far uncertain of their control over them as to use continual severities. A French ambassador, whose guide led him astray near one of these villages, saw all the inhabitants making off to the mountains, mistaking him for a Turkish official. And their houses he says were no better than "gabions couverts." But with these, as with all people who live under a despotism, especially a foreign military one, their chief protection consisted in appearing more miserable than they were; there was no part of Europe where food was better or cheaper; neither did the people treat strangers with the ferocity produced by extreme wretchedness, and at Sofia, in fact, Blount found the opposite extreme—"nor hath it yet lost the old Grecian civility, for of all the cities I ever passed, either in Christendom or without, I never saw anywhere where a stranger is less troubled either with affronts or with gaping."

Still, it was borderland, and mainly Mohammedan; the sea route was common ground and frequented by Christians. But there was a compromise which was often in use — to travel by sea to Zante and thence through Greece, finishing the journey either by sea or land. It might seem that this direction would appeal to a considerable proportion of tourists during the period that is called "Renascence," but the extent to which the acquaintance with, and interest in, Greek thought, first-hand, at this time has been exaggerated may be accurately estimated by the fact that not a single one of these travellers visited Athens except by accident. It must be admitted, however, that things were not made easy for them; one of those who traversed Greece was Dallam, in company with seven others; part of the journey they were stalked by natives trying to arrange with their guide to cut their throats: and every time they slept but once it was in their clothes, either on the ground or on the floor. One of the most interesting places that might be visited on this route was Salonica, a Jew republic under the suzerainty of the Grand Signor, with a training-school for priests; here and Safed near Galilee were the only places where Hebrew was supposed to be spoken.

All these ways to Constantinople have been mentioned in the order into which they fall according to the extent to which they were used by European tourists, the least frequented first. Last comes the most usual, by sea all the way from Venice. And here, however different might be the experiences of this one and that one, two points of interest were invariable. First, they passed Abydos and Sestos, where out must come the note-book, and Leander must be dragged into it. Secondly, Troy. The learned say that these tourists located Troy on the south, instead of on the north, bank of the river, but the more important point is that what they did see stirred their feelings: it was no

mere mild interest. The Trojan heroes were as
real to them as Barbarossa and Don Juan, not
only because no doubts had blurred their individuality, much less darkened their existence, but
because there was less competition for the position of hero owing to the narrower range of their
knowledge. Another characteristic of theirs, was
that Virgil was clearer in their association of
ideas, Homer dimmer, at the moment of seeing
Troy's ruins, than would be the case with a modern tourist: the quotation that arises most naturally in the mind of the finest scholar of them all
was

> Hic Dolopum manus, hic sævus tendebat Achilles;
> Classibus hic locus; hic acies certare solebant.

And so to Constantinople. But not the pilgrims' Constantinople of former days, as marvellous a centre, perhaps, of ecclesiastical civilisation
and dignity, and of relics, as has been seen. St.
Sophia was still there and its doors still of the
wood of Noah's ark, but it was a mosque where
the inquisitive Christian was allowed to look
round on sufferance. Only two churches in the
city were allowed to remain in Western Christian
hands, St. Nicholas and Our Lady of Constantinople, the latter still a place of pilgrimage though
served by one solitary Dominican friar. Gone
was Moses' rod; gone from the neighbouring village of Is Pigas was the fresco of St. John from

whose head, in the first week of each Lent, had blossomed a milk-white rose; gone was the trumpet that sounded at the fall of Jericho and the horn of Abraham's ram. But the last two must be safe somewhere, for they are to be used by the summoning angel on Judgment Day.

As a pilgrim, then, the tourist reached Constantinople only by the way. And setting out thence for Jerusalem, viâ Damascus, he might go by land in one of three ways, either by trading caravan, in which case he should contract with some one in it for all expenses and necessaries by the way, besides engaging a Janizary, necessary under every possible condition, who is to report his passenger's safe arrival to an ambassador or some merchant residing at the point of departure; or he might accompany a governor on his way to take up his duties (and changes were very frequent), in which case the governor had better be required to swear by his head to see the pilgrim safely through; or for the third, and quickest way, on the return journey, accompany the carriers of revenue to Constantinople. But it was far commoner to make a sea-journey of it, which meant taking ship to "Scanderoon" and thence by land, viâ Aleppo, to Damascus. Nobody ever went to Scanderoon except to get to Aleppo; sometimes not even then, for during this period the port of Aleppo was as often as not Tripoli. The objection to Scanderoon was its unhealthiness, lying, as it did, as Peter

Mundy says, "in a great marsh full of boggs, foggs, and froggs"; of the English who went there as apprentices scarcely five per cent lived to go into business for themselves. Aleppo was worth seeing: a pleasant town with its approaches all gardens, like Damascus, and the medley of nations must have been marvellous to watch; a sign of its cosmopolitanism was that Christians were allowed to ride horses there, an unusual privilege in Mohammedan dominion; probably nowhere outside Venice were so many sects represented, whose churches were in what was called the new suburb; two Armenian, a Greek, and a Catholic Maronite were actually side by side, with a Syrian Jacobite church just near. It is not out of place to add that at the Jews' synagogue there was not the usual division of sexes, but that the only separation was that one side was reserved for the families who had been long resident there, the other for strangers: because although the repulsion felt for the Jews was greater at this time than at present, the interest in them was likewise greater, and any information concerning their customs was regarded by the tourist as matter for his readers — a surprising number of these tourists give eye-witness accounts of circumcisions of Jewish babies.

To return to Aleppo; it was equally remarkable for its trade. Dealings to the extent of 40,000 to 100,000 crowns were ordinary, and this implied frequency of caravans to take the pilgrim on to

Damascus. On the way he would pass the district
in which Job was supposed to have lived, which
may well have been so, says Moryson, for no spot
possessed such conveniences for getting robbed,
even of 100,000 head of cattle, nor any better
suited to develop patience.

It was here the pilgrim became acquainted
with the Arabs. How far the latter were independent of the Turks was left an unsettled question,
but it is fairly certain that on many, perhaps
most, of the occasions when a European traveller of the time relates an encounter with the
Arabs, the latter were not the robbers he thought
them but keepers of the roads demanding not
more than treble what they were entitled to. But
it is equally clear that hostilities were perpetual.
In 1601 a caravan guide told an Englishman at
one defile that he had never passed by there without seeing bodies of murdered men; and from
Damascus to Jacob's bridge — so called because
just by was the spot where Jacob wrestled with
the Angel — the caravan travelled by night for
fear of the Arabs and no talking was allowed without the captain's special permission. But there
was much to divert the attention of the faithful
from their trials. At Damascus was Ananias'
house, and soon after starting an ill-informed
tourist would be surprised to see all his fellow
travellers fall on their knees for prayers: it would
be the spot where the conversion of St. Paul took

place. Before reaching the Sea of Galilee they
came upon a field with a little well in it, at which
all dismounted for worship as well as for a drink;
there had Joseph been hidden by his brethren.
Between Cana and Mt. Tabor was a little chapel
to call at, built on the spot where Christ had
multiplied the loaves and fishes, and after this
the road turned westwards to Nazareth and the
church on the site where the Virgin Mary's house
had stood before it had been spirited away to
Loreto; two porphyry columns were standing on
the places occupied respectively by the Archangel
and by the Virgin at the moment of the Annunciation. For those who were not Roman Catholics
there was the actual house there to be identified
on its original site, so far as it had been left intact
by previous pilgrims; Lithgow, the only Western
Christian in the caravan he travelled with, asserts
that his companies carried away above five thousand pounds' weight of the house in remembrance.
Then southward, joining the road from Tripoli,
more frequented, but not by pilgrims, who chose
this Damascus road as passing through Galilee.
And so to Rama, where they may await such as
journey by route 3 from Constantinople viâ Cairo.

Reaching Alexandria it was found to be about
the size of Paris; besides the ruins, the greatness
of which was attested by the intolerable dust
which was all that remained of much of the building materials of the past.

Leaving Alexandria for Cairo, it was a matter
of course to go by river, passing an attractive
town every four miles or so, a very pleasant journey except when the Nile was low, which made it
more practicable for the Arabs to attack. On
landing at Bulak, the port, there would be asses
ready, the wonderful asses of the East celebrated
of old in Western Europe, as the canticle witnesses
which used to be sung at Beauvais cathedral at
the feast of the Circumcision when the ass enters
in the procession.[5]

> Orientis partibus
> Adventavit asinus
> Pulcher et fortissimus
> Sarcinis aptissimus
>   Hez, Hez, sire asne, Hez!!

The asses of Bulak fortified tradition by carrying
passengers into the city, unattended by any boy,
and taking their way back as soon as the ride was
over.

The characteristics of Cairo which impressed
themselves most on the seventeenth-century traveller were its size, and, notwithstanding its size,
its populousness, so great that it was difficult to
move for the press of people. Allowances must
be made, however, for their standard regarding
streets; a large proportion of the ten thousand
streets were in reality passages built over, dark
and dangerous to an extent which probably ex-

ists in few European slums nowadays. The number ten thousand sounds suspicious as a statement of fact, but there was a certain check on it, inasmuch as each "street" was shut at each end by a gate at night and each gate had a guardian as well as a lantern burning; and the number of guardians was twenty thousand besides the four thousand soldiers who patrolled inside the city at night. For the antiquities, there were still to be seen many houses bearing a chalice and two lighted candles, witnesses of Louis IX's captivity in Egypt and the tale of his leaving the sacrament as security for the payment of his ransom on his release; for the rest, knowledge was not in a very advanced state; everything that was not credited to "Pharaoh" was put down to Joseph.

The interest to the tourist centred equally in the excursions. It was but a few miles to Matarea — to use the Italian spelling, preferable with many of the names that occur, especially in this chapter, as a sign of the times — and no Roman Catholic omitted it, seeing that there stood the house where Our Lady dwelt for some years after her flight from Palestine; at Cairo itself was preserved some of the water in which she washed her baby-clothes. Neither, naturally, was any one inclined to pass on without a visit to the Pyramids; no doubt Della Valle's name is still to be found cut on the top of the Great Pyramid on the facet that looks towards Italy. He entered the

Great Pyramid, the only one into which entrance
was effected at this date; but had no opportunity
of saying anything regarding it out of the ordinary; it is when he moved on to what were known
as the "Pyramids of the Mummies" that his
account of his doings again becomes one of the
most remarkable, as well as one of the best written,
of research in Egypt. He made a halt at "Abusir,"
and then after entering one of these minor Pyramids, moved on to "Saccara," the centre for
mummy-hunting, which formed the occupation of
the boys of the village. On Della Valle's arrival
they had a stand-up fight for the privilege of taking him home, and the next morning about fifty
were at his door. A procession having been
formed, all were set to work in different places
probing for tombs, for Della Valle was bent on
examining such as had never been opened hitherto. His trouble and expense were well rewarded,
for the two mummies he brought away intact
were pronounced at Cairo to be the most remarkable that any one there remembered seeing. They
cost him three piastri — less than five pounds in
our money at present values — each, and are now
in Dresden Museum. It was rare for any to be seen
intact, for hunting for mummies was not carried
on for museums, but because of their supposed
medicinal value, greatest, it was thought, in virgin-
mummies; one of the rare qualities of Othello's
handkerchief consisted in its having been

. . . dyed in mummy which the skilful
Conserved of maiden's hearts . . .

Mummies were therefore broken up as soon as
found, and sold piecemeal; sometimes also to
painters, who by means of them obtained certain
shades of brown otherwise unattainable. There
was, nevertheless, an Englishman, named John
Sanderson, who brought one away intact, besides
six hundred pounds of fragments to sell to London
apothecaries, in spite of mummy being contra-
band export from Egypt.

A third, and the chief, excursion was to Sinai
and the Red Sea. It is no exaggeration to say that
for most it was a terrible experience; there were
many who visited Mohammedan lands often and
some who saw Jerusalem more than once, but not
one went a second time to Sinai. No big caravans
travelled that way, few were the merchants who
traded to Suez; it meant, then, being subject to
the pleasure of the Arabs. There privation was
the best that could be looked for, they were dependent for their lives and the endurance of life
on their own enforced liberality and the chance of
forbearance from others; and very thankful must
they have been when they caught sight of the two
great towers, since pulled down, which stood in
the suburbs of Cairo for landmarks to those coming from Suez, although they might expect to receive a welcome, as they had probably had a send-
off, from the boys of Cairo in the shape of dirt,

bricks, and bad lemons. Two Germans were reduced to such a state as to become subject to
hallucinations.

Especially strange did the journey seem to a
Russian who passed by the Cairo route to Jerusalem. So totally different a desert from those he
knew, — neither forests nor vegetation, no people,
no water; nothing but sand and stones, except for
the Red Sea. And it happens that here, in particular, does he show how far more second-hand was
his knowledge of the Bible stories than was that
of other Europeans. The function of the cloud
which is said to have accompanied the Israelites
by day on their flight was, to him, to hide them
from pursuers, and at the Red Sea there were still
visible to him the twelve ways that Moses had
opened up for his people, one for each tribe, marked
on the surface of the water by a deeper tint, and
the prints of Pharaoh's chariot-wheels were as
indelible as ever for him, whereas Christians from
farther west ceased to see them soon after the
beginning of the sixteenth century. Some facts
were even more exclusively his own, as that Pharaoh's soldiers were changed into fish after their
drowning; and were to be known when caught
by having human heads, men's teeth and noses,
though their ears had grown to fins; nobody eats
them. Pharaoh's horses were likewise fishified;
hairy fish with skins as thick as your finger.

It goes without saying that every scene from

Hebrew history was localised to a square foot; but there was, besides, a rock to be seen written over in characters that none could decipher, yet identified by tradition as the writing of Jeremiah the prophet done with his finger. This rock was near the monastery. Hither came the pilgrim, to find the gate barred, whether he had sent word of his approach or not; the monastery was surrounded as a rule by two or three hundred Arabs, howling day and night, and sometimes threatening, for food; let down every now and then from a window high up. Once inside, there was the monks' well to see, the very same one at which Moses watered Jethro's sheep, and a chapel behind the choir built over the spot where had stood the burning bush that Moses saw; with Our Lady and her Baby standing in the middle thereof unharmed, say the Russian pilgrims. Then to bed; and in the morning, after being wakened, maybe, by a monk calling his brethren to "offices" by striking spears of wood and iron with a stick, for bell they had none, a start would be made up what was assumed to be Mt. Horeb, at the foot of which, on the side nearest Cairo, lay the monastery. Not far from the top were four chapels, one dedicated to St. Elijah, at the back of which was the grotto where he hid from Jezebel, forty days, fasting. At the top was the rock behind which Moses lay while God passed, and, hard by, the church of the Holy Summit and a mosque — it was a pilgrimage place for Mohammedans, too. Then down again the farther side to the valley between Mts. Horeb and Sinai, to the hospice where pilgrims stayed the night.

Before reaching Sinai, and after leaving it, these travellers are in the habit of making assertions so flatly contradictory that some of them will be hardly put to it on Judgment Day; but when at Sinai, there is only one opinion — to get to the top thereof was the most terrific struggle they had ever gone through. Only one account has the least suggestion of enjoyment in it, Della Valle's; and yet his ascent was made under worse conditions than any other's.

It was one Christmas. In the night snow had fallen; the morning promised more snow. Only one monk was found to act as guide; but Della Valle was ready, and his servants would go wherever he chose to lead them; two Arabs were bribed into carrying food. So a start was made; Della Valle in the pilgrim's tunic which he always wore in holy places, but tucked up high this time; and all with sticks cut from the tree whence Moses cut his rod. First went the monk, taking the rocks like a young deer; and he must have known his way well, for the stones which marked the way could not have been visible for snow. At first it was just wet; then they met the snow; higher up it came to mid-thigh; still higher, still deeper. Farther still, where in the best of weathers it was

a place for hands and knees, it was all frozen; more
snow was falling and the wind terrific. The interpreter gave himself up for dead, cursed the monk
who encouraged the ascent, commended himself
to God and St. Catherine, remembered his sins,
and forswore meat on every Monday that he
might live to see. However, they did reach the
top, where, once upon a time, the angels laid St.
Catherine's body for a while; and saw the hard
stone which retained the imprint of her body
where she had lain and of the angels' posteriors
where they sat, one at each side of her head, and
one at her feet. They prayed, eat, and forthwith
started to descend, to reach the hospice that
night. What with snow and mist they could often
see but a foot or two before them, and their idea of
descending under the conditions was to toboggan
on their backs; the only risk being, he says, that
of getting buried in snowdrifts, which was no real
risk, because they never all got buried at the same
time. However, once he found himself sitting on
the edge of a precipice with his legs dangling; and
yet, in the end, no casualties occurred except to
one of Della Valle's shoes, and he and his servants,
after buying some of the little rings the monks
provided by way of souvenirs, made of gold, of
silver, and of bone, went back to Cairo to prepare
for the other journey across the desert, to Gaza
and Rama.

Cairo to Gaza was twelve days' journey by

caravan, but an Arab could do it in four days. A merchant-pilgrim who had to rejoin his ship at Alexandria by a certain date in 1601 could find no way of return except under the escort of the Arabs to whom a friendly Moor introduced him. They travelled on dromedaries at first, but he changed to horseback towards the end to save his life from death by jolting. One evening his dromedary ran away, and the two Arabs pursued it out of sight, and there were the Moor and the merchant alone in the desert with night descending on them, not to mention other Arabs who had taken no oaths to respect their lives and pockets, but who eventually postponed beheading them till their guides returned.

An Arab guide meant safety from the chief danger of the desert, that of the Arab bands who laid in wait for every caravan and attacked small ones; in 1611 a caravan of three hundred camels was carried off bodily. The average number of persons in a caravan seems to have been about one thousand and the number of camels three for every four persons, besides the extra ones that would be required for merchandise; a camel carried two persons, and one camel luggage for four, — no small load, for each one had to provide for himself as if he was about to set up housekeeping. The camel had this advantage over the horse, that the latter and his fodder were more coveted by the Arab than the former; and it was all one whether the Arab took horse and fodder or fodder only, for there was none to be bought and the horse would starve if left with the owner. The camels used for caravan purposes were not the small ones the Arabs were accustomed to, but the large ones, on which alone, at that time, at any rate, was it customary to travel in cradles, one cradle slung each side of the camel. They were comfortable, these cradles; comfortable enough to sleep in, hooded and lined to defend the traveller from sun and weather, with a secret pocket in the seat for valuables. The camels themselves were protected against the evil eye by charms written by dervishes slung round their necks in leathern bags; and on special occasions they were painted orange from head to foot, like the Polish horses.

Three of the halts were beside castles maintained by the Turks; elsewhere there was always the chance of an Arab chief enquiring if there were Franks in the caravan and then inviting himself to dinner; after dinner he would want a present, would probably name his needs, and lucky was one particular tourist whose guest only asked for some sugar and a pair of shoes. That the Arab was born to command and the Frank to obey, was an axiom with Franks and caravan-leaders, except to Della Valle, who always showed fight and always won; it is to be hoped that none of the other tourist-pilgrims came to know later how much money they would have saved had they known the effect of gunpowder, even minus the bullet, on an Arab.

At Gaza the caravan would split. The tourist would accompany those who were for Damascus, whose way lay through Rama, where, as already mentioned, all pilgrim ways met. Then to Jerusalem. At the gate the pilgrim's weapons were taken from him and his name registered in a book, to assure that his tribute should not be overlooked. Then the resident representative of his sect took charge of him; if he was a Frank he went to the Roman Catholic monastery of San Salvatore, whether Protestant or not. There was one Calvinist at this time who preferred to deal direct with the Turks rather than endanger his soul; but this meant money to the monks and he found himself in prison, from which he was only released by influence. The fact was that none of the Protestant rulers contributed to the upkeep of any foundation at Jerusalem and all Western Europeans were consequently classed together as in days gone by. At the monastery he would be fairly certain to make the acquaintance of Giovanni Battista, the monastery guide, for by 1612 he had filled that post for twenty-five years; and he it was from whom pilgrims derived most of their information during their stay — in Italian; if their knowledge of Italian was hazy, it probably added one or two marvels to those he meant to tell them. And, indeed, this may be said of most

of these tourists on most of their journeys; much
of the information they retail, in their own books
and in this, they acquired by word of mouth in a
language they only half understood.

Of Jerusalem as a town they say that the walls
were the best part of the building; that there were
three Christians living there to every Turk; that
the Christians dwelled there for devotion and the
Turks for the income derived from the Christians,
and that otherwise it would have been wholly
deserted. Partially deserted it actually was, since
for the scarcity of human beings in its streets it is
compared to Padua, the emptiest city in Europe,
by one Englishman. All the trades driven there
were elementary ones, shoemakers, cooks, smiths,
tailors; and Moryson, on being seen walking about
with gloves and a shirt, was taken for a prince in
spite of his being poorly dressed otherwise; although that did not prevent the natives egging on
their children to leap on to his back from upper
stories and snatch things from him.

But just consider the sights in these streets!
Passing over the localisations of New Testament
incidents (such as where the Apostles composed
the Creed and Christ the Lord's prayer) so exact
and frequent that one must have had to walk
slowly to avoid missing them when the guide
pointed them out, there were besides the houses
of Annas, Zebedee, Caiaphas, Veronica, Dives,
Mary Magdalen, Uriah the Hittite, Pilate, where

nightly were heard noises and whippings and sighs, and of the school which Our Lady attended; the orchard where Bathsheba bathed and the terrace from which David beheld her; the fountain where Our Lady used to wash her baby-clothes; the stone on which the cock stood to crow at St. Peter's downfall, and another which had been the seat of the angel who told the Marys of Christ's resurrection, etc., etc.

These were every-day matters. To see Jerusalem at its best one had to go at Easter, when the concourse of pilgrims was greatest for two reasons: first, the only excursion to Jordan took place; secondly, the descent of the Holy Fire from heaven into the church of the Holy Sepulchre. The incidents of the season are described in detail by George Sandys, Lithgow, Coryat and Della Valle, who were there at Easter in the years 1611, 1612, 1614, and 1616 respectively. On Palm Sunday the warden of the monastery set out for Bethphage in the afternoon and returned riding on an ass, the people shouting "Hosanna, etc.," and strewing the way with boughs and garments. When Lithgow was there they made too much noise to please the Turks and therefore returned black with bruises and somewhat bloody, the warden not excepted. In the evening the warden had recovered far enough to give an address to the Frank pilgrims, entreating the Protestants to refrain from reviling what they did not agree

with, and concluding with the advice that three
things were preëminently needful for a Jerusalem
pilgrim; Faith (to believe what was told him),
Patience (with the Turks), and Money.

On Maundy Thursday came the ceremony of
washing the pilgrims' feet by the warden, and
great was his disgust if he found that he had
washed and kissed the feet of a Protestant. Some
spent the next three nights in the church of the
Holy Sepulchre, some only Easter Eve; a survival
of the pre-Christian idea of the healing influence
of passing a night in a temple.[6] Those who could
not afford, or borrow, the heavy entrance-fee,
never entered but stood outside and wept, or
looked through the round hole in the door through
which food was passed. Inside, it made all the
difference whether or no the Oriental Palm Sunday or Easter Day fell on the Frank Easter.
If so, the Frank would find the number in the
church of the Holy Sepulchre anything between
one and two thousand, many belonging to nations
he had never heard of, all frantic with excitement,
dancing, leaping, and lamenting by torchlight, in
garments that he had never dreamt of, to the
sound of kettle-drums and horns and other instruments as strange to him as their languages
and manner of singing; all combining, with their
flags and banners, in a general cumulative effect
of inexpressible weirdness, without a single touch
to bring it into relation with ordinary life, except

the Turks bringing to reason with sticks those who were really too outrageous even for the occasion. And so the pilgrims spent the three nights, on the floor, in as utter disregard of decency and sanitation, and sometimes of morality, as of silence.

The descent of the Holy Fire was no more than an interesting sight to the European tourist; Roman Catholic and Protestant alike expressed disbelief in its actuality as openly as the Turk.

On Easter Monday the monks journeyed to Emmaus, passing the house of Simeon and the spot where David slew Goliath, returning by another road past the valley where Joshua commanded the staying still of the sun, and the house of Samuel. It was on the Tuesday preceding the Oriental Easter that the great excursion of the year took place, to Jordan; the only one in the year because the danger from the Arabs was considered prohibitive unless an escort of Turkish soldiers accompanied the pilgrims, so strong that only the Easter concourse could pay them. It was more than a day's journey, so Tuesday night was spent in the open, starting again however before dawn at the pace set by the escort's horses; of the poorer pilgrims who could not afford a mount, many died either from exhaustion or from fear. So says Della Valle, and it is confirmed by Lithgow; the latter, who walked, sometimes was up to his middle in sand, and "true it is, in all my travels, I was never so sore fatigued, nor more fearfully endangered than that night." At dawn they arrived where Christ had been baptised, to see the medley of nationalities, all distinct from each other in some striking detail or other, once more in the highest state of excitement; some drinking, some being baptised by friends, some dipping their clothes, some renouncing clothes altogether, scores, perhaps hundreds, of men and women stark naked, there in the chilly spring morning, douching themselves till their teeth chattered and their bodies turned blue, while others who came to pray remained to laugh.

On the way back some diverged to visit Mt. Quarantana, the scene of the forty days' fast; very few ascended it. The way up was a narrow path along precipices; broken by forty-five steps, each from five to ten feet high, where there was little foothold and slipping meant death. This ended at the little cave where Christ was tempted by the Devil; the way thence to the summit, from which Christ had surveyed the kingdoms of the world, was not attempted by any one: Lithgow says he reached the top but proves that he did not; and Della Valle says that the only means of reaching it was that used by Christ, being carried up by the Devil.

Easter, too, gave a good opportunity for a visit to Hebron, for the largest caravan went thither at that time also. But this was as much a Moham-

medan pilgrimage as Christian, and Abraham's
house, another of the remarkably well-preserved
buildings of Palestine, was shut against Christians
and Jews. Of these latter there were many who
journeyed to the Holy Land; how many cannot
be guessed, but they certainly outnumbered the
Christians of the West, and equally certainly were
too many to be omitted from a record of Europeans then, though the only piece of direct evidence
at hand is from the itinerary of one Samuel Jemsel [7] with whom, in 1641, one hundred sailed in one
ship of the regular fleet from Constantinople to
Egypt, some bound for Jerusalem, some for Safed.
They come into notice chiefly when a caravan is
on the move on their Sabbath, when they remain
behind and make up the lost ground as best they
can.

From other pilgrims they differed in this; the
Christian was leaving home, the Jew was going
home. When they reached Palestine, besides,
some of the spots they visited were famous among
Christians; but mostly they were not. In the best
Jewish guide-book in use in 1600, are mentioned one
hundred and sixty-eight of their famous ancestors
whose tombs were localised. If a Christian visited
Abraham's, his duty to the Old Testament was
done with; and even then he invariably omitted
to observe the stone on which the patriarch sat
when he was circumcised. And as for the tomb
of Adam and Eve, and of Jacob and Leah, and

the prophet Hosea (may his memory be blessed), and of Isaiah (may Salvation be his), and of Rachel (with whom be peace), and of the Rabbi Jeremiah who was buried upright, and, at Ras-ben-Amis, of the wife of Moses our master, and of the wife of the high-priest Aaron, and, on Mt. Ephraim, of Joshua the son of Nun and of Caleb the son of Jephunneh (may God, in his mercy, be mindful of them and of all other righteous men) — why, of all these the Ishmaelites knew nothing, nor even that at Rama was to be seen the spot where the Messiah shall appear, nor that there should be rending of garments when Jerusalem is first seen and again on reaching the place where once stood the Temple, now, for our sins, destroyed.

Outside Palestine, too, was much that the un-circumcised knew not of. He passed through Cairo without hearing of the copy of the law of Moses, written by the hand of Esdras the scribe; though, indeed, no man might see it, not even, incredible as it may sound, if he offered the keeper thereof silver (partly because the holy volume had by now been stolen, and lost, with the thief, at sea). And Damascus Hebrew and Frank might equally remember as the city where fresh fruit was never lacking, but only the former remembered that hard by Esdras himself lay buried, any more than the merchant who reached Baghdad heard that there rested Ananias, Mizael, and Azarias, and also, with the river flowing over his

head, Daniel, of glorious memory, — unless the
merchant wished to catch some of the great fish
which swam thereabouts, for fishing was prohibited at that spot lest harm might befall the
greatest fish of all, Zelach by name, who had
abided there since Daniel's own time and was fed
from the royal table.

And if any of the twentieth-century uncircum-
cised hesitate to believe that so much could be
satisfactorily identified, the twentieth-century Hebrew may answer that there are other tests of
identification than those of the "research" that
has achieved such wonders at Stratford-on-Avon
and that tradition can be traced back, unvarying
even in trifles, for centuries.

He might go on to point out that Christian
tradition might well be more stable. It is curious
how much that is mentioned by fifteenth-century
Christians is habitually omitted by those who
came after. That the taking of Rhodes by the
Turks should cause the disappearance of the
basin in which Christ washed his apostles' feet is
intelligible; but why, e. g., should the table disappear from Bethany at which the disciples were
sitting when the Holy Ghost descended? And
why should it have dropped out of remembrance
that the torrent of Cedron had been bridged with
stone by St. Helen to replace the wooden one
from which the wood for the Cross had been taken
and over which the Queen of Sheba had refused

to walk, saying in a spirit of prophecy, that the Saviour of the world was to die on it? It seems as though there had occurred a diminishment of devotion resulting in the concentration of what devotion remained on fewer objects; or else a widening of interests diverting the attention from minor objects. Sometimes, of course, transference took place; which may, or may not, account for one traveller being shown the pillar of salt which had once been Lot's wife at a monastery near Trapani in Sicily in 1639, whereas in 1613 Coryat was told that she existed on the farther side of "Lake Asphaltitis with her child in her arms and a pretty dog, also in salt, by her." Still, no doubt Giovanni Battista and the warden did their best, and the latter was willing, in addition, to confer knighthood of the Holy Sepulchre on all and sundry, with no questions asked as to lineage, not even of a Dutchman in the grocery business; and at least there was the certificate of the pilgrim's visit to Jerusalem to be received — and paid for.

And now the tourist's last and longest journey has been told; he is at home safe, leaving us with nothing fresh to tell except the incidentals of his journeyings, and leaving us, one tourist, at least, with his blessing: "In the meantime I leave thee, gentle reader, travelling towards the heavenly Jerusalem, where God grant at length we may all arrive, Jesus Christ being our pilot and Janizary to conduct us thereunto."

CHAPTER VI

INNS

Servus. . . . Però con licentia, quando quierese ir vuessa merced?	Sed bona venia, quando vult recedere T. D.?
Viator. Mañana, plaziendo à Dios, en caso que pueda madrugar	Cras, si Deo placet, si possim diluculo surgere.
Servus. Paraque no se queda aqui aun algunos dias?	Quare non manet hic adhuc per aliquot dies?
Viator. El huesped y el pesce en tres dias hiede	Hospes et piscis post triduum foetent.

MÜLLER, "Linguæ Hispanicæ Institutio," 1630.

IT is a most unsatisfactory thing — reading about what you would like to see; but if seeing sixteenth-century Europe implied spending the nights in sixteenth-century inns there is much to be said for preferring the experience in print only. Luxury of a kind certainly was to be had. At the "Vasa d'Oro" at Rome were gorgeous beds, hung with silk and cloth of gold, worth four to five hundred crowns each; at the "Ecu" at Châlons silken bedding, too; and Germany occasionally provided sheets trimmed with lace four-fingers'-breadth wide in panelled rooms, while by 1652 Amsterdam possessed a hotel reckoned the best in Europe, every room in which was

floored with black and white marble and hung
with pictures, with one room containing an organ
and decorated with gilded leather in place of
tapestries. But these superfluities did not imply
that a comfortable medium was easily found. In
any case, accommodation divided itself into bedroom and dining-room; of anything approaching
a sitting-room there is rarely a word. The chief
exception to this is the five or six halls, decorated
and furnished like those of a rich gentleman, at
the inn outside Sinigaglia. This was the finest
hotel in Italy when built, shortly before 1578, by
the Duke of Urbino, who allowed no other there.
Its forty bedrooms, with no more than two beds
in each, all opened on to one long gallery by
separate doors.[1]

The Italian host the traveller would often see
before the inn came in sight; sometimes the latter
would have touts as far away as seven or eight
leagues to buttonhole foreigners, carry their luggage, promise anything and behave with the utmost servility — till the morning of departure.
But with all this to expect them to provide clean
sheets was expecting too much, and as the nation
was grievously afflicted with the itch, it was desirable for the visitor to carry his own bedding.
In many cases, too, we find the tourist sleeping
on a table in his clothes to avoid the dirtiness of
the bed, or the vermin. Still, in Italy, you shared
your bed with these permanent occupants only,

as a rule; in Spain you were sure to do so; one man, one bed, was the custom there — a result of the enforcement of the penalty of burning alive for sodomy. In Germany the custom was just the reverse; in fact, if the tourist did not find a companion for himself, the host chose for him, and his bedfellow might be a gentleman, or he might be a carter; all that could safely be prophesied about him was that he would be drunk when he came to bed. The bed would be one of several in a room; the covering a quilt, warm enough to be too warm for summer, and narrow enough to leave one side of each person exposed in winter. This is supposing there were beds: in northern Germany rest for the night would be on a bench in a "stove," as they called the room, because the stove was so invariably part of the furniture that the words "room" and "stove" became synonymous. Windows were never opened at night, to retain the heat in the room; all the travellers lay there, men and women, gentlemen and "rammish clowns," as near the stove as they could manage. The heat was such that the effect on one unaccustomed to it was "as if a snake was twining about his legs." Further, if several met together, says a Frenchman, one might as well try to sleep in a market-place on market-day. In upper Germany, the bedrooms were separate, without fires or the means of making one, and the change from the one temperature to the other was very trying.

As many beds were put in a room as the room would hold; fairly clean ones, however, as the Germans treated them with some disinfectant. In Saxony there were no beds, no benches, no stove, even. All lay in the straw among the cows, the chief disadvantage of which was that your pillow was liable to be eaten in the night. So in Poland, too, where it meant a cold and dangerous night, in the country parts, at least, for any one who did not adapt himself to the custom of the country by using the long coat lined with wolf-skins which served the Pole as cloak by day and bedding by night.

As a relief from the general statements, a particular instance may be quoted to exemplify a night by the way in Poland. The sleeping-room struck the writer as something between a stable and a subterranean furnace. Six soldiers lay on the ground as if dead; the peasant-tenant, his wife, children, and servants, lay on benches round the walls, with coverings of straw and feathers; in one corner slept a Calvinist, a baron's secretary; in another, on the peasant's straw pallet, an ambassador's chaplain, a Roman Catholic; and between the two, to save each, it seemed, from the heels of the other, was lying a huge Tartar, a captain in the Polish army, who had made up a bed of hay for himself. About the room were dogs, geese, pigs, fowls; while the corner by the oven was conceded to a woman who had just given birth to a child. The baby cried, the mother moaned, the tired servants and soldiers snored; and early in the morning the writer rose from the shelf he was sharing with some leggings, spurs, and muskets, and escaped.[2]

Speaking generally, there were no beds to be found in the North. In Muscovy everything had to be carried along; without a hatchet, tinderbox, and kettle there was no hot food for the wayfarer till he reached a monastery or a town, much less shelter; unless by chance he came across somebody's one-story cabin which would have no outlet for the smoke except the door, and accommodation below the level of the average stable, one room shared between the family, visitors, and live-stock. When Sir Jerome Horsey was at Arensberg, in the island of Oesel, near the gulf of Riga, in 1580, snakes crept about bed and table and the hens came and pecked at them in the flour and the milk.

Crossing over to Sweden the absence of inns was equally noticeable, but no disadvantage, for one of the conditions on which the parson held his living was that of showing hospitality to those in need of it. In Denmark, too, while taverns existed for supplying victuals, the wayfarer was dependent on the citizen for lodging, again not to his loss; he was sure of decent food, a clean bed, and a welcome. Foreigners in England are singularly reticent about the inns, except for reviling Gravesend for swindling; which may, perhaps, be taken as confirming Moryson's opinion that the English inn was the best in Europe. As to Ireland, there is the usual diversity of opinion; the absence of inns is accounted for by the traditional idea that the possession of an inn was a disgrace to a town, a slur on the hospitality of its inhabitants; yet the hospitality itself was most uncertain, since the natives were not in a position to believe in the neutrality of a visitor.

The *personnel* question, of course, is one that has to be allowed for throughout. It was in France that this method of discounting dissatisfaction was most in use, but it is in a dialogue printed in the Low Countries, a conversational guide for travellers in seven languages, that the following (an excerpt from the English version) occurs:[3]

"My she-friend, is the bed made? is it good?"

"Yea, sir; it is a good feather-bed; the sheets be very clean."

"Pull off my hosen and warm my bed; draw the curtains and pin them with a pin. My she-friend, kiss me once and I shall sleep the better. . . . . I thank you, fair maiden."

The German host was too apt to think that a heavy meal and honesty were all that could be expected from him. The honesty was indeed remarkable; more than one stranger was astonished by the recovery of property mislaid; sent after him, sometimes, before he had discovered his loss and no reward taken; but it was paid for dearly indirectly through the insolence born of virtue in a class that is naturally below the Ten-Com- mandment standard. The customer was made to feel that the favour was to, not from, him. An exception to this is the experience of Van Buchell, who found German hosts sending hot water up to a traveller's bedroom, if it was noticed he was tired, with herbs in the water, such as camomile, for strengthening the feet; and this even at Frank- furt a/M. in Fair-time as well as elsewhere. But there was no such thing as hastening on, or de- laying, a meal-time, or dissatisfaction with the food; the bill must be paid without question, not a farthing abated.

And generally, indeed, the help of the law did not seem to avail against the innkeeper. Tourists speak of successful appeals to the law on other points and curse the inns without ceasing, but a successful tourist's lawsuit against his host re- mains to be found. In Tyrol, in fact, the plaintiff would find the defendant not only on, but con- trolling, the bench; and in Spain most innkeepers were officers of the " Santa Hermandad," a "Holy Brotherhood" whose forgotten ideal and raison d'être was that of acting as country police, with the result that the complainant would probably be arrested at the next stopping-place on some trumped-up charge. Neither was the local author- ity of assistance so far as prices were concerned in spite of the latter being fixed by it and posted up; because the local authority was open to bribery, and the innkeeper had known that as long as he had been in business. In short, when the bill came to one hundred per cent too much in Spain, the cheapest way was to pay it.

Of all the ill-feeling that the tourists harboured against Spain, the bitterest was on account of the inns; from the earliest, Andrew Boorde, who says "hogs shall be under your feet at the table, and lice in your beds," and another who relates how he preferred to hire three Moors to hold him in their arms while he slept. Those who come midway through the period tell the same tale; at Galleretta, on the border of Castile, a German finds the stable, the bedroom, the kitchen, the dining-room, the pigsty, one and the same room, and a Papal envoy sleeps on straw one snowy night without a fire. The latest writes that the sight of the inns was more than enough. There was but one way to reconcile one's self to the wayside inn of Spain; and that was—trying those of Portugal.

Over all these inns the Turkish "khan" had this advantage, that there was no host. A "khan" was a building which some compare to a barn, and one to a tennis-court, with a platform running round inside the walls about four feet broad and usually three to four feet high, but sometimes ten. At intervals of about eight feet were chimneys. The platform was for the travellers; the inner space for their beasts; the chimneys for each party to cook food at. That was the normal form, seeming to an uninstructed traveller just a stable, in which idea he would be confirmed by the scents in the early morning. The average Christian found that the noises and the lights prevented sleep, but the Turk carried a rug to sleep on, used his saddle as a pillow and his great rain-cloak as a covering and found it comfortable enough till daybreak, when he thought it suitable to get up, greatly to the disgust of the Christians present. Or if the moon was very bright, he might arise earlier by mistake; for he carried no watch, nor believed one when he saw it. Even in the ordinary "khan" there was often a room over the door to which the traveller might retire if he chose, but the Turk seldom used this, preferring to keep an eye on his beasts; and the Frank consequently might remain unaware that there existed any escape from the camels. Most "khans," built of hewn stone roofed with lead, would accommodate from eighty beasts to one hundred and fifty; and practically always had their fountains for the washings prescribed by the Turks' religion: but as time went on, far more magnificent places arose, with covered ways leading to mosques across the road, and many rooms, capable of holding nearly one thousand travellers and their belongings. The finest lay along the road leading from Constantinople to Christendom. The fact that "khan" is indiscriminately applied

to all by most Franks is evidence that they were
not on speaking terms with the natives, to whom
many were known as "Imaret," those, that is,
which provided food free. All lodgings were a
form of good works among the richer Turks, a
practical attempt to disarm the customary sus-
picions of the Grand Signor or the well-justified
wrath of Allah; and free food was an extension of
this appeal. The food was barley porridge mostly,
or of some other grain, with meat in it; and bread,
and sometimes honey; nor was there any idea of
poverty associated with taking it; Jew and viceroy
alike were recipients. Of all the marvellous provision for travellers, and even for the care of stray
animals, in Constantinople, free food, free lodging,
free medical attendance for men of all creeds, as
unfolded in detail by the Turk traveller, Awliyái
Efendí, there is no need to dwell on, since the
Frank knew of its existence but rarely and dimly,
by hearsay only, for he would be lodging over the
water at Pera with his nation's ambassador.

The Turk himself never travelled alone. Had
he done so, he would have found the non-exist-
ence of the innkeeper troublesome. Near Constantinople there was a "khan" for every stage
of every journey; but not so farther away; from
Aleppo to Damascus was nine days' journey and
only five "khans" on the way. But accompanying the caravan, he was taken care of; a quad-
rangle was formed, the travellers inside, among

the waggons; the lines of the square formed by the beasts, their heads tethered inward; and at night-time was an outer line of fires; by the side of the fires, the watch; outside the fires, the patrol, until the three loud strokes on the drum which gave the signal for starting.

For out-of-door lodging, "at the sign of the Moon," as their phrase ran, there was much to be said; but then, how about food? Their guns were short in range; inaccurate within their range; and how much ran about that they might not touch on pain of death. The deer in Germany knew their immunity so well that they would lie in the road and have to be persuaded to leave room for the waggon; and to keep your hand from picking and stealing was an effective commandment where an economical duke of Florence lived who had planted those mulberry trees by the wayside and looked for profits. And so we return to the inns, leaving the bedroom to consider the fare.

But first — how to find them? By the sign when there was one; but supposing there was none? In most parts of Germany inns were distinguished solely by the coats of arms which visitors had put up to commemorate their progresses. The best inns could show, inside and out, as many as three hundred or more. For the signs themselves, it may be interesting to know what were the commonest signs and what were the exceptions. Out of a total of three hundred and fifty-eight

different inns which these travellers mention by
their signs, the "Crown" occurs most frequently
(thirty-two times), mainly as a result of "Ecu de
France" being so favourite a name in France.
"White Horses" and "Golden Lions" seem to
have been about as popular then as now; where
changes have taken place is rather in connection
with ecclesiastical signs. The "Cross" occurs
twenty-two times, eleven of which are "White";
the "Three Kings" (fourteen) and the "Red Hat"
or its equivalents, the "Cardinal's Hat" or the
"Cardinal" (seven), are other examples; but of
saints there are no more than twenty-five altogether, including five of "Our Lady." Barbara
(three), Magdalen, Christopher, and John are the
only other names that are used more than once.
Among those who have but one of the three hundred and fifty-eight inns dedicated to him or her, is
St. Martha, the patroness of those who stay at inns.
The only form that is found coming into fashion
is that of "Town of —— " a fashion set, apparently, by Paris during the first quarter of the seventeenth century, to establish a special clientèle:
the "Ville de Brissac," there, for instance, catered
for Protestants, the "Ville de Hambourg" for
Germans. But there existed at many towns inns
which specialized in this way under ordinary
names. At Lübeck were English inns; at Calais
the "Petit St. Jean" was a meeting-place for
Scotchmen; and Germans in Italy were directed

to the "White Lion" and "Black Eagle" at Venice, the "Two Swords" at Rome, and the "Black Eagle" at Naples. Signs which occur but once and have something picturesque about them are the "Scarlet Siren" ("Serena Ostriata") at Venice, the "Mille Moyens" at Antwerp, the "Good Friend" at Leghorn, the "Fish Cart" of Cologne, the "Bacchus" at Cracow, the "Nereids" at Noyon; Paris had a "Four Winds" and a "Pine-apple," Boulogne a "Tin Pot." Neither should "St. François de la Grande Barbe" at Agen be forgotten, if only on account of the host, who never slept there; every night he was taken away to prison for debt, says the Pole Gölnitz. It is curious, too, that in only one case out of so many should a name come up with any reference to the heroes of romance ("Les Quatre Fils d'Aymon"), which suggests that the acquaintance with them was less common among the lower classes than is generally supposed.

Next, since in nine cases out of ten a sign-board spells a drink, consider drinks. Spaniards and Turks drank water; the rest of Europe thought it unhealthy; in fact, as often as not cleaned their teeth with wine. Still drinking-fountains were not unknown; at Paris Zinzerling sampled sixteen. The consumption of cider, wines, and light beer, and heavy beer seems to have been localized with no material difference from to-day. The Turks alone had coffee and sherbet; and only the Spaniards chocolate, drinking which, however, was no more than a recently introduced fashion for its supposed medicinal qualities; it was only to be had where the most expensive kind of business was done. Among spirits, Irish was reckoned the best whiskey, but was seldom found outside Ireland, where it was known as the "King of Spain's Daughter." In Muscovy aqua-vitæ was the favourite drink; every meal began and ended with it; but for quantity consumed hydromel came first, with mead second. Besides being prepared plain, hydromel was often to be had made with water in which cherries, strawberries, mulberries or raspberries had been soaked for twenty-four hours or more; if aqua-vitæ had been substituted for water with the raspberries, the taste is recommended as marvellous.

For wines, each one was practically confined to the district that grew it. The export trade seems to have been for private buyers, little to inns with the exceptions of Muscovy, where Spanish wine was well known, of Poland (Spanish and Levant) and of Venetian territory, in the various parts of which a considerable variety of wines were grown and between which there had grown up the habit of interchange of products which extended to inn-custom. To be deducted from this is the fact that Greek wine was the name of a kind cultivated as much, perhaps more, outside Greece than within it.

As to the relative quality of sixteenth-century wines there are many independent opinions to be had, and they all agree — Italy was first in that, too. Among Italian wines, preëminent was the Lagrime di Christo ("tears of Christ"), concerning which a Dutchman was heard to lament greatly that Christ had not wept in his country; what has just been said concerning the localization of wines should be modified with regard to this kind which was to be found in many Italian inns outside its native Liguria. Second may be counted Montefiascone, with the help, maybe, of its own particular anecdote, which illustrates the second-hand character of travellers' information, since no two versions of the epitaph agree, and yet most accounts read as if the traveller had read the original. The tale is of a bishop who loved wine, was going to Rome, and had a servant whose taste was to be trusted. The bishop sent him in advance to test the wine at each inn and chalk the door-post with "Est" where the wine was good. When the servant arrived at Montefiascone he chalked "Est, Est, Est"; and so thought the bishop, for he drank till he died. And the servant wrote his epitaph.

> "'Est, Est, Est;' propter nimium Est
> Dominus meus mortuus est."

Drunkenness was infinitely more common than to-day, especially in Germany. Laws had, it is

true, been passed, more stringent, during the past
century, a result of the victories of the teetotal
Turks; but there was no one to enforce them.
Every German's conversation was punctuated
with "I drink to you" "as regularly as every
psalm ends in a 'Gloria,'" says Moryson, and
among a number of princes whom he saw at a
funeral feast, not one was sober. He queries—
what would they have done at a wedding? adding
that during the year and a half he spent there,
attending churches regularly, he never heard a
clergyman say a word against intemperance. The
national reputation abroad was to match; even,
when once some Germans halted at a village in
Spain, there was a riot; the peasants were really
afraid, beforehand, that the price of wine would
go up!

Turning to meals, we find breakfast less of an
established custom than it is at present. In
France it was more, in Germany less, usual than
elsewhere. In fact, in Germany it was not taken
at the inn, but bought in the shape of "brannt-
wein" and gingerbread at shops, existing partly
for that purpose, at the town gates. French
customs generally were more considerate towards
the new-comer; something to go on with would
often be brought him as he dismounted and water
for a wash, just as in Flanders a bright-faced girl
would frequently be ready at the door with beer
or wine, very ready, too, to drink at his expense

and to start first; whereas elsewhere he would be expected to wait till dinner as dusty, inside and outside, as he came in. A French breakfast consisted of a glass of wine and just a mouthful of bread; sometimes, as in Normandy, buttered toast, sometimes even meat was kept ready; but the sole instance of a traveller finding himself expected to eat a substantial meal first thing in the morning was at the inn of St. Sebastian, "the best inn," says Gölnitz, "on the Paris-Lyons road," kept by a mother and two daughters. The English custom of its being taken for granted that the guest saved some of his supper to serve as breakfast next morning, does not seem to have been in use abroad. In Italy it was ordinary to begin the day at a wine-tavern, where boys waited to serve cakes as well as wine, on which foundation the economical Italian would many days last till supper.

Practically, eating resolved itself into two meals a day, just what they were used to at home, and very fortunate it was they were used to it; to us it seems like alternately starving and over-eating. In Germany the latter extreme was the more common; in fact, it is not easy to see how the second meal was fitted in, considering the time one took, three to four hours. At Berne there was a law against sitting at table more than five hours; at Bâle 10 A. M. to 6 P. M. was the maximum, but the town council were unable to practise their own

counsels of perfection and on great occasions finished in private. In Saxony the innkeeper was
forbidden to serve more than four dishes at a meal;
and there public opinion was perhaps some check,
inasmuch as the common saying was to compare
the Saxon dishes, served as they were, one by one,
to the tyrants of Sicily, each one of whom was a
more fearful monster than his predecessor.

Their neighbours, on the contrary, set all on the
table at once in a two-decker on three iron feet;
in the top story was the inevitable sauerkraut and
beneath, roast meat, poultry, puddings, and whatever else was to be had; so that an Englishman
likened this two-decker to Noah's ark, as containing all kinds of creatures. As to these German
"puddings" there is no hard-and-fast rule to be
drawn between them and sausages; and accordingly one cannot say for sure whether it was pudding or sausage which was the food Moryson had
for supper one night near Erfurt; but the description is of no importance compared with the
size, for it was as big as a man's leg, conforming to
the phrase in which the German expressed his
idea of happiness, "Lange Würsten, Kurz Predi-
gen" (long sausages, short sermons). One who
journeyed through Hessen describes his diet as
"mostly coleworts," but a Saxony dinner ordinarily began with stewed cherries or prunes,
continued with poultry or meat, the pot for
which was set on the fire but once a week; and

concluded with bacon to fill up the corners, as important a consideration for the host as any one, for there was no greater reproach to hurl at the host than "Ich hab' mich da nicht satt gefressen" ("I did n't eat my belly-full there").

Bacon was of great account in Germany, so great that the owners were wont to bless their pigs when the latter trotted out of a morning, to ensure their safe return; and told off a servant to wash them as they passed the fountain on their way back, which they took of their own accord. But while a well-fattened sow commanded a fancy price — as much as the equivalent of fifty pounds was paid at Heidelberg in 1593 for one who had become unable to eat a whole raw egg at a meal — sucking pigs were unknown as eatables; an Englishman who bought one for food was forced to kill and prepare it himself on account of the unwillingness of the servants to touch it. What Saxony did lack was everything that was dependent on the yield of a cow; throughout Germany there was little cheese except that made from goat's milk.

A common hors d'œuvre was what were called "Neun Augen" — little lampreys that had nine eyes. Birds other than poultry were unusual: of veal and beef there was a moderate supply, of dried venison rather too much, as was the case at Hamburg with salmon. Dried fish you might expect, with many sauces, all designed to create thirst; fresh fish was expected to be on view alive beforehand in the kitchen; no German inn lacked a wooden fish-tank, kept under lock and key and supplied with running water. Supposing, however, that the sauces failed of their effect, the thirst was sure to come at the end of the meal with the help of little bits of bread, sprinkled with pepper and salt. Fruits were preserved habitually; especially apples and pears, which they halved, dried in the oven, and served up with cinnamon and butter. Black cherries they put in a brass pot, mixed with the best pears cut into small pieces and boiled and stirred till the contents were thick; then pressure was applied which sent the juice through holes in the bottom of the pot; it cooled solid, kept well, and was in every-day use as sauce for meat after it had been liquefied again.

Italians had a sauce of their own, according to Moryson (who has also supplied all the above German recipes), made of bread steeped in broth, walnuts, some leaves of marjoram pounded in a mortar, and gooseberry juice. Much need they had of a sauce, too, for by the "lex Foscarini" it was forbidden to kill an ox until he was unfit for work in the fields. It may be suggested that it is time the "lex Foscarini" was repealed. In the north was plenty of mutton and veal; variety of fish and poultry, mushrooms, snails, and frogs; in Tuscany, kid and boar. First and last everywhere came butter and cheese; everywhere, that is, where any pretence was made of catering for

tourists; at Carrara Moryson found the inns only
fit for labourers, and dined on herbs, eggs, and
chestnuts, while Peter Mundy, near Turin, had to
pay the equivalent of six shillings for "an egg and
a frog and bad wine." De Thou, moreover, using a
main road, that from Naples to Rome, became so
done up through the badness of the inns as to seem
to have completed a long and troublesome illness
rather than a journey. But something might be
said for the average Italian inn as seen from the
street. Through the great open windows — really
open, for there was rarely glass in Italian windows except at Venice — the tables were in view,
always spread with white cloths, strewn with
flowers and fig-leaves and fruits, with glasses set
filled with different coloured wines; during summer, the glasses would be floating in an earthen
vessel, for coolness.

In France, for some reason, Normandy seems
to have made foreigners more comfortable than
elsewhere, yet Picardy, so little distant, was just
the opposite. Picardy, however, at this time was
stamped with the character of border-country
more disastrously than any other district of
France. Nothing remained, indeed, to the country
as a whole, as regards cooking, but a reputation
for entrées, or, as they were called then, "quelques-
choses." "A hard bed and an empty kitchen" was
a common experience in different districts; one
party arrived at Antibes, on the Riviera, in 1606,

to find one melon constituting all the provisions of the only inn.

Comparison of the fare in the various countries of Europe shows no more striking inequalities of supply than is the case with butter: in Poland so plentiful as to be used for greasing cart-wheels; in France so scarce and so bad that English ambassadors used to import theirs from home; in Spain still scarcer, except in cow-breeding Estremadura. A German, when he wanted to buy butter, was directed to an apothecary, who produced a little, and that much rancid, preserved in a she-goat's bladder for use as an ingredient in salves, telling him there was not such another quantity in all Castile.

It was not merely on account of the sleeping accommodation that those who had been to Spain thanked God for their return and wondered at it. The wine, they said, was undrinkable, owing to the flavour imparted to it by the skins that held it; and as for eatables, all had to be bought separately by the traveller and cooked by him when he was tired. A still greater trouble was to find any to buy. One complains that his stomach roared for want of victuals and had to be answered with nothing but roast onions; and so on. But here again can be traced the effects of their buying their experience in the north: what the south thought of the north may be guessed from the Andalusian hero of a picaresque tale recollecting how the food of a Catalan acquaintance of his consisted of hard bread once every three days. The force of prejudice may be exemplified by a note or two from the journal of a courtier[4] who followed after Prince Charles when the latter went incognito to Madrid. His chief complaints as to food are: At the first stopping-place past Santander, whither notice of their coming had been sent a fortnight earlier, they had a plank instead of a table, a few eggs, half a kid burnt black, and no table linen. At a tavern in a wood, the woman laid a cloth on a stool by way of a table, and placed two loaves on it while she fried eggs and bacon for them: enter, from the wood, two black swine who knock the stool over and depart with a loaf each. And yet, although he has noted having enjoyed a good fat turkey at one place and very good hens at another, when he lands at Weymouth he says that there was more meat on the table than he had seen in two hundred miles riding in Spain.

But even in the north different tales are told sometimes. Charles II, when in exile, writes from Saragossa,[5] "But I am very much deceived in the travelling in Spain, for, by all reports, I did expect ill cheer and worse living, and hitherto we have found both the beds, and especially the meat very good. . . . God keep you, and send you to eat as good mutton as we have every meal." Lady Fanshawe is more detailed. "I find it a received

opinion that Spain affords not food either good
or plentiful; true it is that strangers who have
neither skill to choose, nor money to buy, will
find themselves at a loss: but there is not in the
Christian world better wines than their midland
wines are especially, besides sherry and canary.
Their water tastes like milk; their corn white to a
miracle, and their wheat makes the sweetest and
best bread in the world; bacon beyond belief good;
the Segovia veal much larger and fatter than ours;
mutton most excellent; capons much better than
ours. . . . They have the best partridges I ever eat,
and the best sausages; and salmons, pikes, and
sea-breams which they send up in pickle to Madrid,
and dolphins, which are excellent meat and carps,
and many other sorts of fish. The cream, called
'nata,' is much sweeter and thicker than any I
ever saw in England; their eggs much exceed ours;
and so all sorts of salads and roots and fruits.
What I most admired are melons, peaches, burga-
mot pears, grapes, oranges, lemons, citrons, figs,
pomegranates; besides that I have eaten many
sorts of biscuits, cakes, cheese, and excellent
sweetmeats I have not here mentioned."

Both these quotations, it is true, refer to the
middle of the seventeenth century.

England was a land of plenty in these days;
Poland no less so. The sum of the experience of
those who had first-hand means of comparison
suggests that Poland was as great an importer of

luxuries as any country in Europe. Muscovy did
not import, but was well off, nevertheless; plenty of
beef, mutton, pork, and veal, and all the more of
them for foreigners seeing that, with fast-days so
numerous as they were, the natives had become so
used to salt fish that they ate little meat, although
the salt fish, insufficiently salted, was often in a
state like that of the fish which the good angel
provided for Tobit to protect him from a demon,
the scent whereof was so terrible that it drove the
fiend into the uttermost parts of Egypt. In Lent
butter was replaced by caviare. An ambassador's
secretary has a pleasant picture to draw of wayside fare; when they reached a village, the local
priest would appear with gooseberries, or fish, or a
hen, or some eggs, as a present; was rewarded with
aqua-vitæ, and generally went home drunk.

As for food at sea, on small boats no fires were
allowed. Then you were limited, in the Mediterranean, to biscuit, onions, garlic, and dried fish.
On the bigger ships there was garlic again, to roast
which and call it "pigeon" was a stock joke with
the Greek sailors. On an Italian ship of nine hundred tons one traveller fared well: there were two
table-d'hôte rates; he chose the higher one: knife,
spoon, fork, and a glass to himself were provided,
fresh bread for three days after leaving a harbour,
fresh meat at first and afterwards salt meat, and
on fast days, eggs, fish, vegetables, and fruit. An
English idea [6] of victualling a ship included wheat,

rice, currants, sugar, prunes, cinnamon, ginger, pepper, cloves, oil, old cheese, wine, vinegar, canary sack, aqua-vitæ, water, lemon juice, biscuit, oatmeal, bacon, dried neats' tongues, roast beef preserved in vinegar, and legs of mutton minced and stewed and packed in butter in earthen pots; together with a few luxuries, such as marmalade and almonds.

Finally, there is the food to be met with in Ireland, concerning which it is enough to quote:[7] "Your diet shall be more welcome and plentiful than cleanly and handsome; for although they did never see you before, they will make you the best cheer their country yieldeth for two or three days and take not anything therefor."

Except in Italy, fingers invariably did the work of forks; and often of knives, too. The French were the only people who were in the habit of washing before they sat down to table; but this is by no means so much to their credit as it seems at first sight, for it was the result of their getting into such a state previously as to render them intolerable even to themselves. Except for the effects of drunkenness, the Germans appear to have been the pleasantest table companions, in spite of all sitting at one round table; or rather, because of it, for men were the more careful of behaving in a way to which they would have no objection if their neighbours imitated it. Moreover Germans made a practice of having a bath every Saturday night. From this common table no one was excluded in Germany except the hangman, for whose exclusive use a separate table was reserved. The rest of the dining-room furniture consisted of a leather-covered couch for those who were too drunk to do anything but lie down.

As to plates and vessels, no general statement would serve, not even for one country, owing to the rapidity with which the supply of silver increased during these centuries. In 1517 an Italian[8] notes of Flanders that all their vessels, of the church, the kitchen, and the bedroom, were of English brass, but that statement no one confirms later. Wood was common in proportion to the unpretentiousness of the inn; except in Muscovy, where it was almost invariable through the frequency and thoroughness of destruction by fires which caused the use of the most easily replaceable material; the few silver tankards they possessed were rendered unattractive by their custom of cleaning drinking vessels but once a year.

The transition from pewter to silver is most clearly marked in France. The former was in general use as late as Montaigne's time; even he, who owns to making himself in a horrid mess at mealtimes, was glad to escape from its greasiness. By the middle of the next century an Italian priest notes that the inn-utensils were mostly of silver, although the chalices which he was given for mass were mostly tin; and De Gourville, in his autobiography, mentions that, on being asked by the government for an estimate of the total amount of silver in France, gave a higher estimate than the other experts because he based his on what he had noticed in the course of his frequent journeys about the provinces, in the middle of the seventeenth century, how every tavern had spoons and forks of silver and some a basin and ewer. And as silver drinking-vessels were common among the English middle-classes earlier than this, it may be assumed that inns were so provided, too; in fact, in England silver was considered somewhat vulgar for drinking purposes, gentlemen preferring Venetian glass. The Venetians themselves used glass, as did other Italians; likewise the French; Germans drank from pewter or stone, and their plates were often of wood, when they had any; it would give an altogether too high idea of sixteenth-century luxury to imagine that every one was given a plate. Certainly no one had more than one at a meal, though there is nothing to show that he might not turn it over to use the clean side — unless he was at sea, in which case he would risk being thrown overboard, because every sailor knew that a plate upside down signified shipwreck.

Inseparable from the inns are the bathing-places; in most cases the baths formed part of the inn premises. At Abano, near Padua, the chief bathing resort of Italy, were private rooms with a "guarderobbe"⁹ adjoining, through which latter a stream of the water could be turned on. Baden in Switzerland was exceptional in having baths under public control, for poor as well as for rich, besides those in private hands. The inn Montaigne stayed at had eleven kitchens, three hundred persons were catered for each day, one hundred and seventy-seven beds made, and every one could reach his room without passing through any one else's. His party engaged four rooms, containing no more than nine beds; two of the rooms had stoves; and a private bath adjoined. Swiss Baden possessed sixty baths, German Baden three hundred. Spa was much visited, but most of the watering-places have been practically forgotten, so far as the water is concerned, Pougues-les-Eaux, the chief centre in France, for instance, and Aachen, where there existed forty baths outside the town, although the chief ones were within.

The object of the visitors was as much medicinal nominally and as little so really, as might be expected. "Many come thither with no disease but that of love: and many times find remedy." [10] The conditions seem somewhat free and easy: in Rome it was customary to go accompanied by a lady friend in spite of the masseurs being male; of Plombières Montaigne says that it was reckoned indecent for men to bathe naked or for women to wear less than a chemise; from which it may be gathered what ordinary conditions were. The bathing there was "mixed," as at the German

baths where these restrictions were not in force
and where, consequently, the sight of scores of
young couples and parties, some family parties,
some not, in a state of nature, or very nearly so,
amusing themselves with games played at floating tables, or without any help at all, excited the
shame, the interest, and the participation of foreigners from all quarters. Ladies, however, who
needed baths and preferred decency, were provided for at Swiss Baden, where private baths were
for hire, well lighted by glazed windows, painted,
panelled, and clean, with conveniences for reading.
The building of Turkish baths seemed to Della
Valle to afford more likelihood of a chill than the
Italian; but it was, he says, all one could expect
for the price, which was much lower. How much
lower is not clear, but evidently considerably so,
the result of a difference of habit; in Italy the
poor did not bathe, in Turkey the rich bathed at
home.

Quite apart from bathing customs, however,
the position of the lady traveller must frequently
have been embarrassing. Many a nephew, perhaps, may disbelieve that they ever did travel in
the days when no hot-water bottles existed; but
that would be a mistake; there is record of at least
two substitutes: (1) a bag of semolina, or millet,
heated, (2) a dog. A more serious objection is
that the privacy of the bedroom was not respected.
Even in France, a murderer was lodged in Gölnitz's

room for the night together with the six guardians who were escorting him to the place of trial,
and in Picardy bedrooms were merely partitioned
off; doors and windows lying open all night with
no means of fastening them. But a permanently
open window would have been welcome on occasions; as when in 1652 Mademoiselle de Montpensier lodged at an inn in Franche-Comté with
no window at all in her room, and consequently
had to do her hair at the door.

Again, respectable women would not be travelling alone, and as bedrooms were so few they
would always have to be prepared to share the
room with their escort, even if with no other man,
a condition which persisted up to far more recent
times. In 1762, writes M. Babeau, a lawyer,
travelling through Périgord with a lady client,
her son, and a girl, had to put up at an inn which
owned but two beds and those both in one room.
This room, by the way, possessed two doors, one
opening on a meadow, and with joinery so im-
perfect that a dog could have crept in underneath
it; no dog took the chance, it is true, but the wind
did. In the previous century was often reprinted
a "Traité de la civilité qui se pratique parmi
les honnêtes gens" which established the procedure to be followed in these embarrassing circumstances. The escort must allow the lady to
undress and get into bed first, and, for himself,
take care to undress at a distance from her bed

and remain "tranquille et paisible" through the night. In the morning he ought to be well advanced with his dressing before she awoke. But this book was evidently unknown to Sterne when he pursued his "Sentimental Journey," for when he had to share his room with a lady who was a total stranger, they drew up a special treaty which both promised to observe and which each accused the other of breaking.

Of lodgings and "pensions" and houses for hire, it is unnecessary to speak, because apart from the conditions of living that have already been indicated there is nothing to distinguish them from those of to-day; "pensions" are doubtless still to be found in the same variety now as two hundred and fifty years ago at Blois — "dainty, magnificent, dirty, pretty fair, and stinking."

Supervision over the inns was far stricter than at present, especially in Italy. At Lucca and Florence all the inns were in a single street; and in many towns the new arrival was taken before the authorities by the guard at the gates previous to choosing his inn, to which he would be conducted by a soldier. At Lucca, too, was a department of the judiciary, called "della loggia," which was specially concerned with strangers, and to this the innkeepers had to send a daily report on each guest. Yet to judge by the tourists' accounts, the supervision might well have been carried further and reports on the innkeepers required from the tourists. Such a system of double reports would have been a check on the murdering innkeeper, to whom there are occasional references; one had been detected at Poictiers shortly before Lauder's arrival, and at Stralesund, another's tale runs, eight hundred (!) persons had disappeared at one inn. They had reappeared, it is true — pickled. Another kind of innkeeper who ran less risk but was equally dangerous was he who was in league with robbers; it was common enough, if travellers may be believed, for robbers to have spies in the inns. At Acciaruolo, near Naples, another device was practised by the keeper of an atrocious inn. He had an understanding with the captains of coasting-vessels, the result of which was that the latter found it impossible to get any further that night or to let the passengers sleep in the boat.

It must have occurred to the reader that this is a most one-sided chapter: the tourist has been having his say so uninterruptedly that even a clergyman in the pulpit might envy him. What of the innkeepers' side of the question? Fortunately that can be presented, too, with the help of a manuscript so unique that it must be described now instead of being buried in the bibliography. It is nothing less than an account of an Innkeepers' Congress in 1610, written by a delegate. At least, an expert palæographer (whose name I am not

permitted to give for fear of another expert palæographer) affirms it to be in a fairly recent commercial script; and it certainly is in English.
Nevertheless, there can be no doubt as to its genuineness. There is no inn, for example, of the three
hundred and fifty-eight referred to above which
is not mentioned in it; neither is there any inn
that is so mentioned that is not to be found among
the said three hundred and fifty-eight. Subjective
tests, moreover, however dangerous, have their
value, and it will appear that the wealth, and, so
far as it can be checked, the accuracy of detail, the
turns of phrase and of mind, equally characteristic of the innkeeper and the sixteenth century,
leave no more room for doubt here than, to take
a report of a meeting, in the case of the account
of the sayings and doings of the agriculturists in
session of which Flaubert made such instructive
use in his biography of the late Madame Bovary.

The congress was held at Rothenburg on the
Tauber, not so very far from Nuremberg, that
town being chosen because no tourist was ever
known to go there, any more then than now; and
consequently none was better adapted to prevent
more than one side of the question being heard,
— which, as every one knows, means life or death
to a congress.

London was represented by Paolo Lucchese, and
four Englishmen were also present, the four who
saw most of foreigners who had been to England

and of Englishmen who had been abroad: namely, William Cooke of Douay, the host of the "Golden Head" at Calais, another of Dieppe whose name and whose sign are alike illegible, and lastly the notorious Zacharias of Genoa, who told how he had been wrecked in West Indian seas and had swum twenty-two leagues with the ship's carpenter, pushing the latter's tool-chest before him, and how the tinder-box which he put in his hair did not even get wet; all just as he told it to Evelyn years afterwards, until every one got tired of him. The only Scot was Miltoun of the "Croix de Fer" at Paris (Rue St. Martin).

From France the delegates were Robert Buquet of Rouen, Du Peyrat of Loudun, Parracan of Arles, whose inn had no sign because his wine was so good that it needed none, Christopher Prezel of the "Lion d'Or de la Lanterne" of Lyons — but a full list is, after all, of no great interest. It is sufficient to say, to give some idea of the value that attaches to the report of the proceedings, that almost every delegate was a host in himself. For the rest, genealogists in the employ of American millionaires can have access direct to the manuscript; such things are best left in private hands.

The ladies, however, must not be omitted. Old Donna Justina of Venice was there, in spite of its being as much as thirty years earlier that De Thou had been recommended to her as the only innkeeper of the city in whose house none but respect-

able women were to be found. Berenguela de
Rebolledo likewise attended, lady-in-waiting at
an inn at Madrid, cheerful, inquisitive, and a flirt,
just as Pablos de Segovia knew her, with a bit of a
lisp, scared of mice, vain of her hands, and a blush-
rose and gloire-de-Dijon complexion. Then there
was Marie Beltram, who ran the "venta" the
other side of Yrun, and the girl harpist who played
at the inns at Brussels, of whom the appropriate
remark to make was to quote,—

> Haec habiles agili praetentat pollice chordas:
> Tam doctas quis non possit amare manus?

Two elderly parties were likewise present who,
thirty years earlier, had been the two pretty
daughters of the one-eyed host of the "Red Lion"
at Dordrecht, the same host who warned Van
Buchell, the antiquary, when a youngster, against
French girls. They were given, he said, to making advances; once one kissed him, and for a long
time afterwards he did not think he could live
without her.

But the belle of the congress seems to have
been the daughter of the innkeeper at Bourgoin,
the second post-house this side of Chambéry,
since there is a marginal note against her name,
evidently retained from the original, "Ista capit
biscottum." This confirms the account given of
her by Lord Herbert of Cherbury in his autobiography; his friends had told him she was the most

beautiful girl they had ever seen, so he rode over
from Lyons to see her, "and after about an hour's
stay departed thence without offering so much as
the least incivility." Finally there was a widow
from Tours; the one from the "Three Kings,"
known as "La Gogueline"; the other widow of
Tours, of the "Three Moors," stayed at home,
fearing to endanger her reputation as the "mother
of the Germans" by so long an absence. Widow
Gogueline, however, told the writer that the other
was better known as their stepmother and that
there was a rhyme which ran: —

> Quand vostre bourse est trop pleine
> Allez aux 'Mores' en Touraine:
> Je vous jure que vous serez
> En peu de temps en deschargez.

It was taken for granted that the president
must be an Italian; and Francisco Marco of Venice was chosen for that geniality of his that in
years to come was to charm James Howell. He
opened the proceedings with some graceful presi-
dential irrelevancies, commenting on the antiquity
and fame of Rothenburg and so forth, and then
explained the purposes of this Innkeepers' Congress as twofold. Its primary object, he said, was
the advancement of God's glory; secondly, the
furtherance of the interests of innkeepers and
their customers, which, he added, were at bottom
identical. The committee had invited certain of

the delegates who were especially well acquainted with foreigners to explain, or refute, what visitors found objectionable. The assembled innkeepers could then return able to inform, each one his own countrymen, before the latter's departure, what must be looked for in the parts he was travelling towards, and how unavoidable, and even desirable, those characteristics were. The president therefore called upon Messer Bevigliano ("Chiavi d'Oro," Florence) to speak for Italy.

Three things, said Messer Bevigliano, hinder us Italians from doing our best for the community: the licensing system, 'tied-houses,' and labour difficulties. I should be the last to suggest the abolition of our picturesque custom in use when an inn is to be let. At the auction a candle is lighted: the highest bid before the candle goes out wins the business. But the periods of tenancy, one and six years, alternately, in Florentine territory, are inconvenient. Far worse, however, are the prices extorted, especially from those who keep inns outside the gates of towns, the use of which is so necessary to such as are compelled to arrive late, or wish to leave early. Even apart from these, the majority pay 100–150 crowns (£150–£225 present value) for their licenses; some 500 or 600. At Venice wine-shops and inns pay 1000 crowns. The proportion this bears to the rent may be judged from the case of an old widow I know 8 miles from Florence whose rent was 23 crowns

and whose license was 56. Another inn, kept by
a shoemaker, a freehold house worth 6 crowns a
year, pays 20 crowns for license, while the other
license, for shoemaking, only costs a Giulio and a
half.

What I mean by a 'tied' house is one which
belongs to the owner of a large estate who allows
nothing to be sold there except the produce of
that estate.

Lastly, as to labour, the custom of the country
is against the use of women-servants, against even
the host's wife and daughter assisting him. What,
Messer Bevigliano concluded, apart from ordinary
routine-work, would happen to your Fair at Mül-
hausen if there were no girls to serve the drinks?

Next came Francisco Marques of Alicante, well
known to sailors of every nationality. What he
laid most stress on has in the main been antici-
pated by Charles II and Lady Fanshawe, but he
supplemented it as follows: In the towns clean
and comfortable beds were to be had, with meals
ready. Many *posadas*, he admitted, provided nothing but utensils, table-linen, oil, salt, vinegar; yet
travellers were then neither better nor worse
off than in Poland, Bohemia, and Picardy, where
the custom was likewise. As for the wayside inns
which gave nothing but a roof and horse-proven-
der, they barely existed outside Castile and Aragon, and there the wayfarer should prepare accordingly, as the Spaniard did, who journeyed with a

bag full of provisions on each side of the saddle and
a bottle of wine to each bag. As to the supposed
lack of meat, he went on, most Spaniards are vege-
tarians; and considering the achievements of the
Spanish infantry, I do not think any one can find
fault with the principle. Neither does this apply
to the lower classes only, for we have a rhyme
which says: —

> Unas Azeytunas, una Salada, y Revanillos
> Son comida de Caballeros;

and so far from altering our ways, the ancient
rule that a gentleman who has partaken of onions
shall absent himself from court for eight days has
fallen into abeyance. For those who prefer meat,
there is plenty. Fowls, I know, are scarce, and
you are so used to fowls that you think "no fowls,
no meat"; and yet, I remember when I was a small
boy and Queen Anne arrived at Santander to
marry good King Philip II, she was presented there
with two hundred fowls and a calf. As to sheep,
ask the eight Germans who recently ate a whole
one between them; besides, does not the famous
Lazarillo de Tormes tell us that it is the regular
thing at Maqueda to eat sheep's heads on Satur-
days at three maravedis apiece? and on fast days
we have special permission to eat cow-heels and
sucking pigs. Now, how can these things be if we
have no sheep nor cows nor little pigs? On the
contrary, you Germans, who take so well justi-

fied a pride in your bacon at home, how is it you say nothing about it after a week or so with us? Why, we have an author, Lope da Vega Carpio, who will soon be recognised as the greatest writer since Seneca, who always takes a rasher of our bacon before starting to write, as a stimulant!

But I can quote something better than your own experience — the words of the King and of St. Michael. Charles V advised the great Alonzo de Guzman against going to Italy, "Better stay at home and kill rabbits on your own hills and eat them than be killed by the sea and be eaten by the fishes": and when the said Alonzo dreamed that he was dead, St. Michael appeared and sentenced him to return to earth for his misdeeds and eat roast meat and be content; and Alonzo found himself able to arrange for roast duck in summertime and an "olla" keeping hot in the chimney in winter. If I say nothing as to wild boar and partridge, it is merely because it is getting late. But I will just add this in confidence, that people, we find, pay more willingly when the bill is accompanied by a cheerful "Y haga les buen provecho."

The Muscovy delegate, "Cologne Jimmy" of Nerva, had drawn the third place; but being temporarily bereft of his faculties by the number of drinks new to him, a discussion was substituted at the instance of M. Petit, who enjoyed most of the French custom at Rome, on the evil of free board and lodging which various institutions pro-

vided, a most demoralising custom and very hard
on those who wished to gain an honest living. At
Seville and Montserrat, he had heard, things had
come to well-to-do people being given fish as well
as bread, and at Amsterdam foundations were
even being instituted on a secular basis. That
they might be in a better position to take action,
it was proposed to form an Innkeepers' Association, but when an Irish waiter from Madrid suggested as a motto, "Pediculus pro comite jucundo,"
recriminations ensued which soon rendered ad-
journment necessary.

Nevertheless, at the banquet in the evening all
passed off happily in the traditional way.

> In principio est silentium,
> In medio stridor dentium,
> Et in fine rumor gentium.

The next day began well too, with the speech
of Jean Busson ("Le Fardeau" Dieppe), who ex-
cused the faults of the French host as attributable
to the civil wars, and said that whether or no religion was "reformed," cookery certainly was, and
that in future the traditions of Guillot's of Amiens
would be upheld. At the same time he felt he
would be next door to a traitor if he owned to
any serious faults, for supposing that such were
imagined, French chambermaids could be trusted
to keep the visitors happy (great applause). But
he had a proposal to bring forward. He found

they had a custom in Germany, which was also used at Bourges, which deserved extension. He referred to the watchmen who lived at the top of the town belfry and signalled the approach of travellers to those below by means of flags; at Ferrara and Bruges and elsewhere, the signalling was done with bells. Now this ought to be customary everywhere, and whereas here in Germany the watchmen descended at meal-times and made a collection at the inns, surely the municipal authorities ought to pay them. A resolution to this effect was passed unanimously.

The Low Country delegates caused considerable dissatisfaction by their memorial insisting that nobody had complaints to make of their inns, nor would there be any anywhere if pains were taken to be up-to-date and, above all things, clean. But their brethren were grateful for the warning that it was becoming the custom with travellers to slip leaden bullets into the cheese, where they found the custom in vogue of charging for it according to the difference in weight before and after it was set on the table; and agreed with them when they pointed out that the system of putting up a list of things customers might not do and fining them when these rules were transgressed, was breaking down. An innkeeper from Augsburg gave an instance; his request, he said, not to foul the walls was so far from being heeded that he kept one man at work cleaning them.

It was this member from Augsburg who brought
about the unhappy ending of the Congress, for,
in commenting on the Low Countrymen's stric-
tures, he tactlessly quoted the Italian proverb
"Dal hoste nuovo e dalla putana vecchia, Dio ci
guarda," and then went on to lay it down as irre-
futable that nobody grumbled unless he thought
he had been done. This was easily avoided, he
said; treat all alike; no man ever grumbled in Germany except new-comers and unreasonable people. Why? because Germans had fixed prices;
the only system which was conformable with
God's law. By this time the interpreters fairly
trembled as they translated, but when, speaking
as he did in Latin, he went on to apply to the system of variable charges the adjectives that were
in daily use in theological controversy, the others
understood without help and a battle ensued.
First in words, beginning with shouts of "Pese al
diablo," "Voto á Dios," and other Spanish expressions, of which, together with all the Italian,
not even the initial letters could be printed, answered with "Bey Gott den Herrn," "Meine
Seele," "Der Teufel hole dich," "Gottes Kranck-
heit," without, curiously enough, the use of a single one of those employed by historical novelists.
To words succeeded blows; and there the Congress ended.

CHAPTER VII

ON THE ROAD

A journey is a fragment of hell.
AWLIYÁI EFENDI (1611–1679).

WHAT M. Babeau, in his charming "Les Voyageurs en France," says of the history of France since the eleventh century, that it may be divided into three periods, of the horse, the carriage, and the railway, is true of most of Europe. He goes on to point out that the first period synchronises with the feudal system, the second with uncontrolled monarchy. And this was not a matter of chance, for the improvement in the state of the roads implied by the substitution of driving for riding directly resulted from the centralisation of authority. A feudal system tended to keep the roads bad, partly because no one authority received such exclusive and overwhelming benefits from the roads as to be ready to bear the cost of their upkeep; partly because the constant petty warfare which feudalism gave rise to often made neighbours desire that approaches should be difficult rather than easy.

In 1600 the transition was in its infancy; and even during the subsequent half-century is only noticeable in a marked degree in France. Even there, the change was not from bad roads to good, but from very bad to a state of uncertainty. One road, it is true, is mentioned as paved, at any date during these two centuries, that from Paris to Orleans, but by Evelyn's time there were many such in France; while, on the other hand, on the king's highway between Bourges and Lyons the horses of Gölnitz and his companions fell into a marsh, whence they were rescued with difficulty; and on another highway (Paris-Bordeaux) Claude Perrault, the architect of the Louvre, speaks of one occasion when night overtook him before he had reached his stopping-place; and the holes in the road being so deep as to render it almost impassable for his carriage, a quarter of a league took him four hours to cover.

Elsewhere in Europe, things seem to be remaining much as they had been. Here and there in Italy sections of Roman road which had been maintained in fair condition continued to be patched in imitation of Roman methods until they appeared excellent in contrast with the others; what the others were made of travellers do not say, but it may be guessed that they were paved like hell in the proverb. Montaigne might note with sadness how the Via Flaminia had shrunk from forty feet broad to four between Loreto and Lucca, although one may query where he found that it was ever more than fifteen feet across; but no one else had recourse to archæology to make himself grieve. The following is a tale that Riva-deneyra, Loyola's boy-friend and biographer, tells of some of the other early associates during a walk from Venice to Rome. Being Lent, they fasted except for what they received in alms. "And one Sunday it befell that, having tasted no more than a few mouthfuls of bread that morning, they trudge twenty-eight miles of that land on their bare feet; and all the day the rain comes down pitilessly, whereby they find the roads turned into lakes, and that so truly that there are times when the water reaches their chests." He continues, "None the less they feel within them a marvellous contentment and joyousness; and being mindful that they were enduring these troubles of the flesh for love of God, gave thanks to Him without ceasing, singing David's psalms in metre; and even Master Juan Codurí, who was suffering with the itch in both of his legs, was no whit the worse for the trials of this day."

It was always the rain that caused the trouble, although the state of the roads when dry must have been fearful for ordinary wet weather to effect so rapid a deterioration. From Ferrara to Bologna was reckoned a half-day's journey in summer, a whole day in winter. And in 1606 an Italian says of the roads near Strassburg that the mud, stones, and holes compelled the horses to go single file, each one stepping in the tracks of the leader; near

Ypres they found the road often indistinguishable from the fields, and the mud came up to the horses' girths.

In dry weather the only complaint is against loose stones on steep gradients, which latter naturally occur far more frequently on the old roads than on modern ones, keeping, as the former do, to high ground for choice. The fact that by this means traffic was less at the mercy of floods seems to be considered reason enough for the habit, but perhaps it was also found to give greater protection against highwaymen, who were thereby afforded fewer opportunities for attacking from higher ground, and for concealment. One place in particular where these loose stones formed a serious hindrance was Scaricalasino, between Bologna and Florence, so named (scarica l'asino means "unload the ass") because what with the badness of the road and the sharpness of the stones the asses had to be relieved of their burdens at intervals. So, too, the secretary of a Venetian embassy writes that between Terni and Assisi the way was so rough as well as muddy that it cost the party of forty fourteen hours and the deaths of four horses to do twenty miles.[1]

Another difficulty, sometimes a peril, to be faced were the fords. On the main road, for example, from Rome to France, through Florence, there was the river Paglia to cross, which bounded Papal territory in that direction. The passage still remained a ford, although after rain it would be impassable for a week at a time. And where, on the map, north of Venice, you see the Tagliamento divide into seven branches, there, through them, lay the road which joined Italy with Germany. Yet only one branch had a bridge over it, and the fords through the others were dangerous enough to keep guides at work. It is not surprising, then, to find Sir Thomas Browne's son having to engage two men to walk beside his horse upstream to break the force of the current lest it should carry the horse off his feet, since the river was the Var, in the Riviera, and across a less important road.

Sometimes travellers preferred the ford even where a bridge existed, as did one [2] at St. Jean de Maurienne on the post-route from France to Italy because the bridge was in such disrepair as to be unsafe. The same traveller crossed by boat at Otricoli beside the ruins of a Roman bridge which had once been a link in the Via Flaminia. On the bridges the same political reasons that kept the roads difficult had set their mark, accounting as they do for the number of wooden bridges, easier to dismantle in case of a raid. The bridges of Strassburg and Vienna were particularly striking examples of this; the planks were not even fastened down; if one end tipped up, a plank was as likely as not to fall into the river. Neither were there any rails at the sides. That was not excep-

tional, either, in spite of a bridge being worthy of
remark if broad enough for two carts to pass each
other. But whether it was the initial cheapness,
or the habit of precaution, there they were, in
spite of the cost of their upkeep, thirty thousand
thalers yearly in the case of the one at Yarunov
on the Vistula in the middle of the seventeenth
century, when a thaler was nearly equal to one
pound at present value. Yet the traveller[3] who
reports this says his horse trod a hole in it. And
in Hungary, when Busbecq returned from Turkey
by road, the bridges offered so many traps for
horses that robbers laid in wait under bridges for
their best opportunities.

As for stone bridges, Spain seems to have been
the best off before 1600, but subsequently the improvement in bridges became very marked, especially in France. When Zinzerling knew Paris
(1612-16), of its five bridges, only two were of
stone, whereas of the six that Evelyn saw in 1643,
but one was of wood. The only stone bridges in
the empire that are mentioned are those of Schaffhausen, of Ratisbon, and, over the Moselle, of
Coblentz; while two of the finest west of the
Rhine, those of Avignon and Rouen, were impassable owing to gaps which no authority saw
its way to repair. But the test of a first-rate
bridge in 1600 was not how much traffic, but how
many houses, it carried. Judged by this standard,
it was agreed that London Bridge was the finest,

with that of Nôtre Dame at Paris second, considering the latter's houses numbered sixty-eight.
Still, it was with the number of bridges that the
tourist was mainly concerned, in which matter
he would find the Loire the only river across which
passage was fairly easy; the Rhine had no bridge
below Strassburg; the Seine had to be crossed five
times by boat in the first four leagues of road
northwards from Paris; and below Turin there
existed no bridge over the Po except a wooden
one at Ferrara.

Means of conveyance consisted of riding, sub-
divided into post-horses and other beasts; by
cart, either the long, heavy waggon employed by
carriers, or those with two big wheels and no more,
which occasioned the traveller fewest shocks; and
lastly, by litter. Coaches, in the sense of vehicles
which are supposed to be comfortable, can hardly
be said to have existed except among private owners, and even these preferred the litter, especially
in winter. The acme of luxury when on the road
may be represented by Marguerite de Valois' litter
used on her journey to the Netherlands. The lin-
ing was of Spanish velvet, the hangings of silk,
the sides glazed with one hundred and forty panes
of glass, each of which bore a different design.

As for carts, though everywhere one comes
across occasional instances of their use by tourists, this was far more customary in Germany
than elsewhere; even a knight-errant going to

seek his fortune, Sir Anthony Sherley, mentions covering distances in them there without apology. The German "rollwagen" carried six or eight passengers; those of the Low Countries as many as ten, sitting on boards laid across the cart so close behind one another that they resembled geese going to the pond. The chief centre for carrier-arrangements was Augsburg; thence to Venice and back a waggon went each week; between Augsburg and Nuremberg daily. In France conveyances started running more freely as the civil wars slackened, as, e. g. between Troyes and Paris in 1598; a reversion to what had been in force earlier. But in 1584 between Amiens and Paris, and in 1586 between Rouen and Paris, was running what was called the "coche royale," which took passengers.[4] By Zinzerling's time communications of this kind existed between Paris and Orleans, and Paris and Rouen, daily; between Rouen and Dieppe thrice weekly; and between Rouen and Antwerp.

The disadvantages of waggons were more obvious in the Low Countries than elsewhere, since there they never entered towns, depositing the passenger, heavy luggage and all, outside the gate; often, too, a change of waggons was obligatory during the day, whereas an English carter drove straight on, too long, in fact, for his custom was to keep on the move from dawn till sunset. The Dutchman, in addition, was usually drunk

and drove his mares (always mares) like a mad-
man, and passengers found it advisable, besides,
to wear spectacles to protect their eyes against
the sand thrown up by the road-menders. All
waggons were provided with awnings, of cloth or
leather.

In Italy and Spain practically all traffic was
four-footed. Post-horses were always for hire in
Italy, with a bit of fur attached to their bridles to
mark their status. The owner gave the hirer a
ticket to show his host at the end of the day's
journey, who would then take care of the horse
until a return fare was forthcoming; no security
was asked. It was a novel experience for most
foreigners to ride one post-horse all day: in England the stages were ten miles; in France, in the
seventeenth century, four or five, so that a traveller in a hurry would change horses as many as
eighteen to twenty-two times a day. The reason
for the difference lay in the pace, the standard for
which was much lower in a country like Italy,
where mules and asses were habitually used. In
fact, when the pace was set by the mules, as, for
instance, in the Rome-Naples caravans, all who
accompanied which had to keep together for fear
of robbers, a man might be in the saddle all day
and cover no more than twenty miles. As for
wheeled traffic, it may be imagined from the state
of the roads that the pace often sank to nothing
at all. After several breakdowns, one traveller

writes: "Advanced that day as far as the cursed carriages would give us leave, and the rest of the day practised Christian patience. . . . Carts ought to be put in the Litany."

The above must be understood as leaving Muscovy out of account, for that was the one country where the journey itself could, under favourable circumstances, be continued with comfort. Once the ground was hard enough for sledges, the traveller could travel night and day and yet sleep as long as he felt inclined. Nor did the gain end with positive comfort and double the available time, since the diminished strain on the horses enabled them to go at a greater pace for a longer period. Twelve leagues without a change of horses and a hundred leagues in three days represent what was practicable in the ordinary way amid a Russian winter; treble what would be reckoned good for any conveyance elsewhere.

In Dante's "Purgatorio" (II, 11-12) is a comparison well commented on, unconsciously, in these travel-books. It is when he speaks of himself wandering

> Come gente che pensa a suo cammino,
> Che va col core, e col corpo dimora.

Three hundred years later, sign-posts were still as rare as unicorn-horns. One mile north of Rimini, where the road forked, stood a chapel between the two turnings, on one side of it written, "La Strada di Ravenna," on the other, "La Strada di Bologna"; and the roads round Freiburg were planted with trees to mark the way, for the benefit of citizens, however, rather than of strangers, because of the mouths of the silver mines which would otherwise have been man-traps. Something of the kind, too, was put up in Holland when snow hid the roads. More to the point will it be to quote John Smith's account of his escape from Tartary, and how he found pictorial sign-posts at cross-roads, the way to Christian Muscovy being indicated by the sign of the Cross; to Crim Tartary by a half-moon; while a black man with white spots meant Persia; a sun, China; and minor princes' territories were pointed out by the emblems they had adopted. But these were really out of Europe and those of Freiburg and Holland outlined the road rather than indicated directions, as did the poles erected on the Col di Tenda Alpine-pass for a mile together, each pole a spear's length from the next. The Simplon and Mt. Cenis passes were thus marked out also — when the poles had not been blown flat by the wind.

But then, crossing the Alps alone was practically unknown, although only on the Mt. Cenis route were professional guides employed as a matter of course. These guides had their own special name, "marrons" and a special function, to "ramasser" the traveller on his way to France,

down the slope between the summit of the pass
and Lanslebourg, when it was covered with frozen
snow. The traveller took his seat in a rush-seated
chair on runners; one "marron" in front and
one behind. The one in front had a strap round
his chest fastened to the chair; he took a few
steps, and the chair did the rest; if the direction
became amiss or the pace too furious, the "marron" behind the chair guided or checked it with
an alpenstock. The distance was a league; the
time fifteen minutes. Going towards Italy you
would have found fifty or sixty persons coming to
meet you at Lanslebourg, hat in hand, offering
their services as "marrons" or as horse-owners.
Dismounting, one would have held the bridle, one
the stirrup, one yourself. Two or three struggle
for the privilege of taking your horse to the stable
and your trunk to your room, but the latter privilege is not one to be granted lightly; it was not in
sound only that "marron" resembled "larron."
The traveller's own horse was sent on after being
shod with calkins, and he himself followed in one
of the sledges, used in ascents, litter-fashion, by
four "marrons," who carried it, two at a time, turn
and turn about; glasses to protect the eyes from
the snow-light formed part of the stock-in-trade
of the local pedlars.

At the top would be found "La Chapelle des
Transis," the wayfarers' mortuary, not empty
probably; in March 1578 it contained fifteen

bodies.[5] After heavy snowfalls the monks of the neighbouring hospice of St. Nicolas used to send out search parties; corpses discovered were examined for proofs of orthodoxy, beads, for instance, failing which the bodies were left to the beasts of prey.

During this period the Mt. Cenis route came to be used more exclusively for passing between France and Italy than had previously been the case, doubtless as a result of the transference of the capital of Savoy from Chambéry to Turin in 1559, between which towns this route was the most direct. Yet notwithstanding that travellers note here, and here alone, that the population on either side of the pass had no other means of livelihood than by ministering to travellers, the most frequented route must be considered the Brenner. It was the only one which wheeled traffic could pass, though even there the waggon had to be kept from falling off the road "by force of men's shoulders," according to Moryson.

Of the experiences to be met with in crossing an Alpine pass other than the Brenner, there is no better account than that which the Infanta Clara Eugenia wrote home concerning the St. Gothard. Even before reaching Bellinzona the luggage carts had to be exchanged for mules. And at Bellinzona, too, she notes that there was not a woman without an enormous goitre; and, indeed, the frequency with which travellers remark on the num-

ber of those afflicted in this way leaves no doubt
but that the disease was far more prevalent then
than now. It was generally accepted that the
cause lay in the water, but one old resident, at
least, disbelieved this, since he had one himself,
although, as he told a tourist, he had never drunk
water in his life. The worst of the Infanta's journey occupied the four days after leaving Bellinzona; the way so narrow that a horse could scarcely
walk and the litters had continually to be taken
off the mules and transferred to men. This narrow path, of course, lay always with the moun-
tain-side high above it and a precipice and a river
below. The ladies' litters were by no means according to royal standards; just four poles and a
linen seat, from which the royal legs dangled; but
she rode most of the way, feeling no fear of anything but the "snow-bridges," two of which had
to be crossed. On the farther side there was the
"Devil's Bridge" to pass also, or, as she names it,
"Hell Bridge"; which now does not even exist;
twenty paces long above the Reuss, so far above
that the river was out of sight, although the rush
of it resounded so loudly that she could not hear
herself speak. The whole road had been specially
prepared for her passage, and among the preparations was the erecting of railings along "Hell
Bridge"; in the ordinary way there were none,
the wind being so strong in the narrow gorge as
always to sweep them away very soon. He who

passed by the St. Gothard under ordinary conditions, and the Furka, too, wore gloves and boots
studded with nails to preserve his hold; and the
average Alpine bridge answered to the description
which Cellini gives of those he found on the Simplon route, a few tree-trunks laid down. Another
Italian going home that way says the last bridge
was thirty feet by two and bent in the middle; he
crossed it at night, coming as it did among the
"last four leagues"(?) between the summit and
Domodossola, all of which he and his traversed in
pitch-darkness among precipices, the foremost
calling at intervals "Ave Maria" and the hind-
most answering "Gratiâ plena."

Most travellers rode horses or mules where they
could, and led, or crawled with them, the rest of
the way; but sledges were also in use, in which
case, Moryson was told, "it sometimes happens
the sledge whereon the passenger sits is cast out
of the way and hangs down in a most deep valley with the passenger's head downward. Woe be
to him, then, if he let his hold go, or the harness
tying the sledge to the horse should break." Moryson himself had only passed by the Bernina and
the Brenner, the former of which seems to have
ranked third in order of popularity in spite of
the track being no more than a yard wide in
places. The Splügen was used as often, perhaps,
but when the two St. Bernards and the Gemmi
have been added to the list, there is an end of those

frequented by tourists. One used the San Marco and Sir Henry Wotton another, which cannot now be identified, when the ordinary ones were shut against him by plague. But for an instance of some one keeping to the coast between France and Italy, it seems necessary to go back to Beatis in 1518, a man whose narrative is obviously trustworthy; yet, after mentioning that it was so dangerous that few rode, he adds what may sound incredible except in his own words. "Ben vero che questo Camino è di sorte Che in tale giornata di XV miglia solamente le bestie se besognarno ferrare quactro et cinque volte." For all practical purposes, moreover, the mountains near Grenoble must be considered as part of the Alps, lying, as they did, across the route of all who crossed Mt. Cenis, and being no less fearful than any of the Alpine passes themselves. At one point, nearest Aiguebelette, horses and mules were specially trained for the ascent and descent, holes having been cut in the rock which made the way more practicable for animals accustomed to them, but almost impossible to any others, unless riderless.

Elsewhere, wherever mountains have to be traversed, similar conditions prevailed. Near Spalato, it is true, the path was railed in some distance, the only railings of the kind in Europe, apparently; but near Mt. Olympus one looked over the edge of the precipice he had to ride along and saw carcasses of horses, caught as they fell, or fallen, to

warn him to be careful. Says one who knew both,
the road over Pen-maen-mawr in these days was
more fearful than any Alpine way. As for Spain,
there were quite a number of main roads which
allowed nothing more than single file here and
there: the pass into Castile on the road from Ba-
yonne, for instance, and another between Granada
and Cartagena, on entering which it was customary for travellers to tighten their belts and say
an "Ave Maria" for those who had lost their
lives thereabouts. Above San Sebastian ten men
might hold the road against an army and no beasts
but mules could be trusted on it, nor on the pass
from France into Aragon, so steep that no man was
safe there; while south of Santander, according to
Sir Richard Wynn, for two leagues the road was
two feet broad and one hundred perpendicular
fathoms above the river.

Neither were the efforts thus entailed brightened by the idea of mountaineering as a form of
pleasure. Probably the only recorded climb undertaken during this period with no other object
than that of getting to the top is the ascent of "Les
Jumelles," the highest peak near Pau, an ascent
known to us through De Thou. One M. de Candale
started at four o'clock one May morning in the
first half of the sixteenth century. Before half-
way was reached, his younger companions were on
the way down; they had come in their shirts and
found the cold too much for them; M. de Candale

was wearing a fur coat. At half-way the last trace
of a human being was left behind, but he and some
peasants reached the top with the help of ladders
and grappling-irons and took measurements. It
is characteristic enough of the age that De Thou's
comments on the calculated height are a comparison with the reckonings of Apuleius and Plutarch
concerning Olympus, which they considered the
highest mountain in the world. Mediæval opinion put Mt. Sinai first, probably because that was
the only mountain a mediæval Christian ever
tried to get to the top of, a process of reasoning
which may be traced in the guesses of these travellers, and in local opinion, as to which was the
highest of the Alps; it is always one of those
past which they endeavoured to make their way,
St. Gothard or St. Bernard, for which they claim
preëminence. Another fashion of reckoning is to
calculate, not perpendicularly, but according to
the apparent length of the way, which makes Mt.
Quarantana "six miles high"; while one traveller
has a unit of measurement entirely his own, a
mountain being to him so many "towers" high,
the tower in question being the belfry of Malines,
his native place.

There was, nevertheless, one piece of mountaineering that was continually being done under
the guise of a pilgrimage, the ascent of the Roche
Melon, near Mt. Cenis, or, as it is termed in full
as late as 1574,[6] Roche Rommelon; the Latin

name had been Mons Romuleus. Of the origin
of this pilgrimage and the reason for building a
chapel to Our Lady on the summit, nothing has
been ascertained beyond what may be read to-day
in the cathedral at Susa, where is still to be seen,[7]
though unmentioned by Baedeker, a triptych representing a Madonna and Child, St. George,
St. James, and a kneeling warrior, with an inscription to the effect that one Bonifacio Rotario of
Asti "brought me [*i. e.* the triptych] hither in honour of our Blessed Lord and our Lady on September 1, 1358." The word "hither" refers to the
summit of this Roche Melon, to which the picture
is still carried up every year.[8] In 1588 Villamont
made the ascent, which was only practicable in
August, with spikes on his feet and hooks fastened
to his hands, and rather more assistance than a
modern mountaineer would consider dignified.
The feat is the more remarkable inasmuch as the
height (11,605 feet) is more than half as high again
as the highest point of any pass that was used
then.

On reaching the top, Villamont forgot all his
terror and fatigue in the glorious view, glorious
not for the grandeur of the scenery to him, but because it was his first sight of Italy, "the paradise
to gain which they willingly," as another phrases
it, "passed through the purgatory of the Alps."
Such was their opinion of Switzerland. They
spoke of the Alps just as we do of the Channel—

they had had a "good crossing," or the reverse.
More definitely, to quote Howell's words, "the
high and hideous Alps . . . those uncouth, huge,
monstrous, Excrescences of Nature," productive
of nothing useful. Few were those who were free-
spirited enough to enjoy themselves. Of the exceptions most notable are Tasso and the Infanta.
The former mentions the existence of a common
preference for scenes characterised by unbroken
spaciousness, but for himself, he likes a varied
view with much to catch the eye, hills, dales, and
trees, and even, he goes on, "E, che più, la sterilità
e rigidezza dell' Alpi, facendone paragone alla va-
ghezza degli altri spettacoli, suole molte fiate rius-
cire piacevolissima."⁹ The Infanta's own words
are still more remarkable: "Yo dudo que se pu-
diera ver mejor cosa en el mundo ni màs para ver."
Even she, however, when going into detail, gives
first places to the plants that were new to her and
to the waterfalls. When, indeed, somebody else
expresses any degree of pleasure in connection
with the Alps, it is generally the waterfalls that
occasion it. But there is a further exception even
to this, and he, curiously enough, is a popular Pari-
sian poet, St. Amant. Although he writes, in his
"Polonaise," concerning Poland,

> On n'y voit nulle eminence
> Comme on voit en d'autres lieux;
> Cela me charme, et je pense
> Qu'on ne peut dire tant mieux,

he finds the characteristics of the Alps, even in winter, such that they

Sont si doux à mes yeux que d'aise ils en pétillent,

and is even modern enough to speak of

Et cet air net et sain, propre à l'esprit vital.[10]

These three have been entirely overlooked hitherto; the only person of this period whom the modern mountaineer is told to claim as his spiritual brother is the botanist Conrad Gesner; but in claiming him they claim too much — for themselves. It is true that Gesner does write [11] that he never lets a year go by without climbing one or more of the Alps for exercise and pleasure as well as for botany; and that "whoever does not consider towering mountains prëeminently worthy of more than ordinary attention is, to my mind, an enemy of Nature." But he goes on to show that the Alps meant far more to him than this much would prove. He looked on them as an epitome of all Nature's habits and experiments, the key to all Nature's secrets, to geology in the fullest sense of the word, structural, historical, dynamical; and that to a greater extent than is apparent at first sight, inasmuch as problems now treated as solved then belonged to dreamland and problems which seemed soluble there if anywhere are now known to be better studied elsewhere; the internal temperature of the earth, for instance, since it was not recognized in Gesner's day that there was any difference in kind between mountains and volcanoes.

The attitude of the average man of Gesner's time towards the Alps, however, is but the most striking instance of a general attitude towards Nature which circumstances at that time enforced and which different circumstances have since abolished. Further, of all classes of men, it was the tourists who were most oppressed by the circumstances of the past, and it is the tourists who get the greatest benefits from the changed circumstances of to-day. Further still, the difference was, and is, most noticeable by the tourist when on the road. In other words, the absence of enjoyment of the sterner aspects of Nature was the result of their having far more of Nature than an average man can stand. The growth of the size of towns has, so to speak, set a premium on Nature, just as it has, during the past century, created the custom of taking annual holidays; while the successive minimising of the dangers, the discomforts, and of so many of the lesser difficulties of travel has provided the traveller with contrast where once upon a time was none, and leaves him free to find pleasure (sometimes, perhaps, forces him to look for it to avoid being bored), where in 1600 all spelt pain and foreboding. This difference of sentiment culminated then, as it culminates now, when the tourist found himself among the Alps. There, above other places, were his

faculties narrowed by fear and what remained of
them wholly concentrated on self-preservation,
until enjoyment was out of the question.

As to the change of attitude, it is usually credited to Rousseau, but was in progress before his
influence began to be felt; [12] and if the subsequent
development of the idea is considered, the credit
must surely be shared by Napoleon, as to whose
greatness there is no more conclusive evidence
than that of his Alpine roads. Before these were
carried out, men considered themselves at the
mercy of the Alps; he first, and he alone, put the
Alps at the service of men, and in so doing set
free men's sense of beauty when in their midst.

But here, as always when writing about the
prevalence or absence of a point of view, some
reminder should be added as to the effect of literary conventions in exaggerating both the one
and the other; that is to say, that in the former
case it will frequently be expressed when it is little
felt, and in the latter it will frequently be felt
when not expressed. Even as to that binding of
the faculties just alluded to, there is the very definite exception of the Infanta, who was not too
preoccupied to ask questions, thereby learning
that that peak had not been bare of snow for four
hundred years and that this pinnacle was solid
emerald; being considered inaccessible, cannon
had not long before been brought up to shoot bits
off, but without success.

Nevertheless, their turn of mind as regards Nature in general needs some other illustration than from negative evidence alone, or, among positive evidence, from so exceptional a feature as mountain scenery. This may be best taken from their use of the word "desert." A typical instance is in a sentence from Peter Mundy, "the way being faire and plaine, though desert and full of woods." Six times in "As You Like It" is the forest of Arden termed a desert:—

> . . . this desert inaccessible
> Under the shade of melancholy boughs.

"Desert" to them meant deserted by men, and through forests they passed, as often as not, sword in hand. To quote St. Amant's "Polonaise" again:—

> Une taciturne horreur
> En augmente le terreur,
> Et la noire solitude
> Qui dort en ces bois espais
> Fait qu'avec inquiétude
> On y voit leur triste paix.
>
> Là le maistre et le valet
> Roulent, main au pistolet;
> On regarde si le glaive
> S'offre à quitter le fourreau,
> Et dès qu'un zephir se lève
> On frémit sur le carreau.

And yet, if a journey was a " fragment of hell,"

it is comforting to meet some very merry devils by the way. Quevedo,[13] for one, took his troubles lightly. Getting out of a bed in which his legs had been hanging over the end, he and three others left Linares for Condado in a conveyance drawn by ten mules. The road, he says, might have been the road to salvation, so narrow was it, so full of troubles, a purgatory in little. One hill seemed to be reserved for mule-hunting when the carriage had stuck in the mud.

It was February, too; February at its worst. On smaller provocation men have retired to madhouses. It seemed like sleeping in the coach; those who tried to walk pulled their legs out from where they had planted them without hose or shoes; one called out, "You down there, who's pulling off my boots?" After playing at dying for four hours, men arrived to release them from imprisonment, except one whose litter had given way and who was too full of bruises to move, and a clergyman who was missing altogether, the latest news of whom is that men were going round about the marshes calling out his name.

Dallam, too, has a tale to tell. His companions and himself, passing through Thrace, took a house to spend the night in, a two-roomed house, one room above the other. The lower was used as a cellar; a ladder outside led up to a balcony, the balcony to a door, the door to their sleeping room, which was lighted by one small hole. Now, that evening they had gone for a walk and seen "divers sorts of vermin of which we have not the like in England," and, remembering that they had nothing but boards to lie on, gathered plenty of a thick soft moss for pillows. But half an hour after laying their heads down, they discovered that these pillows harboured one more sort of vermin "the which did bite far worse than fleas," with the result that even when the pillows had been thrown away and the room swept, still they could n't go to sleep. So Mr. Glover (afterwards Sir Thomas Glover), who had dwelt long in the country, told them stories about the native vermin, "snakes, adders, and sarpentes." Gradually some dropped off to sleep; the others ceased talking. But one Mr. Baylye had occasion to leave the room; the door was narrow, the wind strong; "so that when he came into the gallery, the wind blew the garter round about his leg; it was a great silk garter and by the force of the wind it fettered his legs both fast together. Our talk a little before of adders, snakes, and sarpentes was yet in his remembrance and the place near where much vermin was. He thought they swarmed about him, but about his legs he thought he was sure of a sarpente, so that, suddenly, he cried out with all the voice he had, 'A sarpente, a sarpente, a sarpente,' and was so frighted he could not find the door to get in, but made a great bustling and noise in the gallery. We that were in the house did think that he said,

'Assaulted, assaulted,' for before night we doubted
that some treachery would happen unto us in that
town. There was fifteen of us in the room — and
it was but a little room. Every man took his
sword in his hand, one ready to spoil another, not
any one knowing the cause. One that could not
find his sword, got to the chimney and trying to
climb up, down fell a part of the chimney on his
head; another that was suddenly awakened, struck
about him with his sword and beat down the shelf
and broke the pitchers and platters which stood
thereon, the room being very dark, for it was
about midnight. Our Janizary, who should have
been our guard and have protected us from all
dangers, took up a loose board whereon he lay,
and slipped down into the vault. As we were all
thus amazed, at the last Mr. Baylye found the
way in at the door. When Mr. Glover saw him,
he said, 'How now, man, what is the matter, who
do you see?' Mr. Baylye was even breathless
with fear, crying out and struggling to get in at
the door; at last he said, 'A sarpente, a sarpente,'
troubled him. When Mr. Glover heard him say
so, he went to the door, and there he found Mr.
Baylye's garter ready to be carried away with the
wind."

Another who was more frightened than hurt
was the Jesuit Possevino, on his way to Muscovy.
Tired out with a day on the main road thither
from Poland, spent handling the axe to clear the

road of vegetation, dragging the waggons by hand, sometimes carrying them on their shoulders, he and his lay down to sleep (in the rain) and were kept awake by Cossacks in among the trees imitating the sounds of wild beasts to terrify them. Pleasanter was it for those in Hungary, where the custom was, when strangers came in sight, to bake some bread fresh in the cinders that served as ovens, and send it to their lodgings by the youngest and prettiest girls, who gathered themselves into a ring and danced round the visitors singing.

Yet another picture is of a Frenchman whose way lay through the Ardennes in time of war; he was journeying on business. Tales were plentiful of bands of peasants in the forests, killing passers-by without distinction. One evening he makes his escape from four men, takes a by-road where the highroad was in particularly bad repute; snow begins to fall, the wind is dead against him; his by-road leads him cross-country, which founders his horse; he sits down on a tree-trunk, back to the wind, and thinks how his brother and four sisters are providing him with nephews and nieces who will never give a guess at the troubles he has gone through in making a fortune, but will take it for granted that they are to have a share of it. The nephews, perhaps, would have told him that it was lucky for him he was in the Ardennes and not outside St. Malo at so late an hour, with the twelve or twenty-four, which-

ever it was,[14] savage English dogs waiting for him,
who were sent out every night with their keeper
to guard the town, "killing and tearing any living
creature they encounter withal." In 1627 a man
did die so. Even without the dogs, at St. Malo
or anywhere else, it was troublesome, or worse, to
arrive late. Gates were closed, and kept closed,
and this applied, of course, to seafarers as well;
one tourist making for Monaco, another for Genoa,
had for that reason to sleep out in an open boat.
In towns where a strict "Reformed" sect had
the upper hand, this waiting might have to be
done in daytime also; gates as well as shops being
shut during sermon-time. But even supposing he
found means to enter at night, it might be wiser
not to take the offer, seeing that he would find
himself wandering about in a pitch-dark maze of
dirty alleys during the hours when it was permis-
sible for the inhabitants to throw "slops" out of
window.

CHAPTER VIII

THE PURSE

A traveller! by my faith, you have great reason to be sad: I fear you have sold your own lands to see other men's.

As You Like It (about 1599).

THE cost of travelling divides itself into two kinds; direct and indirect: that is, into the outlay which the traveller must reckon on and that which he has to reckon with. The first kind, the necessities, consists of fares, food, lodging, passports, tolls, etc., together with loss by exchange of money or by charges on remittances. The second kind, the possibilities, includes loss by robbery, by war, by disease, lack of legal privileges, ignorance of local custom, and such like eventualities in so far as any one was liable to suffer from them through being a stranger in a strange land.

But before considering the most elementary necessaries, some working arrangement must be established about translating payments into terms of English money of the present day. In the first place, between 1542 and 1642 money fell from about nine times its present value to about five times. Dates must therefore be found within which the multiplication figure must become successively nine, eight, seven, six. Suppose the first figure be taken up to 1556, when the States General met at Brussels to deal with Philip II's debt; the second figure thence to 1589, the year when the failure of the Spanish Armada began to tell on economics; seven from 1589 to 1612, at which date the bankruptcy of the Welser firm affected all Europe; and six thenceforward. If these are reasonable fictions, it is the utmost that can be achieved; in so far as they are not, the definiteness of the system makes correction of it easier. Amounts arrived at by these reckonings are given in square brackets. Usually, however, the original amounts have first to be translated out of continental coinage into contemporary English, a process which involves a series of comparisons too long to be tabulated here, and often, even then, needing modification as a result of the context in which the particular statement occurs. This is mentioned only as indicating a fresh source of uncertainty, and possibly of error. A third factor in these amounts as here given is as reliable as the two former factors are unreliable; every original amount represents an actual transaction by a traveller between 1542 and 1642, except where otherwise stated.

Necessities and possibilities are sometimes found considered jointly in general estimates. Sir Philip Sidney considered his brother should have two hundred pounds a year allowed him for travelling. This was in 1578, and he would be reckoning according to the highest standard that a young Englishman would have a use for.

Dallington, a guide-book writer, speaking for Englishmen in France in 1598, estimates eighty pounds a year; if one servant is taken and riding-lessons required, one hundred and fifty pounds; over two hundred pounds is excessive; while another, Cleland, in his "Institution of a Young Nobleman" (1607) considers two hundred pounds a year enough for four persons. Howell (1642) says three hundred pounds for the youngster at Paris, with fifty pounds each in addition for a cook, a valet, and a page; but then Howell had acted as tutor and no doubt hoped to do so again as soon as he could get free from the Fleet Prison, where he lay when his pamphlet was published. Under these circumstances he was likely to be considering his own pocket rather than the father's. Nevertheless, two of the brothers Coligny [Henri II's courtiers], when planning a year's tour through Italy in 1546, were said to have put aside fourteen thousand scudi [£30,000] for expenses; which annoyed their uncle.¹ But within a year or two of this estimate, Evelyn was travelling farther afield than Paris, — he stayed seven months in Rome alone, — keeping one servant throughout, sometimes two, learning under several masters, and making costly and extensive purchases, on less than three hundred pounds annually. Of Sir Richard Fanshawe, again, his wife records that "during some years of travel" (less than seven, for certain) "he had spent a considerable part of his stock"; this stock consisted of what his parents had bequeathed him, fifteen hundred pounds, and fifty pounds a year: his travel lay mainly in France and Spain previous to 1630.

Fynes Moryson, too, gives his expenditure as from fifty to sixty pounds a year, which included the cost of two journeys, one in spring, one in autumn. He was accustomed to the best standard of living at home, but his income was hardly adequate to his social position and by temperament he was a temperate and adaptable man; more so, to say the least, than the son of Davison, the Secretary of State whom Queen Elizabeth made the scapegoat for the death of Queen Mary Stewart.

Father Davison had been told that one hundred marks would suffice for his boy abroad each year, and, consequently, in sending the latter to Italy in 1595 with a tutor, and a servant, allowed him treble that amount, one hundred pounds. The tutor writes, "I never endured such slavery in my life to save money"; if Mr. Davison does not see his way to changing his mind about the one hundred pounds a year, will he kindly find another tutor? As to the "frugal travellers" whose travelling costs them no more than the one hundred marks a year, he does not wish to deny it; in fact, he knows'such men; and very sorry he is for those who have lent them the rest they have spent.

From all this one may conclude that the equivalent of four hundred pounds a year was the minimum for respectable travelling and that the Average Tourist would certainly need at least half as much again. But this is assuming that all who were respectable, or above the need to be so, paid all their own expenses, which was far from being the case. There were plenty of rich travellers who defrayed all charges for a large following. Landgraf Ludwig II of Hessen-Darmstadt [2] even paid a certain knight to accompany him, six hundred florins [£600] down and fifty florins a month, besides expenses and clothes. So when Cardinal Luigi d'Aragona toured Europe, starting May 9, 1517, and arriving home March 16, 1518, and spent about fifteen thousand ducats [£35,000] meantime, in which "eating and drinking were the least costly items," we may conclude that the thirty-five persons he took with him, and the forty-five he brought back, received at least expenses. Another churchman, Johann Gottfried von Aschhausen, bishop of Würzburg, left Strassburg in 1612 with a retinue of one hundred and thirty, twenty-one of whom were young men of high birth. Before he passed out of Germany this number was increased by fifty more. He was away a year in Italy, which cost him thirty-two thousand seven hundred and fifty-four scudi [£40,000].[3]

But since he went as the Emperor's ambassador, this is rather a fresh example of how travelling was facilitated by embassies. For among the advantages of various kinds that rendered accompanying the journeyings of diplomatists the best means of seeing the world, the economical advantages were as important as any. It by no means followed, however, that anything but board and lodging were provided by him; in the detailed accounts of Sir G. Chaworth regarding his special embassy to Brussels is no mention of outlay on anything but necessaries. On the other hand, we find another English ambassador giving one hundred pounds apiece to the gentlemen who were to accompany him, to provide their outfit.[4] In any case, this expedient extended only as far as the ambassador went, a specially important limitation for Englishmen of Queen Elizabeth's day, since she had no ambassador at Venice throughout her reign; and even when James I sent one thither he was, during his first term of office, the only English ambassador in Italy. Bearing this in mind, and turning to other methods whereby the Average Tourist from England might reduce his expenditure, we come upon what is, perhaps, the most remarkable fact of the time in regard to the kind, and the extent, of the usefulness with which travel was credited, namely, that Queen Elizabeth

subsidised it. It is obvious from the life-stories
of all those who served her that they were treated
with extreme stinginess and that employment by
the government meant heavy expense instead of
salaries; and yet, as to travel, these are the words
of Bacon, who had excellent means of knowing the
facts: "There was a constant course held, that
by the advice of the secretaries, or some principal
councillor, there was always sent forth into the
parts beyond the seas some young men of whom
good hopes were conceived of their towardliness,
to be trained up and made fit for such public em-
ployments and to learn the languages. This was
at the charge of the Queen, which was not much,
for they travelled but as private gentlemen." [5]

Ecclesiastics, it goes almost without saying,
received special terms, mainly in the shape of free
lodging at religious houses, although the opinion of
one abbé ought not to go unrecorded, — "avoid
monasteries," because the charities expected
amounted to more than inn-charges. This certainly did not apply to Muscovy, where, if a monastery could be found, it undoubtedly did mean
free board and lodging for the three days, the
usual limit of time, universally, for claimers of
charity. But what with monasteries and special
foundations there must have been far more really
free accommodation than is apparent from tourist-
books, written as the latter almost entirely are by
the class that paid its way. Even apart from the

above there were incidents such as one recorded in 1650, of eight thousand pilgrims to Rome from Spain being fed and housed for three days at Naples at the expense of the Spanish viceroy there. At Compostella, too, for two reals [7s. 6d.] could be obtained a parchment document with a cardinal's seal attached, recommending the bearer for alms as one who was on his way to other places of pilgrimage; and in Italy not even that much was needed, inasmuch as the natives were then so averse to begging that foreigners who had no such scruples found little difficulty in traversing it at next to no cost.

Where a begging-license was necessary, that could easily be obtained also by being, or pretending to be, a student. Loyola lived in term-time at Paris on what he gained by begging at fairs in Flanders and England during holidays. Another useful option open to students, of whatever social position, was the exemption from local tolls, frequently a privilege belonging to all who had matriculated at the university of the district; the graduate of Padua, for instance, was exempt throughout Venetian territory. It so happened that one of these tourists [6] was elected rector of Bologna University during his stay there in 1575, and that during his term of office some students were forced to pay taxes. He and the managing body at once appealed to the Pope, who not only confirmed, but extended, the immunities.

In Italy the tolls were so oppressive that the matriculation fees, twenty lire [£5] at Padua, twelve at Bologna, were soon made good, even supposing them to have been paid; at Bologna, at least, matriculation could be obtained for nothing by applying in formâ pauperis. The examination was no bar worth mentioning. In Germany, moreover, according to Moryson, the tenancy of a house often carried with it the obligation to board and lodge a student free. Another traveller who economised thoroughly was Sastrow, who, on reaching Rome, took service at the hospital of Santa Brigitta, cooked, washed-up, made the beds, and received the equivalent of 2s. 6d. a month, while Jacques Callot, the artist, when he ran away from home, took the way to Italy in the company of those gypsies who appear in those sketches of his which form one of the most vivid memorials of the travelling life of the time. Yet with all these opportunities which presented themselves to the needy, we are told that Turkey was the only country of Europe where poverty was no bar to travel.

Outside Europe fresh estimates have to be quoted. The fare to Jaffa and back by the pilgrim-galley varied from fifty to sixty ducats [say £100]: this included food. Additional expenses brought the ordinary cost of a visit to Jerusalem from Venice under these earlier conditions up to three or four hundred pounds in present-day

values. This, of course, omits the expenses of
the pilgrim between his home and Venice. The
minimum recorded cost for this period is represented by the two hundred and twenty crowns
[£350] spent by one Switzer in thirty weeks, and
two hundred and twenty-eight crowns spent by
another, a barber, in eleven months (1583–84),[7]
of which times only about three months, in each
case, was taken up by the voyage from Venice to
Jerusalem and back, the remainder being devoted
to Italy. The pilgrimage may be considered as
accounting for but little more than two hundred
pounds of the expenditure of each. Many went,
moreover, who never possessed this much, since it
was common for one man to go as deputy for several, who jointly defrayed his expenses; and it was
also a common form of charity for rich pilgrims
to pay for poor ones. Later, in fact, they were
often forced to do so by the Turks when the latter
had reduced to beggary those who had come away
with too little, which led to there arising a custom among pilgrims of showing each other their
money; if one refused, the others avoided his company to escape the possibility of being compelled
to pay for him.

With the cessation of the pilgrim-galley the
cost of the pilgrimage doubled itself, what with
the increased length of the journey due to a roundabout way having to be taken, and, still more, to
its increased duration, owing to the uncertainty;

especially as every day additional brought its own additional risks and extortions. Moryson and his brother spent four hundred and eighty pounds [nearly, if not quite, £3000].

Certain circumstances raised the cost to him above the average, and he was away more than a year and a half, whereas the journey would be done within the year ordinarily. On the other hand, as his brother died near Aleppo, the return-journey represents the expenditure of one man instead of two. How a thrifty man who was used to roughing it would be forced to spend the equivalent of one thousand pounds or more on a journey that would nowadays cost him about sixty-five pounds is partly explained by the exactions of the Turks. When Sandys was at Jerusalem the monks of S. Salvatore had just been compelled to pay eight hundred dollars [£900] for an imaginary offence. When Lithgow arrived late one night after the gates had been shut, the friars let down food to him over the wall; the Turks, being informed of this, insisted they must have been importing weapons, and inflicted another fine, one hundred piasters [£125]. It is not surprising, then, that with expenses like these, and ordinary expenses to match, the monks expected sums from the pilgrims that seem at first sight outrageous. To Lithgow they made a definite charge of a piaster [£1 10s.] a day for board and lodging alone; but their general custom was to

throw themselves on the traveller's generosity
and grumble at the result.

Neither did the Franks suffer from indirect
exactions only. The price for entrance to the
Church of the Holy Sepulchre went on increasing,
from nothing at all in the fourteenth century to
four zecchini [£10] in 1606. Some mention fees
of four times that amount, but this higher sum
included the toll at the city gate, the two being
collected simultaneously and so mistaken for one
charge: the Turks farmed the revenue from the
Holy Sepulchre for eight thousand sultanons [over
£19,000], says Sandys. Extras were almost end-
less, yet very few of them left any change out of
a gold coin; the fee for the certificate of visitation,
without which the poorest pilgrim would not think
of departing, was three zecchini [seven guineas],
while the knighthood, nominally thirty zecchini,
does not seem to have been granted for less than
ten. The monastery servants were liable to excommunication if they accepted a tip, but they gladly
risked damnation for a zecchino, and, indeed, insisted on doing so.

By spending not more than a week at Jerusalem and that at a time which may profanely be
termed out of the season, it was possible to see
the sights of the city itself for the equivalent of
£50; at any rate, that happened in 1676;[8] but to
do as most Franks did, spend Easter there, and
ten days or a fortnight, and accompany the excur-

sions, cost nearly double that. On the journey,
the tributes may be imagined from the fact that
Sandys thought it worth while to pay four shariffs
[£10] for a passport which saved a few of them;
nothing availed against an Arab chief who sent
to demand seven zecchini [sixteen guineas] a head,
and then came in person to demand five more.
Moreover, besides the special outfit to be bought,
the charges themselves were always reckoned on
the basis that a Frank *must* have heaps of money;
from Rama to Jerusalem alone, one day's journey, another seven zecchini had to be paid to the
dragoman, and the same amount coming back.

A considerable saving might be effected by
hiring a Janizary at seven aspers [2s.] a day: his
services more than paid for his keep; and there
were times when even a Frank found himself
living at an easy rate. This happened when he
stayed at a "fondaco," or depôt of Christian
traders, or so it may be inferred from casual remarks backed up by two definite instances in
years far apart. The German Fürer lived so at
Alexandria and Cairo for the equivalent of five
shillings a day in 1565, and in 1625 two Germans[9]
were received for two months free of all charges
at the Venetian "fondaco" at Cairo.

Far above all economies, however, was the system known as "putting-out" money — and this
applied to travel inside, as well as outside, Christendom. The mediæval custom of presenting

offerings before starting had died out; sixteenth-
century tourists only offered prayers, and, for the
rest, often expected to take up, at their home-
coming, all they had left behind them with additions, or even multiplication. They deposited,
or "put out," money before their departure on
that condition. The custom is said to have been
developed in the Netherlands [10] during the first
half of the sixteenth century out of a pilgrims'
practice of leaving a will behind them in favour of
a friend on the understanding that the pilgrim
was to receive double the bequest if he came back.
It would seem from what Moryson says that the
custom was barely known in England till the last
decade of the sixteenth century, and then spread
so rapidly that it fell into disrepute, bankrupts
employing it to reinstate themselves, and actors,
then the scum of the populace, to gain notoriety.
He apologises for his brother Henry doing it, who
put out four hundred pounds to be repaid twelve
hundred pounds if he came back from Jerusalem.
If allusions to the practice in contemporary English literature [11] can be trusted, he drove a bad
bargain; according to them he might have ar-
ranged for his hypothetical profit to be five hundred instead of three hundred per cent, the latter
rate being granted against journeys to Italy. The
only other instance known of an actual transaction of this kind was calculated to yield two thousand per cent [£10 to be repaid £200]; but this

was against a voyage to Russia, near the middle
of the century, from London, whence only one
ship was known to have sailed thither and returned.

Life insurance in its present form was also
adopted by some persons before starting for abroad;
but public opinion condemned every form of life
insurance equally as immoral, and in the Netherlands, France, and Genoa it was forbidden by law,
"travel-wagers" being specially mentioned in the
proclamations. The rate, however, is the point
which specially concerns us here, as indicative of
the risks of travel. At the present day, for all the
parts of the world touched upon in this book, the
safest insurance company will not only lay fifty to
one that the traveller *will* return, in place of the
rate then of three to five to one that he would *not*,
but will further insure him against accidents at a
lower rate than if he became a London butcher.
The system is of interest, too, as marking the transition from mediæval to modern methods of insurance; from "protections" granted by the stronger
to the weaker for a premium which took the form
of personal service, to the capitalist's bond; the
guarantee of redress by force being superseded by
guarantee of reimbursement by a business man,
because the latter had become both more feasible
and more satisfactory.

It is clear, then, that, given the most favourable
circumstances, the traveller might not only make

his journeys pay their own expenses, but might
clear a handsome profit. Yet how far these circumstances were made the most of is a question
that has at present to be decided on negative evidence alone, the verdict on which must be that no
case is made out. In leaving, therefore, the general estimates for details, both have to be put forward as net, subject to the mitigations already
referred to.

The fare from Dover to Calais was five shillings
throughout this period. So invariable was this
charge that when a certain boatman was suspected of being in league with the Roman Catholic seminarists in France because he conveyed
across some ladies who were religious fugitives, he
was considered not guilty on its being ascertained
that he had charged them one pound each for
the passage.[12] This five-shilling charge did not include the cost of boarding and landing when that
required, as so often happened, the use of small
boats, or of porters wading out. Between Flushing and Gravesend 6s. 8d. seems to have been
the fare.[13]

Among the reasons for the preference of travel
by water rather than by land, one was economy.
In the case of tolls, for example, the case has been
exactly reversed. As locks did not exist there were
no river-dues; but of highway-tolls plenty; moreover, it often cost something to cross a bridge but
never a sou to pass under it. As for ferries, the

ferryman occasionally made the passengers pay
what he pleased by collecting fares in the middle
of the river. Yet another reason which raised the
cost of road-travel as against river-travel lay in
the latter affording far fewer chances to robbers,
which also told on the direct expense by eliminat-
ing payments to escorts.

The contrast, of course, between horse and boat
was much greater than between waggon and boat.
In fact, the choice between the latter pair was
many times a matter of comfort rather than of
cost; the fares for both, in all normal cases but
one where they can be exactly determined, varying from three farthings to a penny ha'penny a
mile. To compare this with existing railway fares
we may strike an average and say sixpence a mile;
but the charges will be found to approach the minimum more often on the river than in the waggon.
A typical instance is the five stivers [2s. 6d.] on
the nine-mile canal between Haarlem and Amsterdam, and the lowest, the exception just spoken
of, is the sixteen soldi [3s. 6d.] for the twenty-
four miles by river and lagoon between Venice
and Padua, recorded by Villamont in 1591, and
by Van Buchell in 1587. One disadvantage common to both cart and boat must not be forgotten
— that, to profit by this relative cheapness, the
traveller had to form one of a party; if no party
was ready he had to wait till one collected. Sir
Henry Wotton, to take one example out of many,

once wanted to go by waggon from Brunswick to
Frankfort, about one hundred and fifty miles;
had he started on the spot he would have started
alone and paid at the rate of 4s. 6d. a mile of our
money. He waited a week before two disreputable
specimens turned up to share the expense.

This freedom to choose one's company was a
decided advantage for the traveller who rode, considering that murdering was far less exclusively a
lower-class habit than it has since become. But
he had to pay dearly for the increased respectability and pace. Horse-hire varied from a penny
ha'penny to fivepence a mile, the maximum charge
representing the cost of post-horses in France in
the seventeenth century, the minimum the charge
in Italy for a horse that was waiting for a return
fare, an opportunity that might frequently be met
with. The average was far nearer the maximum
than the minimum rate, since it was often a case
of post-horse or no horse, and post rates did not
sink so very far below the French standard. According to Moryson, the English charged two
shillings a day in London, one shilling a day in
the provinces, for other than post-horses, but he
was a native and the charges to foreigners probably exceeded the charges to natives throughout
Europe in a greater degree then than now; an
Englishman on the way from Calais to Paris
complains that he had to pay £2 15s. where a
Frenchman paid but three pistoles at sixteen

shillings and eightpence each;[14] and that is not an isolated grievance. In fact, as a comment on Moryson's remark about England, when Lionello, a secretary of the Venetian ambassador, went post to Edinburgh and back in June, 1617, besides paying threepence a mile for each horse, he includes in his accounts as usual tips fourpence to the woman and sixpence to the horse-boy, at each stage.[15] In Italy, where several foreigners found the cost of riding less than the average, Villamont reckons that an écu [two guineas] a day per horse covered all horse-charges, while in passing from Germany to Italy the best plan was to buy a horse in Germany, where three pounds would be a fair price, and sell it in Italy, which could be done at double that price.

Travellers' evidence, however, as to horse-charges is less plentiful than might be expected, owing to what may be called the 'vetturino' system. The term 'vetturino' came to be applied, even outside Italy, to the horse-owner or carrier who contracted for the whole cost of a journey, food, lodging, transport, tolls. Their reputation is best illustrated by the tale of an abbé at Loreto about this time, who, in confessing, included among his transgressions a beating inflicted on a 'vetturino.' "Go on," said the confessor, "that does n't count; they 're the worst scoundrels in the world." Nevertheless, the method spread all over Europe during this period with striking rapid-

ity, though far more readily on the road than on
the water. The advantages to the stranger were
recognised at once, the saving of the trouble and
the expense which accompanied repeated bargain-
ing in a state of ignorance as to where and how to
do it, what inns to go to, what extras to put up
with, what the legal dues really were, etc. However dishonest the 'vetturino' might prove, his
victim probably paid no more to him in unintentional commission than his accomplices would have
extorted on their own account otherwise. For the
Lyons-Turin journey, at least, there soon came
into use a regular formula for a written contract, a
formula which has been preserved.[16] The system
has its value for us, too, in enabling us to compare prices. While there are multitudes of figures
apparently available for the purpose of reckoning
cost, a large majority turn out to be, to use one
of their own phrases, no more use than a wooden
poker, the writer omitting one or more of the necessary data. If, for instance, he mentions the hire
of four horses, it leaves us in the dark in reckoning
personal expenses, inasmuch as four horses may
equally well imply two, or three, or four persons.
So likewise, to complete an account of a waggon-
fare, it needs to be stated whether or no it was
what the Germans called "maul frei," that is,
whether the coachman paid for his own food or
not. Or again, riding was so much the rule that
the charge which the wayfarer gives for bed and

breakfast often includes, probably more often than not, the "stabulum et pabulum" for his horse; it is only on the rare occasions when specific statement is made, or when a pedestrian gives prices, that there is any certainty about it. Now the vetturino's charge does away with all this uncertainty. Also as to whether a guide accompanied the party or not — another necessary which cost money; especially a satisfactory one, obtainable only, writes Sir Philip Sidney, " by much expense or much humbleness."

Here again the traveller by waggon went more cheaply than the horseman. What with the absence of sign-posts, the scarcity of persons to ask, the frequent indistinguishableness of the road from its margin and its surroundings, a stranger was practically forced to be guided. In 1648 this brought the cost of a journey from London to Dover to £1 15s. 10d.[17] [say, £8]. In a town this applied to every one who had no friends there. Every single feature on which one depends nowadays was absent, or, if present, present only in embryo, — visible street-names, printed suggestions other than historical, detailed plans, the wide, straight streets which allow the mystified to discover his whereabouts without climbing a church-tower. In short, what was worth seeing was mostly heard of only by word of mouth, and to find it one needed to be led there. Expenditure on guides reached its highest point when the Alps

were snowbound; after a heavy fall he who wished
to pass must wait till others had made fresh tracks
or pay anything up to fifty crowns [£75] to have
it done for him.

To pass Mont Cenis cost in the ordinary way
the equivalent of about £4 10s.; that is, about half
what the 'vetturino' would want to take each
one of several from Lyons to Turin — six crowns,
which latter sum is about ten times as much as
the second-class fare to-day. But then the journey
takes twelve hours now and took seven days then,
with food all the while at travellers' prices.

The length of journeys stands out as the chief
factor in the comparative costliness. Take a typical case, that of the five middle-class men [18] who
left Venice on February 20, 1655, who wasted no
time on the way, reached England on March 29,
and spent one hundred and twenty-five pounds.
Reckoning this as equalling £625, this works out
as the equivalent of £125 each for thirty-seven
days, or £3 7s. 7d. a day. If a man left Venice now
on February 20, he might break the journey at
Bâle, to do things comfortably, and arrive in London at 5.38 A. M. on February 22. Second-class
fare would be £5 10s. 7d.; add £2 for meals and
incidentals, £7 10s. 7d. in all, an average of £3 3s.
a day. The other thirty-four and a half days of the
thirty-seven his food would be paid for at home
rates, say 2s. 6d. a day, £4 6s. 3d., which, added
to the £7 10s. 7d., gives £11 16s. 10d. Now the

daily average of about 7s. higher in the cost of travel apart from food, as above represented, — mainly accounted for by the relative cost of horses and guides as against railway fares,—only comes to £13 in thirty-seven days. On this basis the journey from Venice to London two hundred and fifty years ago cost between nine and ten times as much as it would to-day, solely on account of the difference in speed. That the expenditure of these five middle-class men was very reasonable is easily verifiable, as, for example, by the accounts of Muscorno,[19] another Venetian secretary, whose bill for coming to England, for himself and a servant, comes to three hundred and two ducats [£385]. If there was one place where travelling ought to have worked out relatively cheaply, it was Muscovy, seeing that on the sledges a peasant would take a passenger fifty leagues for three or four crowns; but it does not seem to have lowered the expenses of one Dr. Willes, whose overland journey thither in 1600 cost eighty pounds, including payments to guides. His own share may be reckoned as equivalent to two hundred and forty pounds as compared with the fifteen pounds the same route would cost to-day.

Luggage would frequently entail the same fare as the owner, since an extra horse would be needed to carry a box. Leather trunks were to be purchased which might be carried in front of the rider, but these did not protect the contents against rain. As to what carriers took as free luggage and what as "excess," there is no evidence but that of one Englishman [20] who found he was entitled to five pounds free on the Calais-Paris road and paid ten shillings surcharge on the rest without comment. Any advice the experienced have to offer as regards reduction of luggage for economy is in view far less of carriage than of customs-duties. In Italy the exactions were severest; almost every day's journey would take one over some boundary and at every bridge there were two or three quattrini [twopence] to pay; at every gate six or eight soldi [one shilling], besides baggage dues. Any article carried through Italy would cost its price over again in dues; a sword, for instance, you had to give up at the gate, pay a man to carry it to the inn, where the host took care of it till your departure, when you had to pay again for its carriage to the gate. The Papal states had the lowest scale of charges, yet on crossing their boundary, there was a giulio [3s. 6d.] to pay for the smallest hand-bag; and at Florence even your corpse would be taxed a crown [£1 10s.] if it went in or out of the city for burial. In Germany, where the burden was lighter, Sir Thomas Hoby, coming down the Rhine in 1555, paid toll at twenty-one customhouses between Mainz and Herzogensbosch to fourteen authorities. As a rule, too, the taxes were farmed, which increased the tourists' sufferings from them, inasmuch as they were exacted with

greater rigour and it was the harder to get redress
in cases of extortion, especially when, as in Poland
and Spain, the 'farmers' were Jews or of Jewish
blood. Bribery, however, was often practicable,
and where practicable, economical; one of the best
guides to Spain repeats concerning every custom-
house that the traveller should say he has nothing
to declare and tip the officials only if they take his
word, that is, if they do not do their duty. It is
true there were passes to be obtained from a central authority, overriding the right of search, such
as the imperial pass in Germany, and the indefinite rights of ambassadors, but how far these were
respected seems to have been mainly a matter of
bluff. Navagero, in Spain early in the sixteenth
century, ambassador though he was, had to pay
duties even on the rings on his fingers.

Passports, for one purpose or another, may be
said to have been as much the rule then as they
have since become the exception; an Englishman
must pay five shillings for leave to travel and another five shillings if he wished to take his horse
with him. A Frenchman at Milan speaks of getting a passport, stating his destination and the
colour of his hair; and so on. But few mention
such expenses being entailed as does one Italian,[21]
leaving Dover in 1606. Apparently he had to pay
for separate passports for each of his suite as well
as himself, as these cost forty reals. The "real of
eight" was nearly equal to five shillings English.

The captain of the vessel demanded copies which "cost very dear" and the harbour-keeper, further-more, who had exacted two giuli [six shillings], (each person?) on arrival, required double at departure.

Guide-books seem to have been from two to four times the price of Baedekers, a minor item, but considerable, like food and lodging. It may seem, at first sight, as if food and lodging were far from minor items, and that truly, of course, if only the total expenditure is considered. But in considering, as is being done here, relative cost only, that is, the cost of travel in so far as it has altered since three centuries ago, it has to be borne in mind that the average cost of food and shelter never alters; it is only standards of living that alter. If any one took the average price of meals, say, in Europe then and average prices now, and showed a difference of net cost between them, his calculations must either be based on misleading information, or else would prove that the figure he was multiplying with to equate values was a wrong one. This, of course, refers to necessaries; luxuries must be ruled out for two reasons: first, all attempts to fix a standard or strike an average breaks down for lack of a basis; second, they do not test what any one is called upon to spend but only how much he can spend if he is fool enough to try. Thus, for example, when Montaigne tells us that the charges at the "Vaso d'Oro" at Rome

would be about twenty crowns [£35] a month, we
may conclude that if we ascertain what the average charges would be for the same accommodation
at a first-rate hotel to-day, it is a more reasonable
plan to take the difference as the difference between their money-values and ours than to accept
a surplus in either, according to the usually accepted multiplying figure, as defining an increase
or decrease in hotel charges.

Yet for all this, something remains to be said.
A modern tourist often finds himself in the position of drawing his income from a locality where
money is cheaper or dearer than in the districts
where he is making his payments. Now, three
hundred years ago, he would have met with these
fluctuations more frequently and more suddenly
than would be the case to-day; and when met
with, they would often have been more violent.
In so far as this was the case, so far is the relative cost affected. The causes of these fluctuations may be divided into (1) local custom, (2)
insufficient linking-up of supply and demand.
Hungary may be taken as an example of the latter, Germany of the former, cause; Poland and
Spain of districts where social and economic forces
jib at separate classification. In Hungary and the
districts southeast of it the most seasoned traveller never failed to be astonished at the ideal
natural conditions; "wheat," as Sir Thomas
Browne's son said of Transylvania in particular

a little later, "had no value in relation to the
subsistence of a human being." There was no
outlet for its products; the continual state of war
kept commerce paralysed; Vienna had little need
of it, Constantinople none at all; what the fertility of the soil produced so abundantly was thus
available for local consumption only. Especially
was this the case with products that needed no human tending; the man who ate a whole penn'orth
of fish risked bursting. In Germany prices ruled
low, yet so excessive was the drunkenness, and so
general, that it was a moral impossibility to live
cheaply without cutting one's self off from human
society. Supper over, for instance, the "schlaff-
trinke" was set on the table, and whoever
touched a drop of it had, by custom, to pay an
even share with those who drank till morning.

The Spanish diet, which was such a trial to the
inside if the stranger did conform to it, was equally
a trial to his pocket if he did not. One tried both
ways on one day in 1670.[22] At noon he shared the
landlord's dinner, paying a real [2s. 6d.] for vegetables, dried fish, fruit; but when in the evening he
was one of six who dined on four fowls and neck of
mutton, his bill came to the equivalent of £1 5s.
not including wine. Poland, on the contrary, being the granary of Europe and exporting much
else besides grain, rich in serf labour, and with its
retail trade in the hands of denationalised aliens
who were well under control, could afford to im-

port plenty of luxuries and enjoyed abundance of
necessaries: a goose or a pig for the equivalent of
1s. 6d., a loin of mutton for 1s. — such were prices
in Poland.

A good test of relative cheapness is the value of
the coin most generally useful; in Poland these
were the brass 'banns,' worth about a penny farthing in to-day's values. Of Italy a similar statement may be made; of England just the contrary.
And this presence, or absence, of plenty of small
coins affects the tourist in two ways; partly in relation to his food, because the more common small
change is, the more commonly customary is it to
sell food in quantities suited to a single meal for
one; secondly, the smaller the change, the smaller
the tips. Before leaving the subject of food, an
example may be quoted of the violence of the
fluctuations in prices at that date when the means
of carriage and of making wants known in time
were so crude. Sir Henry Wotton writes, of his
own knowledge, that the price of victuals at Venice was three times as high in 1608 as it had been
in 1604.

Lastly, as regards necessary expenditure, what
did their money itself cost them?

To begin with, the far greater length of time
usually necessary then to prove identity, or to
confirm references, must not be lost sight of, seeing how much it added to the seriousness of the
hope deferred that maketh the pocket empty.

Next, to deal with the ways of remedying this — there were three ways. (1) Carrying cash; (2) depositing money with a merchant, or a friend, who either remits coins or advises an amount; (3) letters of credit.

Carrying cash meant carrying coins. At any rate, not one of these travellers mentions using the bank-notes of the day, the 'segni reppresentativi' just introduced by the Italian bankers, nor even the ancient semi-currency of jewels, unless one includes Henri III, who, when escaping from the throne of Poland to that of France, carried off three hundred thousand crowns' worth. Carrying coins for future use meant, in the ordinary way, sewing them up in one's clothes. The favourite place was inside a waistband of the breeches, a double one designed for that purpose, made of leather or canvas, forming a series of little pockets, all closed by pulling one string. It was so that Lithgow was carrying one hundred and thirty-seven double pieces of gold [probably double pistoles, equal to £500], when he and the gold were seized by the Inquisition at Malaga. Next to the waistband, under the arm-pits was the most usual spot; but it is given as advisable to use one's shabbiest garments in any case for this purpose, as the least likely to be searched thoroughly by robbers. In Muscovy the boots were more often used than other articles. A small reserve might be wrapped round with mending-material, with needles sticking into it to add to the innocence of its appearance; or it might be hidden at the bottom of a pot of ointment. By this latter means Moryson saved himself from utter destitution when robbed, having chosen ointment which smelt, apparently, like the Muscovite's fish. Equally ingenious and successful was another who smuggled all his money past the Mohammedan customs by hiding it in pork. Mohammedans themselves used their turbans.

The advantages of carrying money in this way — that of having it at hand for certain — was outweighed by the chances of robbery or confiscation; the latter by reason of there being legal limits to the amounts that might be taken away from countries and towns. Lyons was the most liberal, allowing sometimes eighty, sometimes one hundred "crowns of the sun" [£144 to £180]. Turin allowed fifty silver crowns [£75], Naples twenty-five; Rome, according to an edict in 1592, no more than five gold crowns [£8]. The rule in Spain was that no gold was to leave the country, and Spanish towns often enforced this against each other; from Murcia in 1617 no more than ten "reals of eight" [£11 5s.] might be taken free, but gold was not confiscated, duty being levied instead.

As for England, Hentzner found the limit of £10 in 1599, as did Gölnitz in some year soon after 1618, although Moryson, writing between

these dates, gives £20. Still earlier, the Frenchman Perlin, who was here at the beginning of
Queen Mary's reign, says that a pedestrian may
take no more than ten crowns [£27], a horseman
twenty, out of the realm; adding, however, that
a man may convert the rest of his cash into goods
and so, by realising these goods later, prevent confiscation; and also, that by accompanying an ambassador one is exempt from search. When it is
remembered, further, that Francis Davison got
inserted in his license to travel a clause enabling
him to carry fifty pounds across with him (for three
persons), that there were trustworthy merchants
who would authorise correspondents abroad to pay
the traveller whatever the latter might have deposited with them, and that these customs concerning the export of gold and silver were in use
throughout Europe, it will be seen that if a traveller suffered loss by confiscation, he deserved his
losses.

By far the greater number had their money
advised at a cost of five to fifteen per cent, usually ten per cent, as against the three-quarters per
cent which would probably represent a maximum
of loss by exchange to-day to tourists. An unknown quantity lay in the differences of values,
which might yield a profit, or might involve heavy
loss. Bimetallism prevailed all over Europe, and
the values of gold and silver both relative to each
other and positive, fluctuated far more violently

than is the case to-day. When Cavendish returned to England after his first circumnavigation of the world, the plunder depreciated gold in London by one twelfth; in 1603 the exchange from Venice to London was twenty-eight per cent in favour of Venice; in 1606 it was six per cent higher London to Venice than Venice to London.

But with all its disadvantages, remitting by advice was the most generally satisfactory and used method. The tenour of an average bill, however, has changed somewhat, "at sight" being the only one of the variable terms equally customary both then and now. Bills not drawn "at sight" were drawn at "usance," "half usance," or "double usance"; "usance" signifying a month as a rule. Exceptions were, of course, for longer distances, such as London and Venice, when "usance" meant three months; and how completely "usance" is a term of the past is shown by the fact that the periods implied by "usance," in the rare cases in which it is still found in use, have not altered since the sixteenth century, in spite of the advance in the quickness of communications. "Thirds of exchange," now nearly as extinct as "usances," were then kept in regular use by the uncertainty of the posts; and in view of the difficulties in the way of identification and the advantage that money-changers were likely to take of them, advices often contained a description of the payee.[23]

Method No. 3, letters of credit, was a more expensive one than remittance by advice, but for places for which no "usance" was established, was obligatory; under favourable circumstances it might cost no more than ten per cent. There is evidence enough to justify conjecture that the English government allowed their credit to be used sometimes for the convenience of tourists in order to facilitate a watch being kept on their movements.[24]

Barter also ought not to be wholly left out of sight. In Norway dried fish was more serviceable than coin, as was tobacco among Turks, the only people prompt to copy the English in the use of it for pleasure; but by the middle of the seventeenth century the same might be said of Western Russia. And there is the case of one Thomas Douglas in 1600 who could not make arrangements for four hundred crowns to be advised for him at Algiers, applying to the English government for leave to take with him duty-free the broadcloth he had bought with the money and meant to realise there, to discharge the ransom which the money represented.[25]

Supposing, however, that all these means failed? The tourist became a beggar till he found friends. He might try, of course, to raise a loan, but only on terms which would possibly induce him to prefer beggary. The "German Ulysses," Karl Nützel of Nuremberg, was robbed at Alexandria of his capital; at Cairo he persuaded a ship's captain to lend him four hundred ducats, undertaking to pay him six hundred at Constantinople. They arrived thither in two months; the interest was therefore at the rate of three hundred per cent.[26] Sir Henry Wotton, when an ambassador, paid twenty per cent for a loan at Venice.

In considering loans we have passed away from necessities into the second half of the subject of cost, — its reasonable possibilities. These consist of the risks and difficulties to which the traveller was liable, nowhere summarised so well as in the English Litany, which was written at this period: —

"From lightning and tempest; from plague, pestilence and famine; from battle and murder; and from sudden death,

"Good Lord, deliver us."

Of the eight risks here mentioned, to most of which an Englishman at least was more liable abroad than at home, all but two have been minimised since. And if we note how in all other clauses of the Litany, only those troubles or desires which have affinity with each other are grouped together, it becomes significant in what company travellers are prayed for; —

"That it may please thee to preserve all that travel by land or water, all women labouring of

child, all sick persons, and young children; and to
shew thy pity upon all prisoners and captives.
We beseech thee to hear us, good Lord."

To take the risk of violence first, and, among
the forms of violence, war, it has to be remembered
that the United Provinces was the only State
whose soldiers were paid punctually. An effect
of this laxness may be traced in the experience
of a tourist in Picardy when the latter had been
reduced to such a state of destitution by war
that the commandants could not wring anything
further out of the inhabitants and therefore
forced contributions from travellers who passed
through. In 1594 Moryson wished to remit from
Venice to Paris, but no one had any correspondence farther than Geneva on account of the civil
wars, in spite of these being nominally at an end.
And they assured him it was twenty to one he
would be robbed by the disbanded soldiers (which
came true), and, if robbed, would be killed, because if they took him for an enemy they would
think him well killed; if a friend, they would kill
him to avoid making restitution; and the mar-
shals were so strictly looked after that they would
kill anyone who seemed likely to make complaints.
The effect on prices receives illustration by comparing Andrew Boorde's experience of Aquitaine
after a long period of peace and prosperity, —
that one pennyworth [say 10d.] of bread will feed
a man a week, and they sell nine cakes a penny,

each cake being enough to last a man a day, "except he be a ravener,"—with a letter from a Venetian gentleman,[27] fifty-four years later, by which time civil war had become chronic. He writes from England, where he found that a good meal could be had for ten soldi [2s. 6d.], comparing this with France, which he had just traversed, where the same could not be bought for less than sixty soldi, or even a whole gold crown [£1 13s.]. As to Germany, in 1623, only five years after the Thirty Years' War broke out, Wotton writes that prices have risen enormously, "insomuch as I am almost quite out of hope to find Conscience any more, since there is none among the very hills and deserts, whither I thought she had fled."

The effect on communications goes without saying. Even worse than that was the danger from those whom the horrible cruelty of sixteenth-century warfare drove half-mad with grief and loss, who shook off civilisation and robbed and murdered recklessly. According to Aubigné, who witnessed the horrors which he dwells on at length in his "Les Tragiques," war demoralised even the dogs in a way that endangered every passer-by. Speaking of those around Moncontour, where was fought one of the battles which left most bodies on the field,

> Vous en voyez l'espreuve au champ de Moncontour;
> Héréditairement ils ont, depuis ce jour,
> La rage naturelle, et leur race enyvrée
> Du sang des vrais François, se sent de la curée.

But it may be objected that the evidence of a sectarian historian is not admissible on any question of fact. Take, then, what a sober correspondent writes from the scene of the Thirty Years' War in 1639, not of dogs, but of men: "It is an ordinary thing in Brandenburg country to eat man's flesh," [28] and he goes on to tell how a judge has just met his death that way.

Again, De Thou, approaching Mérindol, finds not a soul to be seen; all had retired to caves at the sight of armed men. Elsewhere he saw all the peasants at work armed, and of one town nothing remained intact but a fountain and one street; the work of a commander, in the king's name, for the gratification of his private revenge. The state produced is well described by Sir Thomas Overbury in 1609 as one in which there was "no man but had an enemy within three miles, and so the country became frontier all over." What "frontier" meant is well defined by an Italian of this time as country to which a few could do no harm and in which many could not live. The prosperity of the Empire while this was the state of France has been already outlined; what it became, as a result of the civil war, while France was becoming the best organised and most civilised country in Europe, may be guessed from Reresby's description of the district which in 1600 had been the most comfortable in Christendom, that between Augsburg and Frankfurt; villages and towns uninhabited, much ground untilled, no meat to be had, no sheets, sometimes no beds; for drink, milk and water, little wine and that sour and very dear; people so boorish as to resemble beasts. Significant, too, is it that while Sir Philip Sidney, defining the qualities of the dominions of Europe for his brother, writes, "Germany doth excel in good laws and well administering of justice," and while all subsequent travellers for forty years confirm this, a German, Zeiler, compiled his guide to Spain shortly before the date when the correspondent just quoted wrote his letter, and in this guide, in maintaining the claims of Spain on the attention of the student, puts among the characteristics in which Spain excels the rest of Europe, the inflexibility of justice there.

Yet civil war was less detrimental to touring than international war, inasmuch as no nation was barred the country for the time being. Besides, fewer mercenaries were employed. Now, however bad the native soldier may have been, — and how bad that was may be judged from Shakespeare's picture of him in "Henry V" (Act iii, sc. 2), — mercenaries were far worse, seeing that they behaved in the country they were defending as the others did only in that which they attacked. Sastrow followed in the wake of the mercenaries whom Charles V imported; wherever they had passed the way was

strewn with corpses. In one house he found the
body of a man who had been suspended by the
genitals, a usual custom, while they tortured him
to make him reveal his valuables, and released by
a sword-stroke, not on the cord he hung by, but
"flush with the abdomen." From Bamberg they
carried off four hundred women as far as Nuremberg, while Hungarians cut off the feet and hands
of children and stuck them in their hats instead
of feathers. And it is perhaps worth while quoting the effect on Sastrow himself. On his horse
being stolen, he "chose the best nag at hand";
and finding a gentleman's house temporarily
abandoned, he and his companions stole wholesale, not only to satisfy present wants, but also in
order to realise money later.

The effect of all this so far as it concerned tourists may be exemplified by the state of the highroad between Danzig and Hamburg, along which,
in 1600, the only corpses in evidence were those
of criminals. By 1652, in one day's journey, a
traveller [29] could count thirty-four piles of faggots,
each pile marking the spot where a wayfarer had
been murdered. Each passer-by was expected to
add a faggot. Another result was that soldiers
continued to exercise during peace the habits
they had contracted in war. When Lady Fanshawe passed through Abbeville in 1659, the
governor warned her against local robbers, advising an escort of garrison soldiers at a pistole

[£3, 6s. 8d.] each. She engaged ten, and met a band of fifty 'robbers.' The ten parleyed with the fifty, and the fifty retired; they, too, were soldiers of the garrison.

Between the soldier and the robber, in fact, the difference was merely that of official, and unofficial, employment. It was in the latter capacity, of course, that they oftenest had dealings with the tourist; or were supposed to do so. One cannot help being struck by the idea that these travellers were far more frightened than hurt, so far as robbery was concerned. A lady, for instance, between Turin and Genoa, saw the road stained with blood where wayfarers had lately been robbed and murdered, yet passed in safety.[30] One traveller, it is true, was stopped four times between St. Malo and Havre, but more normal experiences were those of Moryson, who suffered so but once in more than four years' travel, and of Hentzner, who encountered robbers once in three years and then escaped. He had warning and hired an escort; but it has to be noted that this escort, for one day, cost more than fifty crowns [£90]. Very similar was the experience of the Venetian ambassador Lippomano on his way to Paris in 1577.[31] A rumour got about that he was conveying a loan of eight hundred thousand francs to the French government, and a Venetian ambassador was easy to get information about because of the red trappings of his mules. He was warned, and so were the towns on the route; with the result that his own company were refused admission on suspicion that they were the highwaymen in disguise; and watched, as they passed, by garrisons on the walls. For six days they marched in continual fear; swords drawn, arquebus-matches lighted. Once they thought the "volori" really were upon them, but out of the cloud of dust galloped nothing but the escort from Troyes to relieve the escort from Bar-sur-Seine. And in the end they were fleeced by none but the escorts themselves.

These escorts were part of the life of the time; important towns kept them as a matter of course, in default of a system of country-police such as existed in Spain, the "Santa Hermandad," who first suppressed the thieves and then took over, and extended, their business. In France, however, towards the end of this period, the highways began to be patrolled regularly by police, in couples, none but whom might carry firearms. Yet this arrangement was in force when of the travellers who followed just behind Evelyn on the Paris-Orleans road, four were killed. And within a few years of this some one tells us how he heard cries issuing from the inside of a dead horse, cut open by robbers in order to give themselves more time to escape by fastening their victim inside it, a dirty trick, literally, for he was pulled out in as untidy a state as it was possible for a stark-naked man to be.

To meet, when alone, with two ruffians, to pretend, being on foot and decidedly shabby, to be
a beggar; and to pass them thus, not only without loss, but with 1s. 2d. towards his next meal
— such was the experience of one Englishman
abroad. But what could he have done had the
beasts been four-legged ones? Here was another
risk to run; and, perhaps, to pay for. There were
plenty to meet. It is not surprising to read of
them breaking into stables and ransacking ceme-
teries in Muscovy, where, by the way, protection against them was supposed to be secured
by the noise of a big stick dragging at the back
of the sledge by a rope; but things were little
better near Paris. Readers of Rabelais may recollect a second narrow escape that befell the six pilgrims whom Gargantua ate in a salad in consequence of their hiding among the lettuces to avoid
being eaten by him as meat. After their miraculous escape out of his mouth, they barely saved
themselves from falling into a snare for wolves. It
was no exaggeration to write so about Touraine;
in the winter of 1653 a pack entered Blois and
ate a child. And just before Evelyn visited Fontainebleau, "a lynx or ounce" had killed some
one passing thither by the highroad from Paris.
The country between Geneva and Lyons, again,
writes one who passed through it, was "mainly
inhabited by wolves and bears."

But we have not finished with people. Slavery

had to be reckoned with, and therefore ransoms.
More than one refers to the "malcontents" of
the Low Countries, unpaid Spanish garrison-
soldiers who wandered about on the look-out for
Englishmen in particular, and esteeming a younger
brother's ransom at twenty thousand crowns of
the sun [£35,000], says Wotton. But the risk of
capture, in the ordinary way, was confined to Mohammedan territory and the neighbouring sea-
shores, with Algiers as headquarters. Many men
who were slaves there at this period have left record of their adventures; of whom Gramaye is perhaps the best to quote from, inasmuch as no one
was a more acute, thorough, and trustworthy observer. He lived at Algiers in 1619, one of twenty
thousand Christian slaves. According to the statistics he gives of the previous twelve years, two
hundred and fifty-one ships had brought in twelve
thousand, two hundred and forty prisoners, of
whom eight hundred and fifty-seven Germans had
apostatised, three hundred English, one hundred
and thirty-eight from Hamburg, "Danes and
Easterlings" one hundred and sixty; Poles, Hungarians, and Muscovites two hundred and fifty,
Low Countrymen one hundred and thirty; besides French and others. Fewest renegades came
from Spain and Italy, because in those two countries alone were permanent systematic collectors
of money for ransoms; the two orders of the Trinity and of Our Lady of Pity paid out sixty-three

thousand ducats [over £70,000], in this way yearly, a drain of gold which does not seem to have been taken into account by economists, although not counteracted, but on the contrary increased, by trade transactions with Mohammedan centres like Constantinople and Aleppo, and added to by all the privately paid ransoms. Sir Anthony Sherley ransomed two Portuguese gentlemen for ten thousand pounds, who had been enslaved sixteen years, and for one of whom three ransoms had been sent, each of which had been captured by pirates. The statement already made about all forms of life insurance being censured as gambling must be modified in connection with slavery, for both the law and public opinion approved of a man paying premiums to assure a ransom being paid, and that promptly, in the event of his capture; and the system seems to have been in frequent use,[32] although it must be admitted that not one of these travellers seems so much as aware of its existence.

The expenses of protection against pirates may be imagined from the estimate for the outfit of the galley intended to carry the Provençal deputation to Constantinople in 1585, referred to earlier. The galley-slaves numbered two hundred; the deputation fifty. Sixty soldiers were to be taken for defence, whose wages for the eight months were to be nineteen hundred and twenty crowns of the sun; in addition to which was their keep, nine thousand and forty crowns, and arms and

gunpowder, five hundred crowns, the total equalling about twenty-seven thousand pounds of our
money.

Of Turkey Sir Henry Blount says that in assur-
ing himself against loss of liberty lay "the most expense and trouble of my voyage." And Blount's
opinion is the better worth having, seeing that
he would have been the last to fail in the exercise
of courtesy and tact, the absence of which is the
commonest cause of martyrdom. Several times
he had to use his knife to avoid being pushed into
a house, and hardly a day passed without his Janizary being offered a price for him. His defences
against it in general were to cultivate or buy
friends and to make a practice of pretending he
had no friends and little money, and that all that
remained to him was wagered against his return,
because enslavement would be more in hope of
ransom than service.

The enslavement of the Jerusalem pilgrim
seems to have been comparatively rare before the
end of the sixteenth century; yet two of the most
striking narratives belong to the year 1565. The
first adventure, however, happened during an
excursion to Jordan without escort, a risk that
none dreamt of running later. A German, named
Fürer, set out in February, with a friend, a eunuch-
interpreter, and a monk-guide. Sitting down to
a meal on the way back, four Arabs appeared,
whom they treated as guests; yet, the meal over,

the Arabs enquired whether their hosts had any money or garments worth stealing. Doubting their negatives, they undressed them, and beneath the monkish outer-garment which each one was wearing discovered on the two travellers underclothing which suggested riches. The Arabs forthwith led all four away into the desert to sell them at Medina, but were induced before long to despatch the monk with two of themselves to the nearest monastery, that of S. Saba, some hours' journey from Jerusalem, for ransom. The remaining three Franks, unarmed, chose their time to attack the two armed Arabs, and after a desperate fight and a fearful journey, wounded, parched, and famished, Fürer climbed up a rope-ladder into the monastery through one of the back-windows, while the two other Arabs were being kept waiting in the front.

The other tale concerns sixty-two pilgrims who sailed from Jaffa in the August of that same year.[33] On October 16 they were shipwrecked off the coast of Asia Minor, one being drowned. On landing six were killed, the rest taken prisoners, a proportion of whom go to Rhodes. These are urged to apostatise — in vain. They offer ransoms; Frau Johanna of Antwerp three hundred ducats [£540], Pastor Peter Villingen three hundred and twelve kronen [which may mean anything from £200 to £800; probably the former]: the total came to three thousand, two hundred and sixty kronen. This does not seem enough to their owners; the Venetian and some sailors get free somehow; the others are sent to the galleys. During 1566 Frau Johanna and six others die. By May 1, 1568, seven more are dead; two have been redeemed for six hundred kronen; two others for four hundred and eighty kronen. Soon after, an Italian was ransomed by the Venetian "bailo." This is all that is known of the sixty-two.

Another risk that was greater on the Jerusalem journey was that of disease, or enfeeblement through hardship. The state of things normal in the Church of the Holy Sepulchre must alone have told on health; one German on his return to Jaffa counted two hundred and thirty lice in his clothes. But, throughout, disease lay in wait for all in a deadlier form than any we meet with. Just as instead of "nerves" they suffered from "inflammation of the conscience," so, instead of influenza, they had plague, infectious in the highest degree and fatal in a few days, or quicker. In Constantinople it was looked on as inevitable and raged unhindered. Yet, says Blount, the Turks' carelessness was less of a hindrance to trade than the Christians' precautions. In Venice, over the doors of the inn-bedrooms was written "Ricordati della bolletta" — "Remember your bill of health." This "bolletta," or "bolletina," also known as "fede" or "patente," had to be obtained, before entering Venice, from the "com-

missari" or "soprastanti della sanità," certify-
ing freedom from plague; failing which, or if a
"fede" obtained elsewhere was not "clean," *i. e.*
not bearing the official counter-signatures guar-
anteeing freedom from plague at the last stopping-
places, the new-comer had to "far la contumacia,"
go into quarantine for forty days. The disinfect-
ants consisted of sun, air, and vinegar, and the
confinement, if not on board ship, was in a spot
chosen for its pleasant healthiness, under shelter
which was clean, roomy, and well furnished, with
a broad verandah on which one's belongings were
to be laid out. This practice was constant at
Venice, where ships were always arriving from
plague-stricken ports; in the rest of Italy it was
frequent but intermittent. Outside Italy a
plague-scare occurred more rarely. When it did
the healthy but tired wayfarers might find themselves shut out of the town where they looked to
find food and rest; perhaps would find the highway itself barricaded [34] by the authorities of a
town which was plague-free and determined to
remain so, and forced to ride all night by dark
and dangerous by-ways [35] — unless they pretended
to be an ambassador and his retinue, as some
English merchants once did.

Too much stress must not be laid on the troubles
of a stranger who fell ill of a less deadly illness.
Perhaps, even, a German with the toothache
might still have the same experience in Spain as

did a countryman of his three hundred years ago. Having tried a cupping-glass himself in vain, he went to the local barber-surgeon; the latter dug the tooth out with a bread-knife! Yet in hospitals a change for the better can be easily proved. The chief hospital at Paris, the Hôtel-Dieu, was visited by an Italian [36] in the middle of the seventeenth century. Three or four men lay in each bed, or two women; and the stench was terrible, even to a seventeenth-century nose. At the galley-slaves' hospital at Marseilles, a boy went in front of visitors with a "pan of perfume." Still more to the point, regarding this particular period, was the predicament of a man at the point of death in a district with a different theological stamp from his own, say, a Protestant in a Roman Catholic country. He would then have the choice of accepting the sacrament in the locally orthodox form or confessing himself a Protestant. In the latter case the priest might cut the heretic off from the help, not only of the doctor, but of the cook also, and if he recovered in spite of this, the Inquisition might be awaiting him. And yet a man of average morality would be far less of an adiaphorist in the sixteenth century than to-day. Some Protestants at Venice resigned themselves at death to the only cemetery-burial — that with Roman Catholic rites; but most chose to be buried at sea off Malamocco, trusting in the phrase, "And the sea shall give up its dead."

As to the "sudden death" of which the Litany speaks, if one regards direct evidence only, there may well be a tendency to think the risk of it somewhat exaggerated, but the balance will recover itself if, to the number of travellers who have left us record of their doings, is added that of the dead men who would have told tales if they could. Mile after mile of loneliest road had to be slowly traversed, many a mile through forest where now is open ground, at a time when existed far less force in conventions to restrain those, perhaps even more numerous then than now, like the murderers of Banquo: —

> . . . I am one
> Whom the vile blows and buffets of the world
> Have so incensed that I am reckless what
> I do to spite the world.

> . . . And I another
> So weary with disasters, tugged with fortune
> That I would set my life on any chance
> To mend it or to be rid on't.

In the towns, the narrow dark streets gave the assassin his opportunity, whether a mistaken one or not. Readers of Cellini's autobiography will recall his remark that he trained himself to turn corners wide and may have noted it as merely characteristic; but before Cellini's book was in print, we find the French tourist, Payen of Meaux, writing of the Venetians, "Quand ils marchent la nuit, ils ne tournent jamais court pour entrer dans une Rue; mais ils tiennent le milieu, afin d'éviter la rencontre de ceux qui voudroient les attendre."

Supposing, however, that a foreigner died in peace, what happened to the money and chattels with him at the moment? According to Zeiler, in Aragon the practice was to notify the authorities at his native place and hold the goods at the disposal of the legal heirs for a year, after which limit unclaimed property was handed to the Brotherhood of Our Lady of Pity to be employed in the redemption of captives. In Rome the custom was for the servant to take the dead master's clothes. In France the State took absolutely everything by the "droit d'aubaine," which was the law wherever feudalism had established itself, though sometimes in abeyance; in Poland it seems to have been completely so.[37] The strictness, on the contrary, with which it was enforced in France is well illustrated by the fate of the library of Sir Kenelm Digby, who died at Paris in 1665. It was forfeited to Louis XIV by the "droit d'aubaine"; he gave it away; the new owner sold it to a relative of the late owner for ten thousand crowns.

This right, based as it was on the same "right to pillage" under which the Jews suffered in the Middle Ages,[38] brings out very clearly one fact which was always liable to affect a traveller's

finances, namely, that in so far as he was a traveller, he had no legal privileges. Two Dutch
gentlemen,[39] for instance, were at Paris at a
time when war between Holland and France suddenly became imminent. They found the financial
agents forbidden to pay them on bills of exchange
or letters of credit, and their goods were temporarily confiscated. It was the ordinary procedure
of the time. Here again is obvious the advantage
of going in the train of an ambassador; the latter's
rights were the fullest protection that an alien
could acquire, except mercantile ones at their
best. Yet even these ambassadorial rights lacked
so much of the fullness and the clearness that
they possess to-day that they were not put forward in a modern form, not even in theory, until
the treatise of Grotius on the subject published
in 1625.[40]

These Dutch gentlemen just mentioned found
themselves in difficulties on their arrival in Paris
in another way also. They had introductions to
good society; fashions had changed while they
were en route; they must stay in their lodgings
till the tailor had done his worst. Even if they
had been going to Jerusalem they would still have
felt the relationship between cost and clothes,
a relationship decidedly closer then than at present. Only in going to Jerusalem it took this form,
that the shabbier you went the less the journey
cost. As to kind, preferably such as were worn

by Greeks, friars, merchants, or Syrian Christians.
The pilgrim's ordinary dress, described in one of
those picturesque snatches of verse with which
Shakespeare's contemporary, Robert Greene,
lightened his tales, —

> Down the valley 'gan he track
> Bag and bottle at his back.
> In a surcoat all of grey,
> Such wear palmers on the way
> When with scrip and staff they see
> Jesus' grave on Calvary, —

was no protection against suspicion of riches.
Yet it was supposed to lessen the risk of being
kidnapped into slavery at Algiers on the road to
Montserrat if one carried the white pilgrim's
staff.

Crossing the Alps, for a northerner who did not
wish to be conspicuously alien, meant a complete
change into black silk; for the brilliant attire
which we see in productions of "Romeo and
Juliet" reflects Elizabethan England, not Italy.
Italy manufactured those multi-coloured materials, it is true, but for export or official use only,
except for the ash colour that betokened a vow
not perfected.

Typical minor incidents were the purchasing
of a new handkerchief in Germany, of light-
coloured silk, and, as to size, somewhat resembling
a saddle-cloth, with initials of some motto worked
in a corner thereof, say D. H. I. M. T. ("Der Herr

ist Mein Trost") or W. H. I. B. ("Wie heilig ist Bruderschaft"), and secondly, the story of a sugar-loaf hat. An Italian priest wore it in Italy — but not in France. Before leaving Lyons he had grown tired of a crowd of children following him about. So far from being able to sell it, it was impossible to find any one who would take it as a gift until he met a man whose business was partly selling a powder which killed mice. The rest of his business was the profession of town-fool. That being so, he could accept the hat; he cut it into the shape of an imperial crown and gave himself out as the Emperor of the Moluccas.

A complete change into French clothes cost this priest two pistoles [£8], and he adds the detail that nowhere was waterproof material to be bought. The waxed cloth which was sold as such cracked wherever it had been folded.

On occasion, too, changes of clothes might be a legal obligation. The sumptuary laws might step in and forbid the new-comer to wear what was perhaps his one respectable garment. Or again, in Muscovy, foreigners used to dress as natives to avoid the jeers of the crowd; but at some date early in the seventeenth century the Patriarch noticed Germans behaving irreverently at a festival and complained that foreigners ought not to seem included in the benediction that was given to the faithful. Foreigners were therefore ordered to revert to their national dress, which produced most ludicrous results until the tailors could finish new garments; inasmuch as the merchants had to fall back on those that had belonged to their predecessors, leaving sometimes a whole generation between the fashions of their upper and nether garments.

All these things might fall on the tourist: each one cost money; some one, at least, of them he would hardly escape. One more source of possible loss existed, one that he was certain to have to face — the money itself. The variety of coins was just as great as the variety of clothes, though with this difference that the clothes were as local as the coins were international — just the opposite of the case to-day. This is not equally true, of course, of all denominations, and the majority may not have circulated so freely as in preceding centuries, but the higher ones seem to have passed about from hand to hand with little more hesitation than Australian sovereigns do in England. When exceptions occurred, they generally had political causes: French gold, for example, being more willingly taken by the Swiss than other foreign gold because they had become so used to it in the course of serving as French mercenaries.

Of the uncertainties of the tourist, however, in relation to coins, that caused by their international character would be the first to disappear. There remained a trinity of diversities to bewilder

him permanently and to deliver him over, de-
fenceless, to the dishonest: diversity of value,
diversity of kind, diversity of inscription.

To take the last first; it might seem that absence was a more appropriate term than diversity,
seeing that the nominal value of a coin in circu-
lation about 1600 was only in the smallest per-
centage of cases stated on its face; and when
one comes to think of it, it is only the tourist
who ever reads a coin for business purposes.
Where the diversity comes in lies in the fact
of certain names becoming popular, such as
"paolo" in Italy, which meant that many different types would be struck, all "paoli" but none
alike. As to variations in value these may be
illustrated from the Venetian zecchino, the Hun-
garian ducat, the sultanon of Constantinople and
the sheriff of Cairo. All of these are reckoned as
equal in one year or other between 1592 and 1620
by one or other trustworthy traveller, yet the
differences of value of one coin or other of the
four vary from 6s. 8d. to 9s.; and this was not a
steady rise. In fact, the difference between the 1592
and 1620 valuations is but fourpence. Moreover,
the settlement of values was far less a commercial
affair merely than it has become; governments
were forever tinkering at it by means of proclamations, all telling against the tourist, since their
object was to attract, or to retain, bullion, which
either depreciated the value of the coin he wished

to change or appreciated that of the coin he had to acquire. Lady Fanshawe mentions a proclamation of October 14, 1664, at Madrid which cost her husband, ambassador there, eight hundred pounds. Since then, paper money has come to absorb all the political dishonesty that used to be exercised on coins, and the far less abrupt modern methods minimise the loss to the tourist. The French government went bankrupt fifty-six times during the seventeenth and eighteenth centuries.[41]

As to the other diversity, that of kind, Lauder saw a proclamation which assessed the values of five hundred coins then current in France.

The whole of the above refers mainly to gold and the higher denominations of silver. Yet these more important coins were a simple matter compared with small change, especially in Italy; for when the tourist had been confronted with soldi, grossi, giuli, paoli, reali, quattrini, susine, denari, cavallotti, cavallucci, carlini, bagatini, bolignei, baocchi, baelli, etc., he could not but feel relieved when, crossing the Alps, he had only to face Swiss plapparts and finfers and the German batz, kreutzer, stiver, copstück, sesling, pfennig, and not many more. The grosch perhaps ought to be mentioned as well if only for the fact that Taylor, the "water-poet," when at Hamburg, noticed that among twenty-three groschen he had in his pocket there were thirteen varieties, owing to the number of local mints. He valued all these at twopence each, but as a matter of fact groschen varied so greatly that to give one away might be either extravagance or an insult. There were, of course, many multiples of these denominations, and besides coins, tokens innumerable, all having but this in common that when one had gone a few miles further they would not be taken in payment. They might be made of base metal, like that of the famous "Mermaid" tavern which is preserved at the "birthplace" at Stratford-on-Avon, or of leather, or almost anything else solid.

In Muscovy were no native coins but silver, and those so small that the Muscovites used to keep dozens in their mouths because they slipped through their fingers — and that without incommoding their speech. In Spain,[42] so far as there was any standard, it was the Castilian real, which you might exchange for thirty-four Castilian maravedis, forty Portuguese rais, thirty-six Valencian dineros, twenty-four Aragonese, and thirty-eight Catalonian dineros. But these Portuguese coins would not be taken in Castile, nor the Castilian in Valencia, nor Valencian anywhere out of Valencia. Along the chief merchants' road in Spain, from Barcelona, you might go one hundred miles, as far as Lerida, and find every place with a different minor coinage, current there only, and in Barcelona one was especially liable to receive coins which no one, not even in Barcelona, would accept.

On the Jerusalem journey the higher payments were reckoned in foreign money usually, the Italian gold zecchini and silver piastri most frequently; smaller ones in brass meidines of Tripoli or of Cairo, equal to about a penny farthing and twopence respectively, or in aspers, about three farthings.

Just as, further, the tourist could examine a coin without being able to find out its nominal value, could ascertain the latter and still be ignorant of its real value, so, too, he was continually having to pay reckonings in coins which did not exist. The Venetian and Spanish ducat, the German gulden, the French livre tournois, the Muscovite rouble, and, later, their altine also, were coins of account only. All these coins were as commonly used in daily business in their own localities as guineas are in English charities; and the ducat and the gulden far outside them. In the seventeenth century the Spanish pistole was actual coin in its own country and coin of account in France; board and lodging on "pension" terms would be reckoned in pistoles in Paris. In fact, the French equivalent for "rolling in riches," "cousu de pistoles," is equally evidence of the international character of seventeenth-century gold and of the method of carrying it.

The tourist in 1600 has done his touring. His money is spent; his pleasure is buried; his wisdom

gathered; and the fruit is ours. And now; was the
pleasure worth the money? was the wisdom worth
the gathering?

The answer is, most emphatically, Yes! — Yes
for them, and Yes for us. But as to the latter
question there were two answers then, and the
subject has suggestions beyond those that have
come up so far. Let us look at this adverse opinion, and one or two of the suggestions.

During the sixteenth century it became a convention to abuse travel, especially travel in Italy;
a convention which may have been more fruitful
in England than elsewhere, but certainly was not
so to the exclusive extent which modern books in
English seem to imply. The difficulty would be
to find a nation whose literature at this time does
not contain examples of it; even in Poland, where
of all places travel was most taken for granted,
this topic was one of the first to be dealt with
when the vernacular was turned to literary account, namely, in the satires of Kochanowski.
When examined, these invectives turn out to have
won more attention than they are entitled to,
written as they generally are, especially in England, by the class whose medium is nowadays the
half-penny paper or the 'religious' novel. We find
among their authors all the familiar figures, from
the hack-journalist who parades a belated morality for the sake of his stomach down to the bishop
to whom the subject, when worn rather thin, is

revealed as a brand-new dummy-sin. It is curious that this very bishop, Joseph Hall, should in describing his own journeys, unconsciously provide the most clear-cut sketch of how not to travel that has, perhaps, ever been written.[43] If, among these types, we miss the retired colonel, we must remember that the title was so recently invented, the times so bloody, that all the colonels were probably either fighting or dead. At any rate, the interest of this type of pamphlet belongs rather to the history of publishing than to that of travel, as dating the time when publishers first discovered what a paying public can be created among the lower levels of Puritanism. The proportion of fact that gave them a starting-point may best be put in perspective by pointing out the parallel that exists between travel in Italy three hundred years ago and modern motoring. Nobody who could afford it went without; everybody who could not afford it abused everybody who did; it killed some, maimed others, benefited most, and brightened the life of many a poor rich man who otherwise would have departed this life little better off mentally than his own cows. These pamphleteers were committing the fundamental error of allowing their attention to be absorbed by the seven eighths of foolishness that characterises everything human instead of concentrating it on the other eighth which provides the justification as well as the driving-force. For a sober, all-round, view of the question as it appeared to a man who was both man of the world and scholar, one cannot do better than turn to a letter written by Estienne Pasquier, a letter of introduction for a son of Turnebus. "Comme il a l'esprit beau, aussi lui est-il tombé en teste, ce qui tombe ordinairement aux âmes les plus généreuses, de vouloir voyager pour le faire sage. . . . S'il m'en croit, il se contentera de voir l'Italie en passant; car ce que Pyrrhus Neoptolemus disoit de la Philosophie, qu'il falloit philosopher, mais sobrement, je le dy du voyage d'Italie, à tous nos jeunes François qui s'y acheminent par une convoitise de voir."[44]

Yet there is one defect of their travels which necessarily escaped notice at the time but cannot fail to strike any one now, which is, how much they passed by without a glance. It is commonly thought that the contrast of travel in days gone by with that of the later times is one of leisureliness as against universal effort to go "faster, farther, and higher" than one's neighbour. But the truth is that in what essentially characterises leisureliness in travelling, the leaving time and energy free for enjoying and studying places on the road, and still more, off it, they were more wanting than we. They went the greatest pace they could; where they stopped at the night they left at dawn; and overnight they had been too tired to explore amid the filth, the dangers, the darkness, the inextricable confusion, of a sixteenth-

century town or hamlet. Yet if you call to mind
the towns seen in passing which you recollect most
vividly, most will probably be those in which your
first walks happened after dark. And is there any
Gothic cathedral, however grand, whose outside
is not commonplace by day compared to its glory
by night?

Moreover, the dearth of information narrowed
not their opportunities merely, but their interests
likewise. Carnac and Stonehenge were no doubt
a long way out of their way, but the dolmen of
Bagneux was no more than three-quarters of a
mile from Saumur, where many of them stayed
for weeks, or even months. Yet not a single one,
apparently, went to see it. As for the opportunities, not only was Pompeii still buried for them,
but Rome itself was, as Montaigne says, not so
much ruins as a sepulchre of ruins. When, again,
some one says of Lyons that the houses are fine
but the streets so ill-smelling and dirty that one
cannot stop to admire them, it may remind us
that much that was nominally visible was practically invisible; whether through being what was,
to them, a considerable distance off their routes,
like Brou or Laon, or, as with most cathedrals,
through houses being built up against them.
Similarly, the Roman amphitheatre at Nîmes is a
case in point; houses having been erected inside
it so freely that in 1682 five hundred men capable
of bearing arms were supposed to be dwelling

there.[45] And along with these conditions of living went ideas to correspond; the total effect being half-prohibitive of the occupations of the artist, the historian, and the archæologist, and this at a period when a larger proportion of the greatest buildings of Europe coexisted than at any other period. In fact, so far as the Loire châteaux are concerned, it is clear that the modern tourist sees far more of some of the finest Renascence work than did its contemporaries, who were restricted here to a visit to Chambord and a glimpse of the outsides of Blois and Amboise.

But after all deductions of this kind have been granted, they may well reply that their concern was not so much with that part of the present which we term the past, but with that which we term the future, their individual futures, in particular; and that their object was achieved; adding, moreover, that travel under these conditions was certainly superior to travel of the twentieth century, considered as a form of education in the wider sense of the word. For not only was it obligatory to share the life of the country and its language to an extent which is optional now, but a traveller was continually being thrown on his own resources and presence of mind in matters which concerned his self-respect, his health, and his safety, whereas now everything is merely a matter of cash.

Turning to the benefit to us in day-by-day

matters accruing from their experience abroad, so many instances have already shown themselves that the burden of proof falls on the other side; whether, that is, any contemporary effort worth making, any contemporary achievement to which we are indebted, has not been in some degree fashioned and vitalized by influences due to travel.[46] If one further instance, typical of much else, is to be chosen, it may be pointed out how almost everything that contributes to the material attractions of Dublin is due to those who, in exile on the Continent, saw the gain that lay in planning a city finely. Further still, their knowledge of languages, acquired at a time when vernaculars were coming into their own, resulted in an infusion into each vernacular of the additions it needed to assimilate to enable it to fulfil its potentialities for the purposes both of every-day life and of life at its best. It is curious and significant that the Pole who has just been quoted as an opponent of travel, Kochanowski, learnt the value and, one might even say, the possibility, of using the vernacular as a medium of literature from associating with members of the "Pléiade" in France.

Far above these and the rest; far outweighing, too, all imaginable drawbacks, was the value of the central idea, that of taking those who were to enjoy the widest opportunities of usefulness and influence, and bringing them, when their conscious receptivity was at its highest, into personal contact with the whole of that world in which, for which, and with which, their lives were to be spent. That was its value at that time. But it had a future as well as a present value, inasmuch as the results of the system were cumulative, more especially in so far as it served the purpose of bringing these younger men into touch with the best teachers and those older men of the finest achievements, to gain acquaintance with whom was always insisted on as an object second to none in importance. As Bacon said, these travellers were "Merchants of Light." They contributed a definite share towards strengthening and widening what is the only effective agency of real advance in civilisation, "that better world of men," of which the contemporary poet Daniel was reminded by the "Essays" of Montaigne.

> . . . That better world of men,
> Whose spirits are of one community,
> Whom neither oceans, deserts, rocks nor sands
> Can keep from th' intertraffic of the mind.

SPECIAL REFERENCES

CHAPTER I

SOME OF THE TOURISTS

1. Purchas, viii, 258.
2. A. Schaube: "Zur Entwicklungsgeschichte der Ständigen Gesandtschaften," in vol. 10 of *Mittheilungen des Instituts für oesterreichische Geschichtsforschung*, 1889. What follows is mainly from "Les Commencements de la Diplomatie," three articles by Ernest Nys in *Revue de Droit International*, vols. 15 and 16, 1883–84. Cf. also V. E. Hrabar's *De Legatis et Legationibus*, 1906, a collection of treatises on the subject up to 1625, some unpublished ones printed in full, with summaries of those better known.
3. Harleian MS. 3822, fol. 599. And *Viaggi* of Gian Vincenzo Imperiale, p. 149, vol. 29 of Atti della Società Ligure di Storia Patria, 1898.
4. *Cf.* Antonio de Beatis, pp. 156, 157.
5. George Chapman, *Tears of Peace*.
6. *Cf.* especially the beginning of Jacopo Soranzo's narrative in Albéri's *Relazioni Venete*, Series III, ii, 212.
7. *Life and Letters*, i, 319.
8. *First Fruits*, p. 18.
9. *Calendars of State Papers*, Ven., v, 109 and 382.
10. Hist. MSS. Com., 1899, vol. 46 (Duke of Buccleugh's *Winwood Papers*, i), 120, 121.
11. Einstein, p. 380.
12. *Operette*, ii, 24.
13. Hantzsch, *Deutsche Reisende*, p. 2.
14. *Cf.* Stählin's *Sir Francis Walsingham und seine Zeit*, i, 79–84.

CHAPTER II

GUIDE-BOOKS AND GUIDES

1. See Faunt's "Discourses touching the office of Principal Secretary of State," in *Eng. Hist. Rev.*, July, 1905.
2. Falkiner, p. 117.
3. Röhricht, "Bibliotheca geographica Palaestinæ," 118. In the London Library is a copy of an edition printed at Ronciglione, 1615, which seems to have escaped the notice of all bibliographers.

4. Bargrave. See under Bodleian MSS. in Bibliography (Rawlinson, C. 799).

5. Quoted by Einstein, p. 101.

6. Printed by Falkiner. See Bibliography.

7. See Cal. S. P. Ven., vol. ii (under "Mole," in the index).

8. Grose and Astle's *Antiquarian Repertory*, 1805, iv, 374–380.

CHAPTER III

ON THE WATER

1. M. Ritter, *Die Union und Heinrich IV*, Munich, 1874, p. 87.

2. Hatfield MSS., ix, 127 (Hist. MSS. Com.).

3. Birch, *Court and Times of James I*, i, 139.

4. See contemporary drawing to scale, reproduced in vol. 5 of Hakluyt's *Voyages*.

5. Hans von Morgenthal (1476) in Röhricht, pp. 14–15.

6. Zuallardo's *Il Devotissimo Viaggio di Gierusalemme*, Rome, 1595, p. 18.

7. Sir Henry Ellis, *Original Letters*, Series III, ii, 277-293.

8. Fahie, *Life of Galileo*, pp. 173–177.

9. Hatfield MSS., x, 43.

10. Harris, *Navigantium . . . Bibliotheca*, ii, 461.

11. W. F. Smith's translation, to which, with Heulhard's *Rabelais, ses voyages en Italie*, 1891, I am indebted for all references to Rabelais.

12. Brit. Mus. MS. Lansdown, 720.

13. R. Symonds (Brit. Mus. MS. Harleian, 943).

14. C. A. J. Skeel, *Travels in the First Century after Christ*, p. 114.

15. Brit. Mus. MS. Lansdown, 720, and Villamont's *Voyages* give more details than any others concerning Italian waterways; but *cf.* Tasso's letter to Ercole de' Contrari comparing France and Italy. All these are ignored by

16. Sir E. Sullivan in *The Nineteenth Century*, August, 1908.

CHAPTER IV

CHRISTIAN EUROPE

Part I — European Europe

1. J. N. Figgis, *From Gerson to Grotius*, 1907, p. 241.

2. Brit. Mus. MS. Harleian, 943, fol. 33.

3. W. H. Woodward, *Studies in Education, passim,* especially p. 172.

4. *Gazette des Beaux Arts,* IIe période, v, 198.

5. Smith's *Wotton,* i, 355, note.

6. His narrative is in vol. 7 of Churchill's *Voyages.*

7. Howell, *Epistolæ Ho-Elianæ,* 1619.

8. Barozzi and Berchet, *Relazioni (Inghilterra),* pp. 34, 35, and 98.

9. Cal. S. P. Ven., xiii, 40, 41.

10. *Harleian Voyages,* i, 1781.

11. Hatfield MSS., v, 462.

12. Barozzi, *op. cit.,* p. 27.

13. Bodleian MS., Rawlinson, C. 799.

14. The following details are taken mainly from T. A. Fischer's *Scots in East and West Prussia* and *Scots in Germany;* the Scottish Historical Society have further information in preparation. For Scots abroad generally, *cf.* W. K. Leask's *Musa Latina Aberdonensis,* Aberdeen University, 1910.

15. Bodl. MS., Rawlinson, C. 799.

16. "La Cena de le Cenere," Dialogo Secondo.

17. De Villers. See Bibliography under "Aarssen."

Part II — The Unvisited North

1. Translated speech to the "Collegio" at Venice, Cal. S. P. Ven., x, 346.

2. Payen of Meaux.

3. Churchill's *Voyages,* iv, 822.

4. Barberini, in Adelung, i, 237.

5. Cf. Dr. Vladimir Milkowicz' *Eastern Europe* (vol. 5 of the translation of Helmolt's *History of the World*), pp. 524, 557, 572, and 610.

6. In Adelung, i, 435.

Part III — The Misunderstood West

1. *Britannia,* Holland's translation, 1610, p. 577.

2. In 1670. — Hakluyt Society, vol. 87, p. 111.

3. Harleian MS. 3822, fol. 604.

4. Erich Lassota; extract in Liske's *Viajes . . . por España* (*cf.* Bibliography under "Sobieski") from R. Schottin's *Tagebuch des Erich Lassota von Steblau* (1573–94), Halle, 1866.

5. Sobieski.
6. Good's account, appended to Camden's description of Ireland (Holland's translation, 1610, p. 142).
7. Chiericati.
8. O'Connor, *Elizabethan Ireland*, pp. 1–4.
9. *Acta SS.* March 17, p. 590.
10. Smith, *Camdeni . . . Epistolæ*, 1691, pp. 68, 69.
11. Cal. S. P. Irish, i, 439, and ii, liii-lv.
12. Jouvin de Rochefort (in Falkiner).

CHAPTER V

MOHAMMEDAN EUROPE

Part I — The Grand Signor

1. Parker Soc., xxvii, 522.
2. Albéri's " Relazioni," vi. 307.
3. Letters, Camd. Soc., p. 61.
4. Hist. MSS. Com., Ormonde Papers, New Series, i, 25.
5. *Works*, 1744, i, 8.
6. Wallington, *Historical Notices*, ii, 266.
7. *Mélanges Historiques*, Paris, 1886, v, 601–638.
8. Hist. MSS. Com., Hatfield MSS., xi, 172.
9. Serrano y Sanz, c. 8.
10. *Cambridge Modern History*, iii, 264.
11. Bodl. MS., Rawlinson, C. 799, fol. 12.
12. "The Three (Sherley) Brothers," 34, 35.

Part II — Jerusalem and the Way Thither

1. Röhricht, p. 314: "Mixolydian"=G Minor.
2. Hakluyt's *Voyages*, v, 204–207, and *Archives de la Soc. de l'histoire de Fribourg*, v, 235–236.
3. Zuallardo, *Il Devotissimo Viaggio di Gierusalemme* (ed. Rome, 1595, pp. 48–50), confirmed by the experiences of Kiechel (Hantzsch, 109, 110) in the same year.
4. Brit. Mus., Egerton MS., 311, fol. 142.
5. Quoted from Egerton MS., 2615, in preface to catalogue of Brit. Mus. Add. MSS.
6. *Nord und Süd*, October, 1887, 52, 53.
7. Printed by Carmoly.

CHAPTER VI

INNS

1. Brit. Mus. MS. Lansdown, 720.
2. Charles Ogier, *Ephemerides*, 1656, p. 327.
3. Quoted by Rye in his Preface.
4. Sir Richard Wynn.
5. Eva Scott, *Travels of the King*, p. 421.
6. Captain John Smith, *Accidence for Young Seamen*, 1626.
7. R. Payne, in *Tracts relating to Ireland*, published by the Irish Archæological Soc., vol. 1, part 2, p. 5.
8. Antonio de Beatis.
9. Brit. Mus. MS. Lansdown, 720.
10. Moryson, who, with Montaigne, contributes most to our knowledge of baths. For Aachen *cf.* Giustiniani and Sastrow.

CHAPTER VII

ON THE ROAD

1. Albéri, *Relazioni Venete*, ii, 3, 89.
2. Brit. Mus. MS. Lansdown, 720.
3. Bodl. MS., Rawlinson, C. 799.
4. Van Buchell, Paris ed., pp. 122, 133.
5. Brit. Mus. MS. Lansdown, 720, the account in which of Mt. Cenis is better than any, except perhaps Villamont's. Besides these two and those mentioned in the text, Montaigne, Hentzner, Locatelli, Reresby, Evelyn, and Lithgow give more details than others.
6. By Audebert.
7. W. A. B. Coolidge, *The Alps in Nature and History*, p. 205.
8. On August 5, Mr. Coolidge says; but Audebert says the festival of the Assumption (15th).
9. *Opere:* Rossini's edition, xiv, 337.
10. *Œuvres*, in *Bibliothèque Elzévirienne*, i, 393.
11. Preface to his *De Lacte et Operibus Lactariis*, 1543.
12. *Cf.* Osenbrüggen's "Die Entwicklungsgeschichte des Schweizreisens" in his *Wanderstudien aus der Schweiz* (Schaffhausen, 1867), i, 1–78; also G. Steinhausen's "Beiträge zur Geschichte des Reisens" printed in instalments in *Das Ausland*, 1893. For a very interesting survey of the subject over a wider

period (2000 years) see vol. I of Friedländer's "Sittengeschichte Roms."

13. *Carta del viage à Andalucia,* in *Obras,* Ibarra's edition, i, 328–331.

14. Peter Mundy, p. 144 and note; and Howell, *Epistolæ Ho-Elianæ,* Jacob's ed., i, 54.

CHAPTER VIII

THE PURSE

1. Whitehead, *Gaspard de Coligny,* p. 25.

2. Röhricht, p. 293. *Cf.* also Solerti's *Vita di Tasso,* i, 137, note 1, for Cardinal Luigi d'Este's expenses in France (1570).

3. H. Weber, *J. G. von Aschhausen, Fürstbischof,* Wurzburg, 1889, p. 30.

4. Smith, *Sir Henry Wotton,* i, 48 note.

5. In Bacon's advice to Villiers, Spedding's *Life,* vi, 43. *Cf.* "She [*i. e.* Queen Elizabeth] hath had many Secretaries that have been great Travaylers," from a dialogue by Sir John Davies, in Grosart's edition of his poems, I, 18.

6. Brit. Mus. MS. Lansdown, 720.

7. Both in Röhricht, p. 269.

8. Bodleian MS., Rawlinson, D. 122, at the end.

9. Röhricht, p. 293.

10. T. Tobler, *Denkblätter,* 1853, p. 569.

11. *Cf.* references collected in Variorum ed. of Shakespeare's *Tempest,* p. 180, and in Ben Jonson's *Works* (1875), ii, 70 ("Every Man out of his Humour"); also Davies' *Epigrams,* no. 42 (Grosart's ed., p. 343). Writers on insurance ignore all these references and usually content themselves with borrowing without acknowledgement what Hendriks wrote in his *Contributions to the History of Insurance* (pp. 35–37) as long ago as 1851. Hamon's *Histoire Générale de l'Assurance* (p. 107) and *Journal of the Institute of Actuaries,* vol. 25, p. 121, give detail previously unprinted. For ransom-insurance, see also Walford's Insurance Cyclopædia, under "Captivity" and "Casualty." Not one of these authors or editors refers to Tobler (see previous note), or mentions any actual transaction, not even Henry Moryson's. For the other transaction here quoted, see an extract from George Stoddard's MS. accounts in H. Hall's *Society in the Elizabethan Age,* p. 53.

12. Hatfield MSS., x, 135.

13. Cal. S. P. For. 1581–82, p. 43; confirmed by Bodl. MS., Rawlinson, C. 799.

14. Brit. Mus. MS. Harleian, 943.

15. Cal. S. P. Ven., xiv, 569.

16. By Gölnitz, pp. 665, 666.

17. Brit. Mus. MS. Harleian, 943.

18. Bodl. MS., Rawlinson, C. 799.

19. Cal. S. P. Ven., 392.

20. Brit. Mus. MS. Harleian, 943.

21. Giustiniani.

22. Hakluyt Soc., 87, pp. 114, 115.

23. Moryson, the main authority for the tourists' money matters, mentions the practice, but an actual instance of its usefulness will be found related by Sobieski in the extract printed by Liske.

24. Hatfield MSS. (1595), p. 184.

25. Hatfield MSS., x, 460; *cf.* Duke of Buccleugh's *Winwood Papers* (Hist. MSS. Com., 1899, 46), i, 188.

26. Röhricht, pp. 273, 274.

27. Cal. S. P. Ven., ix, 237.

28. Montagu Papers (Hist. MSS. Com., 1900, 45), p. 124.

29. Bodl. MS., Rawlinson, C. 799.

30. Brit. Mus. MS., Sloane, 4217.

31. Tommaseo, *Relations des Ambassadeurs Vénitiens sur . . . France*, 1838, ii, 284.

32. See note 11.

33. Röhricht, pp. 248, 249.

34. Bodl. MS., Rawlinson, C. 799.

35. Birch, *Court and Times of James I*, i, 139.

36. Locatelli.

37. J. A. Fischer, *Scots in Germany*, p. 45. *Cf.* also A. Schultze's *Ueber Gästerecht und Gastgerichte in den deutschen Städten des Mittelalters* in *Historische Zeitschrift*, 1908, pp. 473–528.

38. Taylor, *International Law*, *sub voce*.

39. De Villers (see Bibliography under Aarssen).

40. E. Nys, *op. cit.* vol. 16, p. 189.

41. *Cf.* Helmolt's *History of the World*, vii, 122–133.

42. Taken mainly from accounts printed in Morel-Fatio's, *L'Espagne au 16 e et au 17 e siècle.*

43. *Works*, 1839, i, xix–xxiv.

44. *Œuvres*, 1723, ii, 262.

45. Hist. MSS. Com., Various (Miss Buxton's MSS.), ii, 274.

46. *Cf.*, in particular, under " Ideas " in the index.

BIBLIOGRAPHY

O blessed Letters! that combine in one,
All Ages past and make one live with all;
By you, we do confer with who are gone,
And the dead-living unto Council call.
By you, the unborn shall have communion
Of what we feel and what doth us befall.
　　　　　　　　　　SAMUEL DANIEL
　　　　(1562–1619; in "Musophilus").

THE literature of the subject as a whole is absolutely inexhaustible, the contemporary part alone being sufficient to provide any one with recreation — and sleep — for ten years. Including a few whose accounts I have had to read in translation, or even in paraphrase (such as that of Bisoni mentioned below), the number of travellers on whose evidence I have drawn first-hand amounts to over two hundred and thirty; but this number could certainly be doubled, perhaps trebled, by any one who found it practicable to devote to the subject all the time and money it could employ, inasmuch as there are probably few libraries of long standing which do not contain a manuscript account of a journey at this period; some contain them by the dozen. Besides this, there are many printed accounts little less inaccessible than most manuscripts. The most convenient library for consulting contemporary editions of these printed narratives is Marsh's Library, Dublin, where one set of shelves is given up to them; there they will be found by the score, besides having a sub-heading ("Itinera") to themselves in the catalogue.

This appendix, therefore, can concern itself with no-

thing but actual accounts of journeys, and that only in
some abbreviated form. The method followed is this.
First comes a list of the MSS. that I have been able to obtain the opportunities to read (very few, unfortunately);
then another list, of printed books, consisting of those
which are bibliographies or serve as such, and of accounts
of journeys not mentioned in these bibliographical works:
together with some notes on certain recent editions of
books which are there mentioned.

Asterisks indicate bibliographies; square brackets, books
my knowledge of which is second-hand: while, in order
to obviate needless suffering on the part of any who may
feel inclined for a little further acquaintance with these
accounts, the names of the authors of the more readable
are printed in heavier type. It may as well be said that the
value of most of these narratives consists simply in their
having been written three hundred years ago.

The second list is one of authors' names, but topo-
graphical guidance is provided in the index by means of the
abbreviation "BIBL"[iography] added as a sub-heading
to place-names, followed by the names of the authors who
are of assistance with regard to that place; *e. g.:* —
   "Spain"
      BIBL.: Wynn.
After such names will sometimes be found numbers; these
refer back to the Table of Special References. It is taken
for granted that every one of these bibliographical books
will be recognized as adding information about many countries, since however strictly the scope of each may be
limited, it will include travellers who came from, and
went in, all directions.

References to accounts, generally fragments, which
have appeared in periodical form only, have had to be
restricted to the more interesting; most of which are to

Bibliography

be found in the Table of Special References. For further sources not indicated in detail, bibliographies of national history, correspondence, biographies, records of embassies and prefaces to the last-named, especially to the Venetian "Relazioni" edited by Barozzi and Berchet, have all proved particularly useful. All the later publications of the Historical MSS. Commission (the earlier contain indications of MSS. in private hands, but no more than the titles are given) and all the Calendars of State Papers which include the required years, have been examined up to the end of the publications for 1908, at least.

As to non-contemporary sources of information, I have used them only for negative purposes — to decide which of two travellers is the bigger liar, for instance; or to avoid displaying more ignorance than is necessary on those elementary points of geography which everybody is supposed to know and nobody does; etc., etc. Some exceptions to this procedure seemed reasonable; but these are made obvious. Any statement of objective fact, indeed, seems to me impracticable in connection with such a subject as this. My aim has been merely at approximate subjective accuracy; to study, that is, the psychology of the subject, conscious and sub-conscious; and its phenomena only in so far as they are causes of, or symbolize, the psychology. Students are requested to hear this statement with the ear of faith, remembering that all such attempts have to be heavily peptonized if expenses are to be paid, as this one's must be, by those in whom the spirit indeed is willing but the digestion weak. And even students —!

But when all limitations of aim have been granted, it must be admitted further that a summary of the experiences and thoughts of scores of individuals, and of the thousands they stand for, over a period of more than a century and extending over all one continent and into fractions of two others, must be mainly remarkable as an anthology of half-truths.

Further still, to those who may notice that the half-truths are less stereotyped, the detail less hackneyed, than might have been the case, I should like to say that the credit of that is largely due to the London Library, without which this book would probably not have seemed worth writing or worth publishing; and that my debt is by no means only to the books and to the librarian's readiness to add to them, but also to the exceptional ability, and equally exceptional willingness, of the staff to help. It is only fair to mention, too, in speaking of bibliographical assistance, how much I am indebted to that furnished in the numbers of "Revue Historique." Acknowledgments are also due to the owners of the originals of the illustrations. No trouble has been spared to make the book the best illustrated existing for the period dealt with, with the necessary exception of the two quarto volumes of Van Vaernewyck's "Mémoires d'un Patricien Gantois"; all the photographs have been specially taken (except that of Rabelais' receipt) from the best procurable originals, often unique ones. For translations and information from Polish sources my sincere thanks are due to members of the Polish Circle in London, Mr. A. Zaleski in particular; and for help in various ways, which includes encouragement, to many others, especially Mr. Hubert Hall and Professor Gollancz, and, most of all, to my wife.

MSS. USED

Bodleian Library.

Rawlinson, C. 799. R. Bargrave's narrative, already frequently quoted: reliable, & especially useful for economic data. He went to Constantinople (1646), returned overland (1648); went again (1654), returning viâ Venice.

D. 120 Anon. France, Italy, & Switzerland (1648–49).

D. 121. Anon. Italy (1651).

D. 122. John Ashley: account of a stay at Jerusalem in 1675: details of expenses at the end.

D. 1285. Sir T. Abdy. France & Italy 1633–35.

D. 1286. Anon. Italy & Spain 1605–06.

British Museum.

Add. 34177. ff. 22–50. "Account of a journey over Mont Cenis into Italy": 1661.

Harleian, 288. "Direction for some person who intended to travel into France & Italy; being a short account of the roads, chief cities & of some rarities worthy to be seen." (End of the 16th century?)

Harleian, 942/3 and 1278. Note-books of Richard Symonds used in France & Italy (1648–49), no. 943 being the more valuable as containing his diary & detailed expenses.

Harleian, 3822. Journey throughout Spain (1599–1600) by Diego Cuelbis, the author, & his companion Joel Koris. Written in Spanish although the author was of Leipzig.

Egerton, 311. Visits to shrines in Spain, Provence, & Italy in 1587 by a proxy of Philip II.

Lansdown, 720. The frequent references to this MS. will have shown how useful it is. Among many other points that give it value are the excellent drawing of the bust of Petrarch at Arqua, soon afterwards destroyed, and a copy of the subsequently effaced epitaph of Clément Marot at Turin (fol. 37 b). The MS. is anonymous, but the author may be identified as Nicolas Audebert (1556–98), son of Germain Audebert. Beckmann (q. v.) had already established the identity of "le sieur Audeber," whose "Voyage et Observations en Italie" were published at Paris in 1656, with Nicolas Audebert, and that the author of the printed book is the same as he who wrote the MS. is suggested by the relations of both with Aldrovandi (MS. fol. 101 b). More definite evidence is obtainable from an article on Nicolas in the Revue Archéologique (3rd series, vol. 10, pp. 315–322), by means of the dates on his letters written from Italy. In view of this identification it may be worth mentioning that the author's birthday was April 25 (fol. 558) & that he was elected "president de l'Université" of Bologna in Nov. 1575 (fol. 86 b), a year in which the name of the rector has not hitherto been known.

Sloane, 4217. A honeymoon trip, a pilgrimage, & a tragedy combined. Lady Catherine Whetenal, the subject (it is written by her servant, Richard Lascells), after being married at Louvain, travelled to Rome for the year of jubilee, 1650: but on her return journey gave birth to a still-born child at Padua, & there died.

Stowe, 180. Constantinople & the Levant in 1609, as seen by a "Mr. Stampes"; its value consists in its exemplification of the limitations of the ordinary tourist.

Tournay Library.

159. Journey of the Comte de Solre, Sieur de Molenbais, from Solre, near Dinant, in Belgium, to the court of Philip II of Spain 1588: viâ Genoa.

160. Journeys of J. de Winghe, founder of the library (1587–1607). Earlier journeys to Italy, Vienna, & Prague; later ones to shorter distances around Tournai.

PRINTED BOOKS

Aarssen, F. van, belonged to a Dutch family which was accustomed to take part in public affairs (*cf.* especially preface to "Lettres inédites de François d'Aarssen (his father) à Jacques Valcke," 1599–1603, by J. Nouaillac, Paris, 1908), and there is record of some journeying by himself & relatives in the middle of the 17th century, as part of the training of the younger generation. The very interesting "Voyage d'Espagne" (published 1656) attributed to him is now known to have been written by Antoine de Brunel, his companion; but Aarssen's own notes on the preceding journey, through Italy, will be found in vol. 3 of the "Atti del Congresso Internazionale di Scienze Storiche," Rome, 1906. The "Journal d'un Voyage à Paris" of the cousins of the above, the Sieurs de Villers, was published by A. P. Faugère (1862) [and by L. Marillier, 1899].

*Adelung, F. von. "Krit-literarische Übersicht der Reisenden in Russland bis 1700": 2 vols. 1846. The promises implied by the title are fulfilled so thoroughly & so exhaustively that the "Catalogue . . . des Russica" published by the Imperial Library of St. Petersburg in 1873 (Index of travellers thither up to 1700, vol. 2, p. 702) in no way supersedes the former, although it has some additions to make.

*Amat di San Filippo, P. "Biografía dei Viaggiatori

Italiani, colla bibliografía delle loro opere" Rome, 1882. (Società Geogràfica Italiana.)

*Babeau, A. "Les Voyageurs en France, depuis la Renaissance jusqu'a la Révolution." 1885.

Beatis, Antonio de, accompanied Cardinal Luigi d'Aragona through Italy, Germany, the Netherlands, & France (1517–18). His narrative is printed in L. Pastor's "Erläuterungen . . . zu Jannsen's Geschichte," IV, 4, Freiburg, 1905, with a detailed German paraphrase, & notes which add very greatly to its value. A readable English paraphrase will be found in the Quarterly Review, July, 1908. The author was an acute and observant man with wide interests, who travelled under the most favourable conditions. He also came into contact with many of the most attractive personalities in Europe during his journey, among them Lionardo da Vinci, particulars of a long conversation with whom at Amboise he records.

Bertie, Robert (afterwards Lord Willoughby). Letters written while in France (1598–99) are printed in the Earl of Ancaster's MSS. (Hist. MSS. Com.) 1907 (pp. 340–348) together with one from his brother Henry (pp. 390–392; 1617; Constantinople & Italy), and diary of another Robert (1647–49) during travel in France, (pp. 418–421).

*Beckmann, J. "Literatur der ältern Reisebeschreibungen": 2 vols. Göttingen, 1807–10. Contains good notices of many very rare books.

Bisoni, Bernardo, accompanied Vincenzo Giustiniani, Marchese di Bassano, through Germany, the Low Countries, England, and France, in 1606. His MS., now at the Vatican, has been paraphrased into French by E. Rodocanachi (1899) under the title of "Aven-

tures d'un Grand Seigneur Italien à travers l'Europe"
with appendices.

Bonnaffé, E. "Voyages et Voyageurs de la Renaissance,"
1895. In the main a pleasant résumé of accounts
that are common property, but contains much sup-
plementary detail not used by other writers.

*Boucher de la Richarderie, G. "Bibliothèque Univer-
selle des Voyages; 1808; " vols. 1, 2, 3.

Brereton: Sir William. Travels in great Britain & Low
Countries, 1634–35. Printed by Chetham Society,
vol. 1.

Breuning von Buchenbach, Hans Jakob; well known as an
Oriental traveller, also came as ambassador to England, 1595, from Duke Frederick of Württemberg.
Rye (q. v.) refers to him, but was dependent on
Sattler's history of Württemberg & on some letters
among English State Papers; but Breuning's own
detailed account of the journey has since been
printed by the Stuttgart Lit. Verein (vol. 81).

*Brown, P. Hume. "Early Travellers in Scotland," 1891.

Buchell, Arend van, An antiquary of Utrecht, whose
"Commentarius . . . rerum quotidianarum" includes
records of journeys between 1584 and 1591. The
text of his "Iter Italicum" has been printed by
Soc. Romana di Storia Patria (1900–02) with notes by
Rodolfo Lanciani; a translation of the parts concerning Germany begins in vol. 84 of the Hist. Verein für
den Niederrhein, 1907 & of those concerning France
under the title of "Description de Paris" in the
Mémoires of the Soc. de l'histoire de Paris, vol. 26,
1899. Brief selections from the whole in the original
Latin, forming a varied & useful miscellany, will
be found in vol. 21 of Series III of the Historisch
Gezelschap te Utrecht (1907).

Busbecq's letters (see chapter 1) are most conveniently read in Forster & Daniel's "Life & Letters." 1881. All the letters are translated there.

Busino, Orazio; chaplain to the Venetian Ambassador Contarini in England and Spain (1617–18). For an account of the MSS. in which he tells his experiences with exceptional brightness & point, see Barozzi & Berchet's "Relazioni," Series IV, pp. 192–195. Rawdon Brown's translation of what referred to England is among the transcripts he presented to the Record Office in London; a résumé of this was printed in the Quarterly Review, July, 1857. On the latter I have had to be wholly dependent, but part of the translation has just become available in print in the Calendar of the State Papers (Venetian) for 1617–19.

Carmoly, E. "Itinéraires de la Terre-Sainte," 1847. All the itineraries are Jewish ones dating from the 13th to 17th centuries, translated from the Hebrew.

[**Carve**, Thomas; "Itinerarium," mainly in Germany during the Thirty Years' War; but also Low Countries, England & Ireland. Rare, quaint & valuable. In three parts; only complete edition, 1859. Cf. Dict. Nat. Biog.]

Casola, Pietro. M. Margaret Newett's "Canon Pietro Casola's Pilgrimage to Jerusalem," 1907: no. 5 of the Historical Series in the Publications of the University of Manchester. This pilgrimage took place in 1494, but the editor's researches among Venetian archives throw much fresh light on the later phases of the subject.

Cecily, princess; see Roy. Hist. Soc., vol. 12.

*****Chandler**, F. W., "Literature of Roguery," 1899, contains a very full bibliography of picaresque literature & an analysis of much of it.

Chaworth, Sir G., went as special ambassador to Brussels in 1621. His account of the journey & of his preparations for it are printed in A. J. Kempe's "Losely MSS." 1835.

Chiericati, Francesco. His letter concerning Ireland with three concerning England are printed in "Quattro Documenti d' Inghilterra ed uno di Spagna dell' Archivio Gonzaga di Mantova," edited by Attilio Portioli, Mantua, 1868. For further information and more letters see biography by B. Morsolin.

Clara Eugenia, the Infanta. The letter already referred to is printed in the "Boletin de la Real Academía de la Historia," Madrid, vol. 49, pp. 30–50.

*Cobham, C. D. "Excerpta Cypria," 1908. Extracts from the accounts of writers who visited Cyprus, together with an exceptionally thorough bibliography. As so many who went to Jerusalem touched at Cyprus, the book may serve as a bibliography to chapter 5; also for travel generally over a wider period than this.

Courthop, Sir G. (France, Italy, Malta, Constantinople, 1636–39.) In Camden Soc. Miscellany, vol. 11.

Cuellar, Captain, who was wrecked on the Irish coast in a ship which sailed with the Spanish Armada of 1588, wrote a letter describing his adventures in Ireland & Scotland which has several times been translated or paraphrased since the publication of the text in Duro's "La Armada Invencible" (1885). The best version is that in Allingham's "Adventures of Captain Cuellar in Connacht & Ulster," 1897.

*Cust, Mrs. Henry. "Gentlemen Errant," 1909. Annotated & explanatory paraphrases of the experiences of Leo von Rösmital, Wilwolt von Schaumburg, Frederick II, Elector Palatine of the Rhine, & Hans von Schweinichen. The dates range between 1465 &

1602 & the countries visited include most of Europe. Of the bibliography the utmost that can be said is that it is worth consulting; but the rest of the book is valuable as summarizing much that has not been really accessible; and is very readable.

*Dallam, Thomas. See Hakluyt Soc., vol. 87.

"Diarium Terræ Sanctæ," a quarterly periodical beginning March 1, 1908, issued from the monastery of San Salvatore at Jerusalem dealing with the work carried on there, past and present. It came under my notice too late to use.

*Einstein, L. "The Italian Renaissance in England," 1902. The subject frequently comes into touch with touring & the bibliography is very full, especially as regards guide-books.

Falkiner, C. L. "Illustrations of Irish History & Topography," 1904. Contains extracts from the narratives of several travellers of the 16th & 17th centuries who visited Ireland, including that of **Josias Bodley** & some otherwise unprinted paragraphs from Moryson.

Fanshawe, Lady Ann. Two editions of her reminiscences have been published recently, 1905 & 1907. The latter is by far the more fully annotated and authoritative.

**[Farinelli, A. "Apuntes y divagaciones bibliográficas sobre viajes y viajeros por España y Portugal," with a supplement, "Mas apuntes," etc., Madrid, 1903.]

*Fouché-Delbosc, R., published a detailed bibliography of journeys in Spain & Portugal in the "Revue Hispanique," vol. 3, 1896, issued separately in the same year ("Bibliographie des Voyages en Espagne et en Portugal"). It is absolutely indispensable not only as regards travel within those countries, but outside them as well.

Guzman, Alonso de. See Hakluyt Soc., vol. 29.

*****Hagemans, G.** "Relations inédites d'ambassadeurs venitiens dans le Pays-Bas," 1865. Besides the direct bearing on the subject that all such "Relazioni" have, the notes to this book contain references to several still unpublished MSS.

*****Hantzsch, Victor.** "Deutsche Reisende des 16ten Jahrhunderts"; Leipzig, 1895, part 4 of vol. 1 of Leipziger Studien aus dem Gebiet der Geschichte. Brief, lucid notices of many typical adventurers of German blood all over the world in the 16th century. Indispensable by reason of its very full references to books & MSS.

Hoby, Sir Thomas (France, Germany, Italy, Flanders, 1547–64); in Camden Soc. Miscellany, vol. 10.

Khitrowo, B. de. "Itinéraires Russes en Orient." French translations of Russian MSS., published by the Soc. de l'Orient Latin. The promised second volume does not seem to have been issued, but though only a few of the itineraries in this first volume are late enough to be available for questions of fact, the whole is very valuable as a revelation of temperament.

Lauder, J., of Fountainhall. See Scot. Hist. Soc., vol. 36.

*****Łozinski, W.,** "Życie polskie w dawnych wiekach wiek xvi–xvii." ("Polish Life in the 16th & 17th centuries"), 2nd edition, Lemberg, 1908. Contains notices of Polish travel and travellers.

*****Locatelli, S.,** an Italian priest who went to Paris & back (1664–65) & whose narrative has been in part translated from the Italian MS. by A. Vautier ("Voyage de France," 1905), who adds a good bibliography & notes. Its value consists in the author belonging to that type of man who does not hesitate to write what most people are content, sometimes more than content, to keep to themselves. Combined with his extreme

poverty of mind & vanity, this leads him into relating
many trivialities which help to define more clearly
the incidentals, & the psychology, of contemporary
touring.

Maulde, François de (Modius); for the adventures of this
learned Fleming (1556–97) mainly in Germany, see
two articles by A. Roersch in the Revue Générale.
May & June, 1907, based on his MS. autobiography
at Munich. [Also P. Lehmann's "Franciscus Modius
als Handschriftenforscher," 1908, in Quellen und
Untersuchungen zur lateinischen Philologie des Mittelalters, III, 1.]

Montaigne, Michel de. English translation of his Journal
by W. G. Waters, 1903. [Latest edition of the text
edited by L. Lautrey, Paris, 1906.]

*D'Ancona's edition (Città di Castello, 1889: 2nd ed.
1895) contains an excellent critical bibliography
concerned with foreigners' travel in Italy.

Moryson, Fynes, published his "Itinerary" in 1617 in a
form that has proved the equivalent of a burial. A
fine reprint, the only one, was issued in 1907, in
a series which includes other travel records of this
period. The better part of what Moryson himself
left unprinted appeared under the editorship of C.
Hughes under the title "Shakespeare's Europe" in
1903. See also under "Falkiner."

*Mundy, Peter. For his travels in European Europe
(1608–28) see Hakluyt Soc., Series II, vol. 17, to which
a useful bibliography of MSS. & printed works is
appended. A second volume will be partly concerned with northern Europe.

Possevino, the Jesuit, besides his "Moscovia" (1587)
wrote letters to his superiors while engaged on his
mission thither (1581–82), as did his brother-Jesuit

Campan. A contemporary digest of these letters was printed by Father Pierling (Paris, 1882) under the title "Missio Moscovitica." In the editor's other books on the relations between the Tsars & the Popes will be found indications of other travellers, notably in his "L'Italie et la Russie."

*Röhricht, R., "Bibliographia Geographica Palæstinæ," (2nd edition, 1890) a chronological bibliographical list of all accounts of visits to Palestine

    and

*"Deutsche Pilgerreisen nach dem Heiligen Lande" (2nd edition, 1900), another work of extraordinary research, giving the names of every German whom the author has found to have visited Jerusalem between 1300 & 1700, with an account of the journey whenever remarkable. To a 26-page introduction are appended 377 notes, with an enormous number of detailed bibliographical references, a large proportion of which are to MSS. located all over Europe.

*Rye, W. B. "England As Seen By Foreigners in the Days of Queen Elizabeth & James I," 1865. Annotated extracts prefaced by a long and valuable introduction containing all that has since become, in England, the commonplaces of the subject. In view of this latter fact, I have quoted as exclusively as is reasonable from writers whom Rye overlooked or who visited England outside the dates within which Rye confined himself.

*Saint-Genois, J. L. D. "Les Voyageurs Belges." 2 vols. 1846. Biographies, in several cases drawing on MS. sources.

Sastrow, Bartholomew. [Latest (modernized) edition of the text of his autobiography, vol. 2 of Schultze's "Bibliothek Wertvoller Memoiren," Hamburg, 1907.]

An English translation, by A. Vandam, exists under the title of "Social Germany in Luther's Time." Sastrow's journeys, however, reached as far as Rome.

*Serrano y Sanz, M., "Autobiografías y Memorias" 1905, a volume of the Nueva Biblioteca de Autores Españoles. The long introduction on Spanish autobiographies mentions many travellers of whose accounts I have been able to make practically no use owing to my not knowing of the book in time (see pp. 49, 50, 62, 63, 86, 89, 94, 97 (2), 109, 123, 124, 125, 142, 148; and bibliography of Jerusalem pilgrims' accounts, 55–58). Several of these, however, exist only in MS. in Spain. Great Britain & Scandinavia receive little attention, but plenty of valuable material seems to be included for every other part of Europe; certainly this is so in the narratives (16th–17th centuries) which the author prints.

Sobieski, Jakób, Marshal of the Polish Diet, travelled throughout Europe (1607–13 & 1638). An incomplete MS. was printed by E. Raczynski (Posen, 1833) & the missing portion by A. Kraushar (Warsaw, 1903) from the autograph at the Imperial Library at St. Petersburg. The only part that seems to have been translated is that relating to Spain, in Liske's "Viajes de Extranjeros por España" (a book, by the way, that no one who is interested in 16th century history can fail to be assisted by).

*[Szamota, István, " Régi utazások Magyarországon és a Balkán-félszigeten, 1054–1717 " ("Travellers of the past in Hungary and the Balkans, 1054-1717") Budapest, 1891.]

Taylor, John (the "water-poet"). Both his continental journeys — one to Hamburg, the other viâ Hamburg to Prague — have been reprinted by C. Hindley in

Taylor's "Works" & also by the Spenser Soc. (vol. 4, pp. 76–100): that to Hamburg only, in Hindley's "Old-Book-Collector's Miscellany."

Vargas, Juan de, contemporary with Alonso de Guzman & Sastrow, both of whose narratives he supplements very closely. As a soldier under Charles V in Germany, his remarkable experiences illustrate the present subject: he also saw the wildest life in Hungary & Vienna, & slave-life in Constantinople & Africa. Still more remarkable were his experiences in S. America as a "conquistador." His capacity for telling us what we most want to know, & for telling it well, are so much beyond what might be expected from an uneducated soldier as to raise doubts about the genuineness of the narrative. But the abundance of detail is past invention. It is unmentioned by Serrano y Sanz; the only edition seeming to be the French translation by the owner of the unpublished Spanish MS., C. Navarin, "Les Aventures de Don Juan de Vargas" in the Bibliothèque Elzévirienne, 1853.

Wotton, Sir Henry. For all references to Sir Henry Wotton (& for much else) I am indebted to his "Life & Letters" by L. P. Smith (1907). Both his life & his letters come into touch with the travel of the day from various points of view, & frequently; & the same mellowness & intimacy characterize both the reminiscences of Sir Henry Wotton & the comment of his biographer.

Wynn, Sir Richard, followed Prince Charles from England to Spain in 1625. His account of his journey has been printed by Hearne as an appendix to his edition of the "Historia vitae . . . Ricardi II," 1729; illiterate & prejudiced, but valuable for its frankness.

Halliwell-Phillips reprinted it at the end of his edition of Symonds D'Ewes' autobiography.

Zetzner, Johann Eberhard, a descendant of the Strassburg printers of that name, left an autobiography consisting largely of accounts of his journeys in Germany, along the coasts of the Baltic, in England, Scotland, France, & Spain. A paraphrase of the more interesting parts has been printed in three instalments, in French, in the "Revue d'Alsace" [1905–07 ?] and reissued separately under the titles "Idylle Norvégienne d'un Jeune Négociant Strasbourgeois" (1905), "Londres et l'Angleterre en 1700" (1905), and "Un Voyage d'Affaires en Espagne en 1718 (1907)," all published by the Librairie Noiriel, Strassbourg, edited by Rodolphe Reuss, who has put together in a very readable form matter which is of considerable value not only as a record of things seen, but also in connection with finance & commerce. In spite of the dates being so much later than those of the rest of the books I have used, it seems desirable to include these pamphlets here as containing much that illustrates conditions equally normal a century earlier, & as being, too, of such an out-of-the-way character that they are liable to be overlooked.

INDEX

All names of travellers are indexed, but only those towns concerning which some distinctive detail has been given.

Aarssen, F. van; 395.

Abdy, Sir T.; 393.

" Acta Sanctorum " quoted; 179.

Allen, Cardinal; as protector of English at Rome, 111.

Alps; *see* Mountaineering.

Ambassadors; *see under* Embassies, Busbecq, Chaworth, Chiericati, Contarini, Fanshawe, Foix, Glover, Guicciardini, Lionello, Lippomano, Muscorno, Myszkowski, Navagero, Pindar, Sherley, Willes, Wotton.

Amsterdam; 117, 281, 329.

Antwerp; 122, 252, 291.

Aragona, Luigi d' (cardinal); travelling expenses, 317; itinerary, 396.

Art; an "Ephesus" statue of Diana, 149; art-student abroad, his difficulties and advantages, 150–1, 376–7; Turkish arts and crafts, 191.

Aschhausen, J. G. von (bishop of Würzburg); travelling expenses, 317.

Ashley, John; 393.

Aubigné, Agrippa d'; his "Les Tragiques" quoted, 349.

Audebert, Nicolas; 140, 145; his MS., 394.

Augsburg; 119, 141, 152, 291, 350.

Average Tourist (*see* Education, and Tutors, and, for examples, Aarssen, Audebert, Bertie, Browne, Coligny, Davison, Hoby, Lauder, Raleigh, Rohan, Roos, Sobieski, Wotton); the special type of the age, 25; and its development, 26, 319; psychology of, 29, 30, 32, 378–9; instructions to, 37–9, 48, 57–8, 95; and Protestantism, 53–6; objective, 95, 100–1, 114, 118, 130, 132; what he would have to spend, 314–8; subsidized by Queen Elizabeth, 319.

Awliyái Efendi; quoted, 249, 284.

Babeau, A.; his "Voyageurs en France" quoted, 270, 284.

Bacon, Francis; quoted, 3, 148, 319.

Barbaro, Giosaffate; 29.

Barberini, Rafael; 383.

Bargrave, R.; 393.

Bassompierre, François, Maréchal de; 108.

Bathing-resorts; of western Europe, 3, 267–9; Turkish, 196; the Jordan, 235.

Battista, Giovanni (pilgrims' guide at Jerusalem); 230, 239.

Beasts of prey; risk from, 355.

Beatis, Antonio de; 396; quoted, 162, 299, 381, 385.

Bergamo; 114.

Bernini, the artist; 98.

Bertie, Robert and Henry; 396.

Bisoni, Bernardo; 396.

Blount, Sir Henry, philosopher-errant; his aims, 8; quoted, 33, 182, 187, 202–3, 213, 358, 360.

Bodley, Josias; 51, 400.

Bologna University; 103, 310–1, 394.

Boorde, Andrew; his "Introduction of Knowledge" as marking the beginning of the period here dealt with, 26; quoted, 27, 50, 154, 173, 247, 348.

Bosio, Antonio; his re-discovery of the Catacombs at this time, 108.

Bouchet, Jean (Rabelais' " Xenomanes"); 56.

Boyle, Robert ; 185.

Brereton, Sir William; in Holland, 83, 116, 140, 397.

Breuning, von Buchenbach, H. J.; 397.

Bridges; 82, 288–90, 328.

Brittany; neglect of, 144.

Brooke, N.; (18th century), 191.

Browne, Edward (son of Sir Thomas); 288, 339.

Brunel, Antoine de ; 395.

Bruno, Giordano ; at Geneva, 112; in London, 134.

Buchell, Arend van, antiquary; 246, 275, 329, 385, 397.

Busbecq, A. G. de; Imperial ambassador at Constantinople, and in France, 14; his letters, 14, 398; tries to naturalize camels, 140; quoted, 20, 81, 187, 192, 289.

Busino, Orazio; 398.

Cagots; 138.

Cairo ; largest city then known, 8; Bulak asses, 220; and other details, 221, 237, 325; usual excursions from, 222–7.

Callot, Jacques, the artist; 321.

Camden, W.; quoted, 41, 119, 164.

Campan, the Jesuit; 403.

Captivity and Ransoms (*see* Pirates); 56, 71, 101, 201, 203, 346, 356–62, 366.

Caravans ; 216–9, 228–30, 235–6, 249, 292.

Carve, Thomas ; 398.

Casola, Pietro ; 398.

Cecily, princess (of Sweden) ; marries on condition her husband takes her to see Queen Elizabeth, 11 ; her journey, 11–3 ; and narrative, 398.

Cellini, Benvenuto ; adventures, 81, 298 ; quoted, 363.

Chamberlain, John, the letter-writer; 63.

Channel-crossings ; havens, 60–2; experiences of, 12, 60–4 ; size of vessels, 64 ; charges, 328.

Chapman, George ; quoted, 25.

Charles II ; his experience of Spanish fare, 262.

Chartres ; a pilgrimage to, 20.

Chaworth, Sir G. ; outlay on his embassy to Brussels, 318 ; his account of it, 398.

Chiericati, Francesco ; 384, 399.

Cirot, G.; his biography of Mariana quoted, 48.

Clara Eugenia, the Infanta ; journey from Milan to Brussels, 11, 399 ; quoted, 135, 296–7, 303, 306.

Cleland's estimate of annual cost of travel ; 315.

Clothes ; 37, 133, 359, 365–8.

Coaches and Waggons ; 79, 290–3, 333.

Coinage ; small change and its bearing on expenses, 341 ; substitutes for, 346 ; multiplicity of, a great hindrance to travel, 368-72.

Coleridge, S. T. ; quoted, 45.

Coligny, Francis and Gaspard de ; their estimate for a year in Italy, 315.

Communications; *see under* Bridges, Caravans, Coaches, Escorts, Ferries, Litters, Locks, Mountaineering, Riding, River-travel, Road-travel, Seatravel, Sign-posts, Vetturino.

Compostella ; 173–4, 320.

Constantinople ; 122, 194–7, 200–1, 215–6.

—— **Bibl.;** MSS. Rawlinson, C. 799 ; Stowe, 180 ; and Bertie, Busbecq, Carmoly, Cobham, Courthop, Dallam, Khitrowo, Moryson, Mundy, Röhricht, Vargas.

Contarini, Tommaso ; takes peat from Flanders to Italy, 140.

Conversation - difficulties; *see* Linguistics.

Coryat, Tom ; in Palestine, 232, 329.

Cost of Travel in 1600.

—— **Direct** (*see* Coinage, Fares, Finance, Food, Guides, Licences, Lodging, Luggage, Outfit, Passports, Pilgrimage — Jerusalem, River-travel, Tolls); estimates of annual, 314–7; means of economizing, 318–25; foreigners more liable to overcharge then than now, 330; "conducted" travel, 216, 331–2; crossing the Alps, 332–4; duration of journeys the chief factor in expense, 332–5; in relation to food and lodging generally, 338–41.

—— **Indirect** (*see* Beasts of Prey, Captivity, Clothes, Droit d'aubaine, Escorts, Illness, Legal Status, Manners and Customs, Pirates, Plague, Robbers, Touring — greater strain of travel, War); defined, 313 ; epitomized in "Litany," 347.

Courthop, Sir G.; 399.

Cuelbis, Diego ; 393.

Cuellar, Captain ; 175–6, 399.

Dallam, Thomas ; 9, 65, 214, 308, 400.

Dallington's estimate of annual cost of travel; 315.

Daniel, Samuel ; quoted, 379, 389.

Dante ; did not add to the attractions of Florence, 103 ; quoted, 293.

Danzig ; 131, 155, 211.

Davies, Sir John ; quoted, 177, 386.

Davis, William ; a Protestant sailor, cared for at Rome, 112.

Davison, Francis ; cannot live abroad on 100 marks a year, 316 ; quoted, 344.

Della Valle, Pietro ; a model traveller, 6; life-story, 7; his many interesting experiences on the way to Jerusalem, 205–35; quoted, 50, 88, 90, 191–4, 198, 200, 269.

Denmark ; 155, 244.

Digby, Sir Kenelm ; dies in Paris, confiscation of property by "droit d'aubaine," 364.

Douglas, Thomas ; remits broadcloth to Algiers as a substitute for money, 346.

Dresden ; 120, 149.

"Droit d'aubaine"; enforcement and disuse of, 364 ; its equivalent in Turkey, 196.

Education ; as related to travel (*see* Average Tourist, Ideas, Touring — uses of, and, — causes of, Universities), growth of the idea, circ. 1542–1642, as constituting the unity of subject of this book, 25, 26, 158 ; then and now, 377.

Elizabeth, Princess (James I's daughter); a visit to, 129.

Elizabeth, Queen ; sends an organ to "Grand Turk," 9; is visited by Princess Cecily, 12 ; her twofold attraction for foreigners, 125–7; as a linguist, 47; and "der Einlasse," 141; subsidizes travel, 318 (*cf*. 346 and 386).

Embassies (*see* Ambassadors, and Spies) facilitate touring to the point of becoming the chief cause of it, 15 ; system of resident ambassadors developed in 16th century, and why, 15–6; economical advantages to the tourist, 318, 337, 344, 365; French maritime towns send one to Constantinople, 186, 197, 357.

Empire, the; communications in, 80, 289, 291; sub-divisions for tourist purposes, 117; characteristics of, 118–21; inns, 242–3, 245, 250, 255–9, 268–9, 283; expenditure in, 336–7, 339–40, 349–53; coinage, 370.

—— **people** of ; popularity of travel among, 29; as seen by foreigners, 118–21, 255, 265, 366.

—— Bibl.; MS. Tournay 160, Beatis, Bisoni, Breuning, Buchell, Carve, Clara Eugenia, Cust, Guzman, Hoby, Maulde, Montaigne, Moryson, Rye, Sastrow, Sobieski, Taylor, Vargas, Wotton, Zetzner; IV. 1. note 14, VIII. notes 28 and 35.

England (*see* London); as seen by foreigners, 123–30, 267, 343–4; their reasons for coming, 125–6; and usual route, 127; inns, 245; communications, 291; expenditure in, 330–1, 337–8, 349.

—— Bibl.; Bisoni, Brereton, Breuning, Busino, Cecily, Einstein, Rye, Sobieski, Zetzner.

English abroad; 346, 356, 386 note 5; increase in their numbers and its significance, 25–8; in Italy, 28, 74, 112; innkeepers, 273–4.

Ens, Gaspar; one of his guide-books quoted, 49.

Escorts (*see* Communications); 38, 353–4, 357; Janizaries, 198–9, 216, 325.

Espinel, Vicente; his "Marcos de Obregon" quoted, 49.

Este, Luigi d' (Cardinal); 386.

Evelyn, John; visits the Catacombs, 109; goes to see a prisoner tortured, 137; his credulity, typical, 146; cost of his "Grand Tour," 315; quoted, 18, 80, 95, 99, 140, 274, 285, 354.

Executions, etc., as "sights" (*see* Robbers); 136–7.

Exile; as a cause of travel; 23–4, 26.

Fairs; 114, 144.

Fanshawe, Ann, Lady; her journeys and memoirs, 13, 400; quoted, 79, 170, 262, 352, 370.

——, Sir Richard; 13, 315, 370.

Fares (in Europe); 328–36.

Ferries and fords; 287–90, 329.

Finance (*see* Coinage, Cost, "Putting-Out"); equation of money-values, how reckoned, 313-4; methods of ensuring supply of ready-money, 341–2; how coin was carried, 342–3, 372; legal limits to amounts carried and how to evade them, 343–4; fluctuations in values, 338–9, 344–5, 369; remitting by advice, 344–6, 348; letters of credit, barter, and loans, 346–7.

Finland; wizards on the coast of, 75.

Flagellants; 138.

Florence; as attractive then as now, 103; its Zoos, 139; inns, 271, 277.

Florio, John; his "First-Fruits" quoted, 27.

Foix, Paul de; 13.

Food; on board ship, 66, 68, 79, 264–5; in Turkey, 249; drinks, 252–5, 263; meals and meal-times, 255–66, 278–80, 333; cost, 338–41, 349.

France; routes, 84, 115, 122; on the rivers in, 79, 82–5; attractions of, 114–6, 268; inns, 255–6, 260, 266, 270–2, 274, 276, 281; on the road in, 285, 289, 291–2, 300, 330, 354; expenditure in, 315, 330, 348–9.

——Bibl.; MSS. Rawlinson D. 120, 1285, Add. 34177, Egerton 34, Harleian 288, 942/3, 1278, Lansdown 720, Tournay 159, 160; Aarssen, Babeau, Beatis, Bertie, Bisoni, Buchell, Busbecq, Busino, Courthop, Cust, Fanshawe, Hoby, Lauder, Locatelli, Montaigne, Mundy, Zetzner; IV. 1. note 4, VIII. note 45.

Frederick II (Elector Palatine); 399.

Fürer, Christopher, pilgrim; 325, 358.

Galileo, G.; 72, 97.

Galley-slaves; treatment of, 76, 137–8, 362.

Games new to travellers; 153.

Genoa; 99, 143.

Germany; *see* Empire.

Gesner, Conrad ; as a mountaineer, 304.

Giustiniani, Vincenzo (Marchese di Bassano) ; 396.

Glover, Sir Thomas ; in Thrace, 309.

Gölnitz, Abraham ; quoted, 129, 252, 256, 269, 285, 343, 387.

Good, ——; an Englishman in Ireland, 384.

Gourville, J. H. de ; "Mémoires" quoted, 266, 311.

Gracián, Jeronimo, St. Teresa's confessor ; enslaved, 186.

Gramaye, J. B.; at Algiers, 356.

Greece ; lack of interest in, 213.

Greene, Robert ; quoted, 366.

Gresham, ——(?); obtains news from hell at Stromboli, 91.

Gruberus ; a typical guide-book writer, 35, 204.

Guicciardini, Francesco ; 16; on Spain, 170.

Guide-books ; general characteristics of, 35–40, 42–3, 333; itineraries as guide-books, 43–6; advice from, 57–9; doggrel from, 106, 121, 154, 204; a Jewish one, 236; cost, 338.

—— **Bibl.**; Einstein.

Guides (*see* Escorts and Tutors) ; 333 ; in Mohammedan lands, 210.

Guzman, Alonzo de; his autobiography, 23, 401; quoted, 51, 280.

Hall, Joseph (bishop) ; his abuse of travel — in word and in deed, 374.

Harington, Sir J.; 142.

Hentzner, P.; typical character of his "Itineraria," 44; quoted, 60, 120, 343, 353.

Herbert, Lord, of Cherbury; 61, 275.

Hoby, Sir Thomas ; 336, 401.

Holland ; *see* United Provinces.

Horsey, Sir Jerome; 244.

Howell, James ; his "Instructions for Foreign Travel" taken as marking the end of the period here dealt with, 26; estimate of cost of travel, 315; quoted, 36, 71, 122, 276, 303.

Hungary ; 156, 289, 311, 339.

—— **Bibl.**; Szamota, Vargas.

Ideas of the Day in relation to travel : — **influencing travellers** ; political (monarchical), 25, 31, 33, 95, 115–6, 118, 164; historical, 40, 109, 110, 166–7, 185, 206; æsthetic, 103, 214, 302–7; lack of sympathy or sentimentality (*see* also theology, intolerance), 136–7, 144 ; critical, 145–6, 148, 214–5, 239, 301 ; pedagogic, 38–40, 58, 60, 95, 378–9 ; relating to the Empire, 119, 351 ; to Spain, 162–70, 261–3, 351 ; to Ireland, 175–9; to the Turks, 182–9, 193; to Jerusalem, 205–6; to Italy, 95–100, 103, 302; to the fascination of Queen Elizabeth, 125–7 ; where to stay, 101, 163.

—— **modified by travel** (*see* Touring, uses of); 27; historical, 33, 105, 167; town-planning, 117, 378; economic and domestic, 113, 116, 120, 140–2, 169–70, 201–2; political (democratic), 119, 120; trustworthiness of relics, 19 ; Scottish opinion of Scots, 32 ; concerning Italy, 100; and Venice, 105 ; of Christians about themselves, 171, 199 ; Turkish craftmanship and character, 191.

Illness (*see* Plague, and Touring, hardships of) ; provision against, 66, 360–2; mortality at sea, 67–8; and on the Alps, 295–6 ; hospitals, 112, 362 ; abundance of vermin, 59, 67–8, 121, 241, 309, 360.

Imperiali, Gian Vincenzo ; 381.

Inns (*see* Food, and Lodging) ; 46, 351, 372; the best, 240–1, 268 ; inn-signs, 240, 250–2 ; innkeepers, 241, 245, 273–80; and their case against the tourists, 272–83 ; the personnel, 245, 275, 281 ; utensils, 266–7 ; government supervision strict, 271–2 ; town watchmen notify innkeepers of new arrivals, 282 ; "Khans," 247–50 ; free quarters, 249, 265, 280–1, 319–20, 325.

Ireland ; 175–181, 378 (Dublin) ; scarcity of knowledge about, 41, 179–80 ; accommodation, 245, 265.

—— Bibl. ; Carve, Chiericati, Cuellar, Falkiner, Moryson ; vi. note 7.

Italy (*see* English abroad) ; high reputation in 16th century, 6, 95–100, 254, 302 ; adverse criticism, 100, 373 ; communications in, 82–3, 85–7, 285–94, 329–32 ; usual routes through, 102, 114 ; inns, 241, 252, 256, 259–60, 271–2 ; baths, 267–8 ; expenditure in, 330–1, 336 ; coinage, 369, 372.

—— people of ; 114, 366 ; travelling coming into fashion with Venetians, (1603), 26 ; courtesans, 106, 143.

—— Bibl. All but a very few entries refer to Italy to some extent.

Jemsel, Samuel ; a Jewish pilgrim (1641), 236.

Jerusalem (*see* Pilgrimage) ; relation to mental life of the time, 205–7 ; monastery of S. Salvatore at, 210, 230, 323 ; as seen by foreigners, 230–4, 360 ; extortion at, 323–5.

—— Bibl. MS. Rawlinson D. 122 ; Carmoly, Casola, Cobham, Diarium, Khitrowo, Moryson, Röhricht, Serrano.

Jews ; interest in, 8, 217 ; as linguists, 50 ; their badges, 139 ; centres, 214, 236 ; as travellers (to Palestine), 235–8.

Johanna, Frau (of Antwerp), a pilgrim ; enslaved, 359.

Jonson, Ben ; as tutor, 56 ; quoted, 103.

Jouvin de Rochefort ; 384.

Jusserand, J. ; his "English Wayfaring Life" and comparison of its types with those of 1600, 17.

Kiechel, S. ; 384.

Knight-Errant ; of fiction as a cause of travel, 22 ; typified by Alonzo de Guzman, 23 ; one in a cart, 291.

Kochanowski, Jan ; Polish satirist, 373, 378.

Koris, Joel ; 393.

La Brocquière, Bertrandon de (15th century) ; quoted, 99.

Lascells, Richard, pedagogue ; 394.

Lassota, Erich ; 383.

Latin ; see Linguistics.

Lauder, John, of Fountainhall ; his diary, 31, 401 ; studies law — and other things — at Poitiers, 31–2 ; seasick, 77 ; quoted, 49, 53, 272, 370.

Legal status of the traveller (*see* Droit d'aubaine) ; 246, 271, 365 ; at Geneva, 112.

Leipzig ; 4, 136.

Levant Company ; 8.

——, Islands of the ; particularly attractive to travellers, 88 ; some details, 88–94.

Leyden ; 4.

Licences to travel ; *see* Passports.

Linguistics ; Latin, its uses and limitations, 46–49, 215 ; Italian and French as international languages, 49, 50 ; "lingua franca" and other hybrids, 50–1 ; misunderstandings, 46, 49, 51, 52, 230–1, 249 ; tourist-pronunciation as a guide to phonology, 52 ; towns, etc., in favour for purity of language, 103, 115, 121 ; Jews as linguists, 50 ; books as aids to conversation, 52, 245 ; ignorance of, and lack of interest in, Greek, 213 ; in Turkey, 193, 249.

Lionello (secretary to Venetian ambassador); expenses, London, Edinburgh, 331.

Lippomano, G.; in Poland, 132; in France, 353.

Liske, K.; his " Viajes . . . por España " quoted, 383, 387, 404.

Lithgow, William ; becomes a bad traveller and a worse writer, 10; extent of his travels and consequent value of his comparisons, 10–1, 89, 123 ; quoted, 54, 72, 88, 179, 203, 219, 232–5, 323, 342.

Litters the least uncomfortable method of travel ; 290.

Locatelli, S.; 401.

Locks (on rivers) ; then being introduced, and where, 82, 83, 116.

Lodging ; towns the stopping-places, 101; monasteries, 225–6, 230, 319; downstairs, 143, 244, 247, 266; upstairs, 37, 59, 240–50, 265, 269–71.

London and Londoners ; 120, 134, 140, 153, 289.

Loreto ; 107–8.

Loyola, Ignazio ; journeys to England and Flanders as a beggar, 320.

Lübeck ; 120, 152, 251.

Ludwig V of Hessen-Darmstadt; pays a knight to journey with him, 317.

Luggage; (*see* Outfit); 291, 335–6.

Lyons; 84, 343, 376.

Madrid; 165, 174.

Malta; 91, 113, 399.

Manners and Customs (*see* Droit d'aubaine, Inns, Theology, intolerance, Vetturino, and under the various nationalities); in the Levant, 88–90; treatment of foreigners, 111–2, 132–5, 159, 170–1, 176, 197–8, 213, 231, 296, 311, 330, 343–4; drunkenness, 133, 160, 192–3, 242, 254–5, 291, 340; odds and ends, 135–54, 171, 174, 190, 246, 250, 277, 282, 312, 321, 332, 366; carrier-pigeons

and incubation in use among Mohammedans, 193.

Manwaring, —— ; an Englishman ill-treated at Aleppo, 198.

Maps and Plans; 52, 333; rivers marked, but not roads, 78.

Marlowe's " Tamburlane "; quoted, 185.

Maulde, François de (Modius); 402.

Mechanical devices as "sights"; water, 151–2, 174; other kinds, 141, 152.

Messina; its municipal bank, 113.

Milan; 100, 147, 337; its importance then, 102, 120.

Mines; 155–6, 294.

Missionaries-errant; scarcity of, 24.

Mole, John, a Protestant tutor; imprisoned thirty years at Rome, 54.

Money-matters; *see* Cost.

Montaigne, Michel de; as a traveller, 3–4, 105; usefulness of his knowledge of Latin, 47; his theory of travel, 57; his narrative, 402; quoted, 43, 107, 138, 186, 266, 268, 285, 338, 376.

Montpensier, Mlle. de; 270.

Montserrat; 19, 173, 281, 366.

Morelli, Jacopo; essay on little-known Venetian travellers quoted, 29.

Morgenthal, Hans von; 382.

Moryson, Fynes; his journeys, 4–5; writings, 5, 402; at Rome and Geneva, 111; expenditure, 316, 323, 348; quoted, 52, 65, 78, 100, 120, 131, 137, 140, 142, 153, 179, 186, 192, 198–9, 201, 231, 245, 257–60, 296, 298, 321, 326, 330, 343, 353, 385.

——, Henry; journey to Jerusalem, death and epitaph, 4–5 ; " puts out " money, 326.

Moscow ; 157.

Mountaineering ; Alpine passes in use and details of crossing, 294–9,

306, 332, 334; other passes, 212,
299, 300; ideas about, for and against,
300–6.

—— ascents; Horeb and Sinai, 226–
7; Quarantana (Palestine), 235; Les
Jumelles (Pau), 300; Roche Rommelon (Alps), 301–2.

Mundy, Peter; 14, 402; quoted, 82,
217, 260, 307, 386.

Münster; his "Cosmography," 43,
146.

Murder of travellers; *see* Robbery.

Muscorno (secretary of Venetian ambassador in England); cost of journey
thither, 335.

Muscovy; 156–62, 327, 342; communications in, 80, 156, 293, 355;
lodging, 244, 266, 319; fare, 253,
264; an innkeeper of Nerva, 280;
expenses of an Englishman's journey
thither, 335; coinage, 371.

—— people of; hostility to travel,
159, 367; as seen by foreigners, 159–
61, 346; on the way to Jerusalem,
211, 224–5.

—— Bibl.; Adelung, Khitrowo,
Mundy, Possevino.

Myszkowski, Marshal of the Polish
Diet; in England, 128.

Naples; 7, 113, 120, 138, 252,
292, 320, 343; a St. John's Eve
ceremony at, 145.

Nashe, Thomas; quoted, 33.

Navagero, Andrea; in Spain, 48, 337.

Netherlands, Spanish; 122.

——Bibl.; MS. Tournay 159; Beatis,
Bisoni, Breuning, Buchell, Carve,
Chaworth, Clara Eugenia, Cust,
Hagemans, Hoby.

Newberie, John; his tale of the Isola
dei Diavoli, 93.

Nîmes; its amphitheatre in 1682, 376.

Noë, Father; his guide-book, 42–3;
quoted, 77.

Northumberland, ninth earl of; letter to his son about travel, 58.

Norway; 346, 406.

Nützel, Karl; ("the German Ulysses") pays 300% for a loan, 346.

Ogier, Charles; 385.

O'Sullivan, Philip, the historian;
quoted, 179.

Outfit; (*see* Clothes and Luggage), 37,
135; for Jerusalem pilgrimage, 66,
325.

Overbury, Sir Thomas; quoted, 350.

Padua; (*see* Universities), 4, 231,
320–1, 329.

Paris; 115, 145, 153, 251–2, 289–
91, 362, 372, 397.

Parsons, Robert, the Jesuit; at Geneva, 112.

Pasquier, Etienne; his verdict on
touring, 375.

Passports and Licences; official
restrictions, 54–5; "charte-partie,"
76; licences to wear weapons, 135;
in Mohammedan lands, 198; Jerusalem "Placets," 209; licences to beg
used by tourists, 320–1; cost of English ones, 337–8; "bills of health,"
360–1.

Patron Saints; of travellers, 44; of
those who stay at inns, 251; of seafarers, 75.

Payen of Meaux; quoted, 363,
383.

Payne, R.; 385.

Perlin, a French visitor in England;
quoted, 344.

Perrault, Claude, architect of the
Louvre; sticks in the mud, 285.

"Picaro"; a special 16th century type
of vagabond, 21–3.

—— Bibl.; Chandler.

Pilgrimage (*see* Chartres, Compostella, Loreto, Montserrat, Saumur,

Theology); consecration for, 7; an epidemic in France, 20; to what extent in vogue, 18–20, 179, 208, 320; relics to be seen, 145–8, and chap. v. part 2; the degree and kind of attention relics received, 145–8, 239; to St. Patrick's Purgatory, 179.

—— to Jerusalem; (*see* Jews, Passports, Sea-Travel — pilgrim-galley) the most popular guide-book for, 42; routes, 207, 209–14; and their characteristics, 210–30; information bureau at Venice, 209; motives for, 208; decline of, and why, 208–9; licences for, 209; finance of, 209, 216, 229, 321–6, 365; at Jerusalem, 230–4; Easter excursions to Emmaus, Jordan, and Hebron, 234–6; Knighthood of the Holy Sepulchre, 239; lodging, 247–50, 323; enslavement of pilgrims, 358–60.

Pindar, Sir Paul; 13, 14.

Pirates; the chief centres, 72; frequency of, 72–74; tales of, 74, 106, 185–6.

Plague; 201, 299, 360–1.

Plotius; a typical guide-book writer, 35.

Poland; 130–2, 263, 303, 337, 364, 373; inns, 243–4, 278; bridge at Yarunov, 289; expenditure in, 339–41.

—— Bibl.; MS. Rawlinson, C. 799; Adelung, Cust, £osinski, Moryson, Mundy, Possevino, Zetzner; iv. 1. note 14; vi. note 2.

Possevino, Father (the Jesuit); 51, 310, 402.

Prague; 140.

Psalms; in use by travellers, 44, 64.

"Putting-Out" money (travellers' insurance); 325–7, 357–8; for mortality among travellers, *see under* Illness, and Robbers.

Quevedo Villegas, F. G. de; quoted, 21, 275, 308.

Rabelais; quoted, 44, 57, 77, 139, 355, 382.

Raleigh, (Sir Walter)'s son abroad with Ben Jonson; 56.

Reresby, Sir John; quoted, 149, 350.

Retz, Cardinal de; quoted, 76, 94.

Riding (*see* Communications); 44, 333; Bulak asses, 220; camels, 228–9; post-horses, 292, 330–1.

Rivadeneyra's "Cisma de Inglaterra" quoted, 41; life of Loyola quoted, 286, 320.

River-, and Lake-Travel; 79–87; frequency of, 156; relatively cheap, 328–9.

Riviera, the; unvisited, and why, 101, 260, 312.

Road-travel (*see* Communications, Luggage and Riding); inconveniences of, 79, 84, 328–9; on the way to Jerusalem, 210–30; transition-stage of, 284–5; anecdotes (state of the roads, etc.), 285–7, 308–12.

Roanne; starting-point for navigation on the Loire, 79.

Robbers and Murderers (*see* Executions); in south-eastern Europe, 212, 214, 289; Arabs, 218, 220, 223, 225, 228–9, 234, 323, 359; at inns, 272; highwaymen, 287, 292, 329–30, 348–54, 363; a by-product of war, 311, 348–54.

Rohan, Duc de (1600); his narrative typical, 33, 119; quoted, 117.

Rome; as seen by visitors, 108–12, 116, 252, 280, 292, 343, 364, 376; numbers received into English College there, 28; Protestants at, 54, 110–1; hôtel Vasa d'Oro at, 240, 338.

Roos, Lord; 54.

Rösmital, Leo von; 399.

Russia; *see* Muscovy.

St. Amant, the French poet; quoted, 303, 304, 307.

St. Malo; guarded at night by savage dogs, 311-2.

Sanderson, John; smuggles mummies, 223.

Sandys, George; quoted, 28, 91, 92, 113, 187, 232, 323-5.

Sarpi, Paolo; quoted, 60.

Sastrow, B.; his autobiography, 20, 403; quoted, 133, 321, 350-1, 385.

Saumur; 20, 115.

Schaumburg, Wilwolt von; 399.

Schweinichen, Hans von; 399.

Scotland; 5, 124, 127.

—— **Bibl.**; Brereton, Brown, Cuellar, Moryson, Zetzner.

Scots abroad (*see* Lauder and Lithgow); 131 (and note), 274.

Sea-sickness; 12, 59, 63, 77-9.

Sea-travel (*see* Channel-crossings, Levant, Pirates, Sea-sickness); size of vessels and accommodation, 64, 65; Eastward-ho! from Venice, 68; incidental difficulties, 69, 70, 267, 312; water preferable to land, 70, 71; daily service, Genoa-Rome (1588), 71; coasting the usual practice, 71-2; storms, 11, 74-6; sorcerers and good weather, 75; the need of the "chartepartie," 76; a "funeral" at sea, 93; Turkish sailors, 197, 201.

—— **pilgrim-galley** (Venice-Jaffa); arrangements in theory and practice, 66-8, 208, 210; concerning the date of its cessation, 207-8.

Seville; 172, 174, 281.

Shakespeare's knowledge about Italy, 86, 112, 114; a conjecture about "Othello," 188; Rosalind on the cost of travel, 313; quotations, 154, 222, 307, 363.

Sherley, Sir Anthony; 291, 357.

——, Sir Robert; his many journeys, 13.

Sicily; 113, 147.

Sidney, Sir Philip; abroad, when, where, and why, 27; quoted, 35, 58, 100, 314, 333, 351.

"Sights"; *see* Art, Bathing, Executions, Fairs, Flagellants, Galley-slaves, Games, Levant, Locks, Manners and Customs, Mechanical devices, Mines, Pilgrimage-relics, Unicorn horns, Volcanoes, Women, Zoos, and names of towns.

Sign-posts; 293-4.

Sigonius, the Italian scholar; could not speak Latin, 48.

Sinigaglia; inn at, finest in Italy, 241.

Smith, Captain John; 294, 385.

Smith, L. P.; his life of Sir Henry Wotton, 104, 405.

Sobieski, Jakób; in France and England, 128-30, 384, 387, 404.

Solre, Comte de (Sieur de Molenbais), 394.

Spain; 162-74, 261-3, 343, 364; the usual itinerary through, 163; communications in, 85, 289, 292, 300, 354; inns, 242, 246-7, 261-3, 278-80; expenditure in, 337, 340; coinage, 371.

—— **people of**; the women, 170; the men, 171; few know Latin, 48; a Spanish dentist, 362.

—— **Bibl.**; MSS. Rawlinson D. 1286, Harl. 3822, Egerton 311; Tournay 159; also Aarssen, Busino, Chiericati, Fanshawe, Farinelli, Fouché-Delbosc, Guzman, Sobieski, Wynn, Zetzner; I. note 3, VII. note 13, VIII. note 42.

Spenser, Edmund; as foreign correspondent, 17.

Spies; qualify for their work by travel, 16; numerous but not communicative, 17.

Stampes, ——(?); 394.

Strassburg; 119, 133, 152, 286, 288.

Students; (*see* Universities, and, Average Tourist), 121, ''

Sweden; 155, 244, 406.

Switzerland; *see* Mountaineering.

—— Bibl. MSS. Rawlinson D. 120, B. M. Add. 34177; VII. notes 5 and 12.

Symonds, Richard ; 393.

Tasso, Torquato ; quoted, 141, 303, 382.

Taylor, John (the " water-poet ") ; 80, 137, 370, 404.

Theology in relation to Travel (*see* Pilgrimage) ; as a cause of travel, 24; a "religious test" for tutors, 53–4 ; examples of intolerance, 28, 53, 75, 111–3, 133, 171, 362; attractions of Mohammedanism, 55–6 ; increases the interest of volcanoes, 97 ; in Spain, 167.

Thou, J. A. de ; accompanies de Foix to Italy, 14 ; interview with Sigonius, 48 ; nearly drowned on Lake Wallenstadt (?), 81; quoted, 97, 180, 260, 274, 300, 350.

Tolls and Duties; 320, 328, 336–8.

Touring, [1542–1642] ; spread of the idea, 25–30, 158 ; bibliography of, 29, 389–91 ; estimates of amount of (*see* Constantinople, English abroad, Ireland, Pilgrimage, Scots abroad), 29, 236 ; towns the stopping-places, 101; hardships of, and their effect (*see* Illness), 102, 163, 173, 179, 223, 242–4, 260, 286, 310–2, 375–6 ; official supervision of (*see* Passports), 131, 158, 271–2, 343, 346, 351 ; compensations, 377–9.

——for and against (*see* Ideas, modified by travel); opinions of Bacon, 3; of Montaigne, 3, 57; of Pasquier, 375; new ideas and knowledge brought home, 14, 140, 378–9 ; otherwise unobtainable, 17, 40, 140 ; opposition to, 36, 158–9, 373–4; how far reasonable, 375 ; some weak points, 375–7 ; tourist-books as a source of knowledge for us, 52, 72, 82, 86, 118–9, 124, 154–6, 162, 175, 189, 193, 202, 213–4, 232, 350.

—— special causes of (*see* Average Tourist, Embassies, Exile, Pilgrimage, and Tourist, types of)); commerce, and lack of means of communication at a distance, 18 ; exploration, 18; difficulty of obtaining information from abroad, 17, 25, 40–3 ; current fiction, 22 ; theological, 24; Philip Sidney's reason, 27 ; historical, 28, 284 ; the chief cause, 34.

Tourist, types of, in 1600 (*see* under names mentioned in pages here following, and also, Average Tourist, Pilgrimage, and Tutor) ; Subjective, 3–4 ; Objective, 4–5 ; Perfect, 6 ; Philosopher, 7 ; Unintentional, 8 ; Intolerable, 9 ; Feminine, 11–3, 59 ; Ambassadorial, 14, 130–1 ; mediæval types, and how far they survived, 17–23 ; Spy and News-Gatherer, 17 ; Commercial, 20, 131, 321 ; Vagabond, 21–3, 321; Exile, 23; Missionary, 24, 286, 320, 402–3; Various, 24, 92 ; Journalistic, 80.

Transylvania ; cheapness of food there, 340.

Travellers and Travelling; *see* Tourist and Touring.

Turberville, George ; on Muscovy, 159.

Turks ; relation to European States, 8, 182–9, 197, 204 ; Christians' fear of, 22, 85, 113, 117–8, 188 ; conversions by, 55–6, 356; learn navigation from renegades, 73 ; Danube mainly a Turkish river, 81 ; increase of their sea-power during this period, 106, 184–6 ; as seen by tourists, 90, 189–91, 200–2, 269, 343, 346, 360; their teetotalism, 93, 190, 192; likeness to the Japanese as contrasted with Christians, 191, 321 ; signs of decay, 192 ; other characteristics, 90, 189–91, 200–2, 269, 343, 346, 360; " Khans," 247–50; coinage used by, 369, 372.

—— their ruler, the Grand Signor ; Dallam and, 9 ; as an employer, 55; supposed to possess a complete Livy, 194) ; diversions of, 196 ; how to see his palace, 196–7; audiences with, 197.

—— Bibl. ; *see* Constantinople and Jerusalem.

Tutors ; 37, 180, 316 ; Hentzner as, 43–4 ; qualifications, 53 ; Ben Jonson as, 56.

Ulm ; 120.

Unicorn horns ; fact, fiction, and prices, 149, 150.

United Provinces; 116–7, 348; communications in, 83, 291, 294, 329.

—— people of; 132, 143.

—— Bibl.; Beatis, Bisoni, Brereton, Buchell, Cust, Hagemans, Hoby, Moryson.

Universities (*see* Bologna, Padua, Saumur, Students, Wittenberg); Alcalá and Salamanca, 48 ; Italian ones idealized, 103; Orleans, 115.

Vagabond; *see* " Picaro."

Valois, Marguerite de; 152; her litter, 290.

Vargas, Juan de; 405.

Venice; 4, 136, 149, 153, 291, 329, 341, 360–2; more English there than in the rest of Italy, 28; as a model State, 100–1; attractions of, 103–6; small boys of, 133; inns of, 252, 274, 276–7.

Verona; 113.

" Vetturino-system " ; what it was, 331; its rise and services, 332–4.

Vienna; 121, 147, 188, 288, 395.

Villamont, Sieur de; quoted, 65, 87, 104, 143, 302, 329, 382.

Villers, MM. de; 365, 383, 395.

Villingen, Pastor Peter, pilgrim to Jerusalem, 1565; enslaved, 359.

Vinci, Leonardo da ; a conversation with, 396.

Volcanoes; 91.

Waller, Edmund ; 80.

War; (*see* Robbers); decreases use of Latin, 47; even distribution of war and peace in this period, 124, 350; as affecting tourist finance, 348, 364.

Weston, Sir Richard ; learns much from the Dutch, 116.

Whetenal, Lady Catherine; 394.

Willes, Dr.; cost of journey, England, Muscovy, 335.

Wilson, Arthur; 63.

Winghe, J. de (of Tournai); 395.

Wittenberg; 121.

Women and Travel;(*see* Cecilia, Clara Eugenia, Fanshawe, Johanna, Whetenal); at Rome in 1600, 18; advice concerning, 59; in a seven-day Channel-passage, 63; position of, in Italy and United Provinces, contrasted, 142–4; Jerusalem " Placets " not granted to, 210; embarrassments of, when abroad, 269–71; of Chios, 88–9; Russian, 161; Spanish, 170; Irish, 177–8; Turkish, 200.

Wotton, Sir Henry; quoted, 26, 71, 154, 299, 329, 341, 347, 349, 356, 405.

Wunderer, Johann David; at Pskov, 162.

Wynn, Sir Richard; 385, 405.

Zeiler, Martin; guide-book to Spain quoted, 48, 351, 364.

Zetzner, Johann Eberhard ; 406.

Zinzerling, J.; his itinerary as a guidebook, 46; quoted, 122, 134, 138, 150, 252, 291.

" Zoos " of Europe; 139, 140, 174, 196.